'An accomplished, forth[...] history from its very ear[...] A challenging, robustly [...] round, reminding one o[...] complexity of the present) but at the same time of its – yes indeed – romance'

Adolf Wood, *Literary Review*

'The reach of this elegant, angry essay is astonishing ... it is Johnson's withering depiction of the new black government, 10 years in power, that provides the hardcore excitement ... Johnson's *South Africa: The First Man, the Last Nation* will not please the thought-police. It may be burnt perhaps, along with images of its author, in some public place, as a warning to others. And that is precisely what makes this book – for those who love South Africa – absolutely essential reading'

Christopher Hope, *Sunday Times*

'The South African saga is a magnificent drama. It is told in this remarkable book with clarity and skill by a man with the courage to speak out on a continent where the fate of the bringers of sad news is not usually comfortable'

Trevor Grundy, *Glasgow Herald*

'The first nine chapters of this book are a lucid and engaging romp through the first 3.5 billion years of South African history, from blue-green algae to Nelson Mandela's release from jail in 1990. But it is the last chapter that really makes the book worth buying. R.W. Johnson is a historian, but also a polemical journalist, and he writes with most passion about the present. He provides a robustly liberal critique of the new South Africa'

*Economist*

'Johnson manages to sustain a remarkably even hand in tracing the key determinants of South Africa's 20th-century history, and especially the machinations that brought about the doomed ideology of apartheid, and finally the irresistible rise of the African National Congress (ANC). For the most part, Johnson's judgements are extremely astute'

Richard Synge, *Independent*

'This book is determinedly polemical, but it is academically rigorous in its understanding of South Africa's history ... This is a well-written and necessary book which challenges the myths draping the rainbow nation'

Justin Cartwright, *Daily Telegraph*

R.W. Johnson was born in 1943 and educated at Natal University, from which he won a Rhodes Scholarship to Oxford. Unable for political reasons to return home to South Africa for many years, he was a Fellow in Politics at Magdalen College, Oxford from 1969 to 1995. In 1995 he returned to South Africa as Director of the Helen Suzman Foundation, a post he held until 2001. His books include *How Long Will South Africa Survive?* (1977), *The Long March of the French Left* (1981) and (edited with Lawrence Schlemmer) *Launching Democracy in South Africa* (1996). He has written for journals and newspapers all over the world and is currently the South Africa correspondent of the London *Sunday Times*. He lives in Cape Town.

*By R.W. Johnson*

How Long Will South Africa Survive?
The Long March of the French Left
The Politics of Recession
Heroes and Villains: Selected Essays
African Perspectives (*ed., with Christopher Allen*)
Shootdown? The Verdict on KAL 007
Launching Democracy in South Africa
(*ed., with Lawrence Schlemmer*)
Ironic Victory: Liberalism in Post-Liberation South Africa
(*ed., with David Welsh*)
South Africa: The First Man, the Last Nation

# SOUTH AFRICA

## THE FIRST MAN, THE LAST NATION

# R. W. Johnson

PHOENIX

A PHOENIX PAPERBACK

First published in Great Britain in 2004
by Weidenfeld & Nicolson
This paperback edition published in 2006
by Phoenix,
an imprint of Orion Books Ltd,
Orion House, 5 Upper St Martin's Lane,
London WC2H 9EA

1 3 5 7 9 10 8 6 4 2

A CIP catalogue record for this book
is available from the British Library.

ISBN-13 978-0-7538-2100-8
ISBN-10 0-7538-2100-1

Typeset in Great Britain by
Butler and Tanner Ltd, Frome and London

Printed and bound in Great Britain by
Mackays of Chatham plc, Chatham, Kent

The Orion Publishing Group's policy is to use papers that
are natural, renewable and recyclable products and
made from wood grown in sustainable forests. The logging
and manufacturing processes are expected to conform to
the environmental regulations of the country of origin.

www.orionbooks.co.uk

# CONTENTS

# PREFACE

History is not written in a vacuum; every history is a thing of its time. But in South Africa history has itself always been a site of political struggle, an effect multiplied by the fact that the country has often seemed like a vast social science experiment, a theatre in which much of the rest of the world finds echoes of its own struggles. This has the happy effect of giving its history a wider than national significance but it also leads to some fairly large misunderstandings. After 1994 one frequently met black Americans who had come here as to the promised land: a land of six-lane highways, computers, jet planes and the recognisable Coca-Cola culture, presided over by Nelson Mandela. This was, they surmised, the Africa they had been looking for all this time, a place much like America but where Martin Luther King had become President. Such visions did not long survive South Africa's protean realities. For although the world often seems to catch echoes of itself in South Africa's reflection, it is a place all of its own. A friend who often visits Australia always says on his return that Australia is a fine country but, after South Africa, a little bland. It is, he says, a relief to get back to abnormality.

Many ironies have been at work in South African historiography. With history writing so politicised, there has been enormous pressure for even the best historians to bow to all manner of sacred cows, to indulge in an ever-changing game of praise and blame and to observe a great deal in silence. Yet oddly, one has to go back half a century and more to find a time when history writing was more or less congenial to what the ruling group in the country would have liked. And even when jingoistic historians were singing the praises of Cecil Rhodes and were willing enough to see South Africa solely through the eyes of the whites (the rest being social anthropology and 'native administration'), theirs was a view which would have been angrily rejected by many Afrikaners, let alone by brown and black intellectuals.

Afrikaner nationalism naturally aspired to set the record straight about 'the century of wrong', as they referred to the period of British rule over South Africa. The result was historiographically peculiar, for at just the moment when in the rest of Africa a huge work of historical revision was beginning in which pride of place was given to the African majority instead of the ruling white elite, in South Africa the historical mythology of Afrikaner nationalism was now placed at the centre of the political canvas. The sacred cows of this new history were 'the Afrikaner nation', the 'civilising role' of the white man in Africa, the simultaneous arrival of whites and Bantu on South African soil, the righteous grievances which underlay the Great Trek, its civilising and pacifying mission and, above all, the terrible suffering of these god-fearing whites at the hands of those other whites, the treacherous English.

Afrikanerdom, however, lacked an intelligentsia able to contest on equal terms the histories produced by English-speaking South Africans or English speakers worldwide. The former had the fatal advantage not only of a far longer and wider intellectual tradition but the possession of an international language. So while Afrikaner nationalism produced history textbooks for school and university consonant with the ruling view, liberals of one sort or another continued to occupy the historical high ground. This was reflected not only in the work of de Kiewiet, Eric Walker and the *Oxford History of South Africa* but of those writing from America such as Jeff Butler, Leonard Thompson and Donald Morris. (And even Alan Paton's *Cry the Beloved Country* was written in a sleazy motel in middle America.) Naturally, Afrikaner nationalism sought to redress this situation: from 1948 on, when the National Party gained power, money was poured into Afrikaans universities and a new intelligentsia was brought on at speed. But intelligentsias aren't created on command and although South Africa's English-speaking universities were utterly embattled – those of us who came through them at that period cannot forget – they continued to outperform the Afrikaans universities in everything to do with the creative spirit, including, of course, writing and research. It was only at the very end of the apartheid period that this ceased to be true and by then even many leading Afrikaner intellectuals were liberals too.

However, during the 1970s and 1980s the liberal tradition of historiography was itself increasingly displaced by a more radical and often Marxist school of history with powerful adherents in both South Africa and (particularly) Britain. This new school had many strands – an insistence on the primary place of class analysis and thus the down-playing of race as an explanatory factor; the allowance of 'nation' as a political entity only, the view that 'ethnicity' was an invented and imposed construct, used essentially for purposes of manipulation; a determination to view history from below and a concern to rescue those 'forgotten by history'. Neither tradition nor culture was really thought to exist except as created, manipulated categories. The whites were now seen as the true savages of African history while blacks were either victims or the heroes of struggles against white oppression. Even Shaka's atrocities were claimed either to have been a fiction or attributed (wrongly) to the indirect effects of white penetration.

Naturally, this new school was deeply sympathetic to black aspirations and aimed to redraw South African history as African history rather than as a drama between Boer and Brit. In some cases this led to an open identification with the views of the African National Congress and the South African Communist Party – particularly in the frequently argued contention that apartheid and capitalism were inextricably connected so that one could not be abolished unless the other was too. Extraordinarily, when apartheid was abolished and capitalism happily continued, not one of those who had argued this point so vociferously wrote to explain how this could have occurred. For – and this was the point – such historians had taken to its logical conclusion the contention that history was one of the political front lines of the anti-apartheid struggle. Those who did not go along with the new line were judged to be pariahs, sell-outs or worse. South Africa ended up with two different historical societies publishing their separate journals and having no communication with one another.

After 1994 this Marxist school quietly collapsed, unwilling to face the new world it had helped create. When President Mandela balanced off the different tribes in his appointments and when President Mbeki emphasised that in South Africa there were 'two nations, the poor black and the rich white' there was no comment from this school about this clear resurgence of ethnicity. It remained silent when Mbeki appealed not only to African 'traditions' and 'culture' but, quite straightforwardly, to anti-white racism. Nor, indeed, was one word uttered about the obvious class basis of ANC rule although the situation cried out for a Marxist analysis. But by this time it was anyway assumed that all history written before 1994 was wrong, if not racist, because it had been written by whites. The history departments of the English-speaking universities which had been in the forefront of the ideological struggle soon themselves came under pressure.

Undoubtedly the central institution of the new wave history of the 1970s and 1980s had been the African Studies Institute at Wits

University under the directorship of Charles van Onselen. The university was nervous of Van Onselen who was uncomfortably to the left – he had already been declared a prohibited immigrant from Rhodesia by Ian Smith's white minority regime. The apartheid security police, aware that Van Onselen associated with ANC exiles when abroad and that the ASI was a centre of Marxist thought, paid the Institute a good deal of attention. Moreover, the ASI had distinguished black scholars on its staff such as Es'kia Mphahlele and Chabani Manganyi at a time when this was extremely unusual. Many more younger blacks were employed as research assistants and translators, though the ASI rigorously insisted that they also be registered for degrees, for it wanted to train young black historians and also to avoid any claim that it had benefited unequally from their labours. Wits, uncomfortable at the ASI's reputation and its penchant for hiring radicals, made difficulties over the hiring of blacks but could not quarrel with the Institute's productivity – in under twenty years of Van Onselen's directorship it saw over twenty-five major books produced, together with countless articles. Perhaps the greatest strength of the ASI lay in its recognition that much African history existed in oral form only: accordingly it became the country's greatest centre for the capturing and recording of oral history.

With the end of apartheid and the advent of democracy it might have been expected that the ASI (now renamed the Institute of Advanced Social Research – IASR) would come into its own. For while the radicals who had struggled against apartheid had often had scholarly aspirations, so that the anti-apartheid struggle produced a vast and often distinguished literature – in politics, economics, sociology and biography – there was no doubt that the outstanding achievements of this radical intelligentsia had been in history and that the IASR had been the central focus of that effort. Its emphasis on recapturing the lost history of the African people and its stress on oral history – inevitably central if one is capturing the history of often illiterate people – meant that it was perfectly positioned to provide the new history which the democratic regime would surely want.

In fact, the new political climate proved to be insidious, though at first in a benign way. Suddenly South Africa was fashionable and South African scholars were acceptable around the world. At the same time the ANC announced that it was time to quit the ivory tower and get one's hands dirty by helping build the new society. The result was a torrent of international invitations and air tickets on the one hand and recruitment into government on the other. Whenever one met radical scholars in that period they were either off to workshops in Jakarta, a conference in Leyden or a seminar in Stockholm, or they were working on the umpteenth draft of the ANC's Reconstruction and Development Programme. The result was that many were too busy travelling and talking to do much work, while the others largely wasted their time on policy proposals which got discarded (like the RDP).

Tougher times soon arrived. At Wits, Van Onselen and twelve other leading scholars found themselves ranged in opposition to the leading Africanist intellectual, Deputy Vice-Chancellor William Makgoba, whom they accused of having partially falsified his CV and of having misadministered his office. The affair became a cause célèbre and the thirteen found themselves branded as white racists (though one of them was black). Memorably, Makgoba announced that each morning he rubbed himself all over with lion fat the better to confront his enemies. He illegitimately appropriated the private personnel files of the thirteen and issued a series of allegations of financial and other malfeasance against them, all of which charges were later admitted to be without foundation. Under extreme pressure from the university, nine of the thirteen were forced to reach a compromise deal with Makgoba. Despite his disturbing behaviour, Makgoba was later made head of the Medical Research Council and then Vice-Chancellor of the University of KwaZulu-Natal. All four who opposed him to the end left Wits, two of them emigrating.

Thus the IASR, far from coming into its own, found itself under fire from the crude new wave of Africanism. It was immediately clear that any amount of intellectual achievement or meritorious past service counted for nothing if one got on the wrong side of the new elite, which was willing to use charges of racism as an all-purpose method of getting its way. So, instead of the IASR leading the way for a new wave of history writing, Dr Colin Bundy, the Marxist historian who briefly became the new Vice-Chancellor of Wits, had the IASR shut down altogether.

This demolition of the country's only institute for historical research was accompanied by a great deal of hostile press publicity about Van Onselen who was routinely – though absurdly – vilified as a racist, some even going so far as to claim that his own monumental achievements as a historian had resulted from unfair exploitation of black research assistants. One might have expected Wits to point out that this was the exact opposite of the truth and, indeed, to seek to protect Van Onselen, one of their few scholars of top-flight international calibre, from some of the grosser assaults on his reputation. But the university was far more concerned to curry favour with the new elite. Not only was no attempt made to keep Van Onselen but when he left after twenty years of running the IASR there was no farewell, no send-off, no speeches, no acknowledgement of any kind. The IASR, which had played a unique role in South African historiography, was closed down without any celebration or even recording of the remarkable work it had done. Even amidst the general decline in higher education in the post-1994 era this act of intellectual vandalism stands out.

But Van Onselen and the IASR were not a unique case. Every history department in the country felt the pressure and many fine historians underwent similar if less publicised traumas. Like many other academics, they found themselves fighting a rearguard action for the universalist values on which higher education depends: intellectual merit as the key criterion of the whole enterprise, the right to express dissident views and blindness to race and colour. Instead, a crude new Africanism washed over the universities: race was made the key criterion for appointment and promotion in the interests of 'transformation'. Individuals with the 'wrong' views or 'wrong' skin colour got short shrift. The then Minister of Education, Kader Asmal, openly threatened the imposition of racial quotas on universities which did not bow the knee fast enough – for the new government quickly made it clear that it cared little for academic freedom, let alone university autonomy. The values asserted by this new wave were symbolic, parochial and based on racial solidarity: there was no pretence that what was being asserted could ever pass muster in the academic world outside South Africa. The alarming assumption behind all such policies is that the government can simply force through the development of a new black intelligentsia to staff the universities – to order and within a generation. The fact that it took far longer for Afrikaner nationalism, under far more favourable circumstances, to produce a competitive intelligentsia suggests that this policy is bound to fail. It is a truism that by introducing Bantu Education the Afrikaner Nationalists did lasting damage both to education and the wider society but it seems all too possible that African nationalism may, by these ill-conceived attempts at social engineering, inflict at least equal damage.

The new government showed little sign of knowing much history itself but seemed convinced that the subject was still generally taught in a white racist fashion. Endless speeches were made calling for history departments to stop teaching only European history and the story of the Great Trek, to drop such Eurocentric notions and teach African history instead. When historians rushed forward to point out that actually African history had been the main focus of their departments for many years past, they were met with a stunned silence but before long one would hear the same speech being made again. Bashing Eurocentricity was far too important a political exercise for it to cease simply because it did not fit the facts. With all previous South African history under attack by the new black elite as intrinsically racist, it was not surprising that history was downgraded throughout the nation's educational system. History ceased to be a compulsory school subject, a change which caused the numbers of those choosing to study history at university to plummet: there was no longer a need for history teachers and thus no jobs. Within universities history shrank sharply and at the same time a strange new bastard subject was born, Heritage Studies, whose content suggested it was mainly useful for training tourist guides.

Meanwhile President Mbeki had announced his belief in the African Renaissance – a theme which proved popular among the new elite, which repeated this phrase as a virtual mantra. Bizarrely, at several universities African Renaissance institutes and centres were set up – though nobody had the first idea what the term might mean. There seemed to be a vague sense that the age of colonialism had been equivalent to the Dark Ages and that now that all Africa was decolonised there could be some return to the promise of a lost golden past and that peace would replace Africa's chronic civil strife: indeed, Mbeki frequently announced that the twenty-first century would be 'the African century'. Quite why this was supposed to happen was left unclear: after all, the end of colonialism had seen civil strife increase, not decrease, in many African states. But lack of clarity was the essence of the exercise not only because there had never actually been such a lost golden past but because the proponents of the African Renaissance were in any case not historically trained or aware. Serious historians passed over the phrase 'African Renaissance' in embarrassed silence. The occasional celebrations of the African Renaissance which took place did not much help one to understand what was meant. Typically such occasions would include some African song and dance and a lot of assertive speechifying, a sort of appeal to cultural history with the history left out. With Heritage Studies entering stage right and the African Renaissance stage left, one was truly in the land of the lost.

Most striking of all, there was no new history. There was not even an attempt to understand apartheid properly: a visit to the Museum of Apartheid in Johannesburg shows that this is already quite mis-understood. What bedecks the walls of the museum is actually a history of the struggle against apartheid and particularly the history of the ANC. If there is a new trend, this is it: instead of reinterpreting, say, the last century, the tendency is just to represent the history of 'the struggle' and obliterate everything else. Even those who might have produced a new history seemed little interested in doing so. Thus in 2003 Eddie Maloka, Director of the Africa Institute, launched an attack on all previous schools of South African history – colonial, liberal and Marxist – because virtually all the historians were whites who had somehow prevented the emergence of younger black historians, though the only evidence he could adduce was his own failure to get his Ph.D. published. He concluded that a number of historians ought to have been hauled before the Truth and Reconciliation Commission to confess their ideological and racist crimes.

We stand at the juncture of the crude historical myths of the apartheid period and new myths propagated by an African nationalism with little intellectual content. When, in October 2003, J. M. Coetzee was awarded the Nobel Prize for literature, Xolela Mangcu, the Director of the Steve Biko Foundation and a leading black intellectual, immediately denounced the award as racist, claiming that Coetzee had only got the prize because he was white. Such crude abuse was typical of what African nationalism had come down to after less than a decade of ANC power, a mirror image of the old white settler abuse of 'kaffirs'. This is no way ahead any more than the deliberate dumbing down of school exams in today's South Africa represents real educational progress. To be sure, it produces more passes in the matriculation exams but only at the cost of selling the nation's children down the river.

This sort of cynical betrayal can only happen in the new South Africa because there is, on every hand, a willingness, even a determination, to pretend. Telling the truth is the hardest thing. Intellectuals who refuse to pretend – J. M. Coetzee is a shining example – have been vilified by the ruling party and have often ended by emigrating. But the enemy is not those who expose pretence, it is the pretending itself. We have to face the sad truth that South Africa, with the end of apartheid, exchanged one set of authoritarian, hegemonic nationalists for another and that many of the hopes of liberation have faded as the similarities between these two hegemonies have multiplied. One has to be frank about history. The job in hand, here in the southern tip of Africa, is to live through this period and to tell the truth about it so that we can, one day, go beyond it.

One can see why apartheid bureaucrats clung to Verwoerd's vision, mad though it was. For the demise of apartheid's historical myths was also accompanied by the disappearance of clarity. Today's picture of what went on, where and when, is much more complicated than it used to be and historians themselves do not make this new past easier to understand. Many use different terms for the same phenomena. Some avoid using any terms at all or invent new terms in order to avoid those that are now stigmatised, while others make their texts impenetrably complicated. It is difficult to avoid the impression that in their eagerness to satisfy the demands of the new political correctness some are even willing to obscure facts which do not fit into the new historical dispensation. At the same time the ANC and African intellectuals in general tend to treat the country's history as if it were simply and only the history of suffering under colonialism and of the liberation struggle. There is little recognition that history goes back much further than that; that even white rule had its own history quite apart from its oppression of blacks; and that far from the ANC's conquest of power being the end of South African history, it too is merely a phase. Hence the need for a new history.

History is also not written in a personal vacuum. It is only fair to tell the reader that the author is a political scientist and journalist as much as a historian; that he happily bears the distinction of being the only Oxford don to resign his fellowship in order to return to South Africa; and that his own political history belongs in roughly equal measure to the ANC, the British Labour Party and to the variously named strands of South African liberalism. My overwhelming debt is to a historian friend who generously contributed knowledge and advice. However, the views expressed and whatever mistakes I have made are all my own.

R.W. Johnson
Cape Town, March 2004

# CHRONOLOGY

**6–8 million BCE** Early hominids (Australopithecus), walking upright, populate south and east Africa

**2.5 million BCE** Earliest man, *Homo Habilis*, populates east and south Africa

**1.8 million BCE** First hominids leave Africa to colonise Eurasia

**500,000 BCE** First *Homo Sapiens* (Neanderthal) men populate Africa

**300,000 BCE** *Homo Sapiens Sapiens* (i.e. modern man) emerges in southern Africa

**100,000 BCE** First men cross from Africa to the Levant

**38,000 BCE** Stone Age ancestors of the Khoisan begin to populate south Africa

**25,000 BCE** First San rock paintings

As the Common Era begins, the Khoi introduce sheep-herding to the Cape

**300** First Bantu peoples move into south Africa from east Africa

**900–1000** Bantu develop Iron Age technology and large-scale mining. First south African state, Mapungubwe, emerges

**1488** Circumnavigation of the Cape by Bartolemeu Dias

**1497–8** Vasco da Gama reaches India via Cape, naming Natal en route

**1652** Jan van Riebeeck founds Cape colony for Dutch East India Company

**1689** Arrival of Huguenot settlers

**1739** Last Khoi resistance crushed

**1778** First frontier war

**1795** The British take the Cape

**1803** Cape returned to Dutch rule

**1806** The British retake the Cape

**1807** Abolition of the slave trade

**1819** Shaka defeats the Ndwande, establishing Zulu kingdom

**1824** Port Natal (Durban) founded

**1828** Shaka assassinated

**1833**  Abolition of slavery

**1834**  Executive and Legislative Councils established in Cape Colony

**1836–8**  The Great Trek leaves the Cape

**1838**  Piet Retief, Gert Maritz murdered by Dingane. Boers victorious at Blood River

**1845**  Natal annexed as British colony

**1854**  Republic of the Orange Free State proclaimed

**1857**  The great cattle killing of the Xhosa

**1859**  South African Republic (Transvaal) proclaimed

**1860**  Indians begin to arrive in Natal

**1867**  First diamonds discovered at Hopetown

**1878**  Ninth (and last) frontier war ends

**1879**  Anglo–Zulu War: battles of Isandlwana, Rorke's Drift and Ulundi

**1886**  Gold discovered in Transvaal

**1899–1902**  Anglo-Boer War

**1906**  Bambatha rebellion in Natal

**1910**  Union of South Africa proclaimed, Louis Botha first Prime Minister

**1912**  South Africa Native National Congress (ANC) formed

**1913**  Native Land Act ends African private ownership of land

**1914**  South Africa invades and occupies South-West Africa (Namibia)

**1922**  The Rand revolt

**1924**  Hertzog's National Party wins power

**1933**  Hertzog and Smuts form 'fusion' coalition

**1934**  D. F. Malan breaks away to form National Party

**1944**  ANC Youth League founded

**1947**  ANC and SA Indian Congress form 'Doctors' Pact'

**1948**  Malan's Nationalists defeat Smuts and come to power

**1949**  Population Registration Act, Mixed Marriages Act. ANC accepts Programme of Action

**1950**  Immorality Act, Group Areas Act, Suppression of Communism Act

**1952**  Defiance campaign

**1953**  Separate Amenities Act, Bantu Education Act, SACP founded

**1954**  Johannes Strijdom succeeds Malan as Prime Minister

**1955**  Congress of the People, Kliptown, adopts Freedom Charter

**1956**  Disenfranchisement of Coloureds

**1956–60**  Treason Trial of 156 people, including Nelson Mandela

**1958**  Hendrik Verwoerd succeeds Strijdom as Prime Minister

**1959**  Separate Universities Act

**1960**  Shootings at Sharpeville and Langa

**1961** South Africa becomes a republic outside the Commonwealth. Umkhonto we Sizwe launched

**1963** Rivonia trial. Detention without trial introduced, torture becomes common

**1966** Verwoerd assassinated, succeeded by John Vorster

**1969** Steve Biko founds SASO, ANC Morogoro conference

**1974** Independence of Angola and Mozambique

**1976** Transkei independent. Soweto riots

**1977** Biko murdered by police

**1978** Vorster succeeded by P. W. Botha as Prime Minister

**1980** Zimbabwe independent, Robert Mugabe takes power

**1983** Tricameral constitution introduced, UDF launched

**1985** ANC Kabwe conference. COSATU launched. Botha's 'Rubicon' speech: foreign loans called in, collapse of Rand

**1986** Influx control abandoned. KwaZulu-Natal Indaba launched

**1989** F. W. de Klerk succeeds P. W. Botha. Namibia's independence election

**1990** De Klerk abandons apartheid, Nelson Mandela released, bans on ANC, PAC, SACP lifted, exiles return

**1991** Constitutional talks begin

**1993** Chris Hani assassinated

**1994** ANC wins first democratic election, Mandela becomes President. Restitution of Land Rights Act

**1996** De Klerk's Nationalists leave government, GEAR launched. Land Reform (Labour Tenants) Act

**1997** ANC Mafikeng conference: end of reconciliation

**1998** Equity Employment Act reintroduces racial criteria for employment

**1999** ANC increases electoral majority. Thabo Mbeki President. DP becomes main opposition party

**2000** Zimbabwe referendum: Mugabe defeated. Mbeki rallies to his support. Mbeki's Aids denialism becomes apparent. Equality Act introduces 'equality courts'

**2002** SACP spokesman Jeremy Cronin denounces 'Zanufication' of ANC

**2003** One millionth Aids victim dies, 5.3 million now infected. Unemployment at 42 per cent

**2004** ANC returned with two-thirds majority in third democratic election, DA makes large gains

# ABBREVIATIONS

**AFL-CIO** American Federation of Labor-Congress of Industrial Organisations
**ANC** African National Congress
**APO** African Political Organisation
**ARM** African Resistance Movement
**ASI** African Studies Institute
**AU** African Union
**AWB** Afrikaner Weerstandsbeweging (Afrikaner Resistance Movement)
**AZAPO** Azanian People's Organisation
**BC** Black Consciousness
**BCE** Before the Common Era
**BEE** Black economic empowerment
**BOSS** Bureau of State Security
**CAD** Coloured Affairs Department
**CE** The Common Era
**COD** Congress of Democrats
**CODESA** Convention for a Democratic South Africa
**COSATU** Congress of South African Trade Unions
**CPSA** Communist Party of South Africa
**CUSA** Council of Unions of South Africa
**DA** Democratic Alliance
**DP** Democratic Party
**FDI** Foreign direct investment
**FLN** National Liberation Front (Algeria)
**FOSATU** Federation of South African Trade Unions
**GAA** Group Areas Act
**GDP** Gross Domestic Product
**GEAR** Growth, Employment and Redistribution policy
**GMS** German Moravian Society
**GNU** Government of National Unity

**HNP** Herstigte (Restored) National Party
**IASR** Institute for Advanced Social Research
**ICU** Industrial and Commercial Workers Union
**IFP** Inkatha Freedom Party
**ISCOR** Iron and Steel Corporation
**LP** Labour Party
**MK** Umkhonto we Sizwe
**MP** Member of Parliament
**MPLA** People's Liberation Movement of Angola
**MU** Miners Union
**NEC** National Executive Committee (ANC)
**NEPAD** New Economic Partnership for African Development
**NRC** Natives Representative Council
**NGO** Non-governmental organisation
**NIC** Natal Indian Congress
**NP** National Party
**NNP** New National Party
**NUM** National Union of Mineworkers
**NUSAS** National Union of South African Students
**OB** Ossewabrandwag (Ox Wagon Sentinel)
**OFS** Orange Free State
**ORC** Orange River Colony
**PAC** Pan Africanist Congress
**PNP** Purified National Party
**PP** Progressive Party
**PR** Proportional representation
**RDP** Reconstruction and Development Programme
**RENAMO** National Resistance Movement (Mozambique)
**SACP** South African Communist Party
**SACTU** South African Congress of Trade Unions
**SAIC** South African Indian Congress
**SANLAM** Suid Afrikaanse Nasionale Lewens Assuransie Maatskappy
**SANNC** South African Native National Congress
**SANTAM** Suid Afrikaanse Nasionale Trust en Assuransie
 Maatskappy
**SAP** South Africa Party
**SAR** South African Republic
**SASM** South African Students Movement
**SASO** South African Students Organisation
**SWAPO** South-West African People's Organisation
**TRC** Truth and Reconciliation Commission

**UCT** University of Cape Town
**UDF** United Democratic Front
**UNITA** United National Independence Movement of Angola
**UP** United Party
**UWUSA** United Workers Union of South Africa

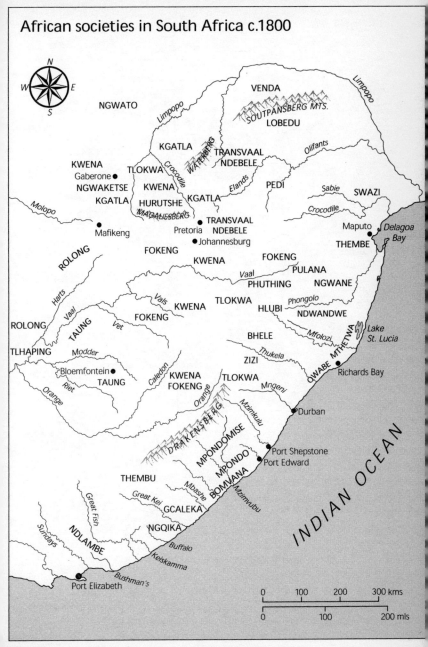

# African societies in South Africa c.1800

N
W E
S

NGWATO

VENDA

Limpopo

SOUTPANSBERG MTS.

LOBEDU

KGATLA

WATERBERG

TRANSVAAL
NDEBELE

Olifants

KWENA

Gaberone ●

TLOKWA

Crocodile

NGWAKETSE

KWENA

KGATLA

Elands

PEDI

Sabie

SWAZI

KGATLA

Molopo

HURUTSHE

MAGALIESBERG

Crocodile

Mafikeng ●

Pretoria ●

TRANSVAAL
NDEBELE

Maputo ● Delagoa
Bay

ROLONG

FOKENG

Johannesburg ●

THEMBE

Harts

KWENA

FOKENG

Vaal

PULANA

NGWANE

PHUTHING

Vals

TLOKWA

Phongolo

Molopo

ROLONG

TAUNG

Vet

FOKENG

KWENA

HLUBI

NDWANDWE

Mfolozi

Lake
St. Lucia

TLHAPING

Modder

BHELE

Thukela

MTHETWA

Bloemfontein ●

Riet

KWENA
FOKENG

TAUNG

Caledon

ZIZI

TLOKWA

Mngeni

QWABE

Richards Bay

Orange

Orange

Mzimkulu

Durban ●

DRAKENSBERG

MPONDOMISE

Port Shepstone
Port Edward

THEMBU

MPONDO

Great Kei

Mbashe

BOMVANA

Mzimvubu

Great Fish

GCALEKA

Sundays

NDLAMBE

NGQIKA

Buffalo

Keiskamma

Port Elizabeth ●

Bushman's

INDIAN OCEAN

| 0 | 100 | 200 | 300 kms |

| 0 | 100 | 200 mls |

Modern place-names such as Johannesburg, Pretoria, Port Elizabeth, etc. have been added.

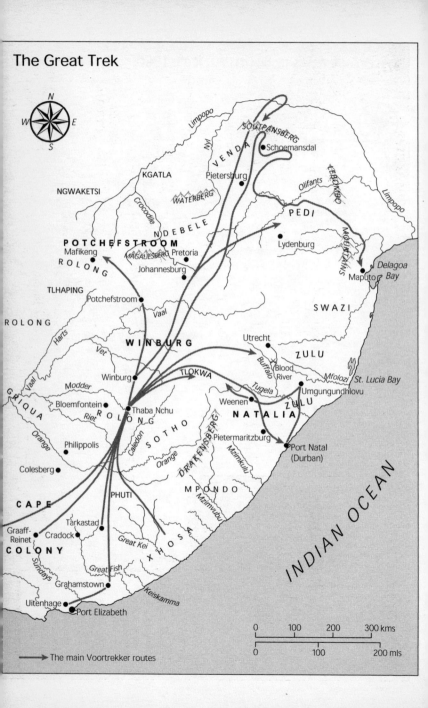

# The Great Trek

N
W E
S

*Limpopo*
SOUTPANSBERG
Schoemansdal
KGATLA
VENDA
Pietersburg
*Nyl*
NGWAKETSI
WATERBERG
*Olifants*
*Limpopo*
LEBOMBO
N D E B E L E
PEDI
**POTCHEFSTROOM**
Mafikeng
MAGALIESBERG
Pretoria
Lydenburg
R O L O N G
Johannesburg
MOUNTAINS
Delagoa
Maputo
Bay
TLHAPING
Potchefstroom
*Vaal*
SWAZI
**ROLONG**
*Harts*
*Vet*
**WINBURG**
Utrecht
ZULU
Winburg
*Modder*
TLOKWA
*Buffalo*
St. Lucia Bay
ROLONG
*Vaal*
*Rietr*
**ROLONG**
Bloemfontein
Thaba Nchu
SOTHO
Blood
River
*Mfolozi*
GRIQUA
Weenen
*Tugela*
Umgungundlovu
*Orange*
Philippolis
*Caledon*
DRAKENSBERG
**NATALIA**
ZULU
Pietermaritzburg
Colesberg
*Orange*
Port Natal
(Durban)
*Mzimkulu*
C A P E
PHUTI
M P O N D O
Tarkastad
Graaff-
Reinet
Cradock
*Great Kei*
*Mzimvubu*
**COLONY**
X H O S A
*Sundays*
*Great Fish*
Grahamstown
*Keiskamma*
Uitenhage
Port Elizabeth

INDIAN OCEAN

| 0 | 100 | 200 | 300 kms |

| 0 | 100 | 200 mls |

→ The main Voortrekker routes

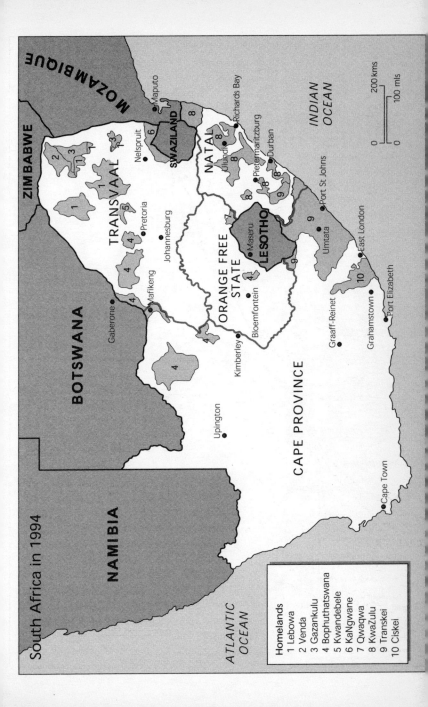

South Africa in 1994

**Homelands**
1 Lebowa
2 Venda
3 Gazankulu
4 Bophuthatswana
5 KwaNdebele
6 KaNgwane
7 QwaQwa
8 KwaZulu
9 Transkei
10 Ciskei

MOZAMBIQUE

ZIMBABWE

BOTSWANA

NAMIBIA

Maputo

SWAZILAND

Nelspruit

TRANSVAAL

Pretoria

Johannesburg

Mafikeng

Gaberone

Upington

ORANGE FREE STATE

Bloemfontein

Kimberley

LESOTHO

Maseru

NATAL

Ulundi

Richards Bay

Pietermaritzburg

Durban

Port St Johns

Umtata

East London

Graaff-Reinet

Grahamstown

Port Elizabeth

CAPE PROVINCE

Cape Town

ATLANTIC OCEAN

INDIAN OCEAN

0    100 mls
0    200 kms

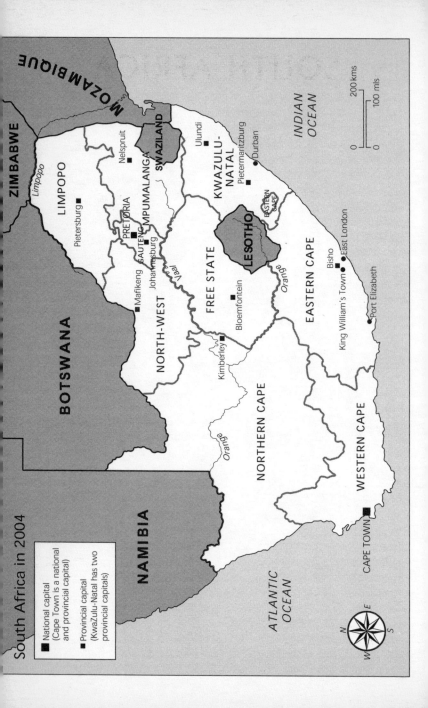

South Africa in 2004

- ■ National capital
  (Cape Town is a national
  and provincial capital)

- ■ Provincial capital
  (KwaZulu-Natal has two
  provincial capitals)

NAMIBIA

BOTSWANA

ZIMBABWE

MOZAMBIQUE

SWAZILAND

LESOTHO

LIMPOPO

Pietersburg

NORTH-WEST

Mafikeng

GAUTENG

PRETORIA

Johannesburg

MPUMALANGA

Nelspruit

KWAZULU-
NATAL

Ulundi

Pietermaritzburg

Durban

FREE STATE

Bloemfontein

Kimberley

NORTHERN CAPE

EASTERN CAPE

Bisho

King William's Town

East London

Port Elizabeth

WESTERN CAPE

CAPE TOWN

Limpopo

Vaal

Orange

Orange

EASTERN
CAPE

INDIAN
OCEAN

ATLANTIC
OCEAN

0    100 mils
0    200 kms

N
E
W
S

# SOUTH AFRICA

# I

## CONTESTED ORIGINS

ⓐ ⓐ ⓐ

U nder apartheid South Africans were taught that before the advent of the white man South Africa was mostly uninhabited. According to this version of history the only Africans the whites encountered when they settled at the Cape after 1652 were scattered groups of hunter-gatherers, whom the settlers called Bushmen, and the Hottentots, regarded as slightly more civilised because they herded sheep and cattle. Both these groups were said to consist of multiple interrelated 'tribes', each with its own particular language and culture. These cultures and languages were regarded as constituting the effectively fixed and unchanging identity of each group. Then, in the middle of the seventeenth century, 'more civilised' Bantu tribes arrived, having perfectly timed their appearance in the north-eastern part of contemporary South Africa to coincide with the disembarkation of the first Dutch settlers in the south-east. These Bantu were agriculturalists and pastoralists who possessed weapons and technology superior to anything the Hottentots or the Bushmen had and so the latter were either conquered or cruelly hunted down, the few survivors fleeing into the desert as the Bantu moved forcefully through South Africa's interior.

This picture of South Africa's past was not the creation of apartheid propaganda alone but was based on widely shared notions current right from the beginning of the colonial era. Apartheid historians merely turned these crude notions of cultural anthropology into a doctrine and thus extended their existence by several decades.

With later research – and the changing political climate – this picture crumbled. It became clear that South Africa's history was much longer than had been thought, that neither languages nor cultures had been fixed either to specific groups or to one another so that neither could be unchangeably associated with a particular physical bearer, that is, with a particular 'tribe'. The new anti-colonial orthodoxy claimed that the whole notion of a 'tribe' with a specific culture and language had been created by colonial anthropologists and historians, and did not truly exist. Naturally, this more recent research also showed that both the geography and chronology of the area's settlement by various groups was dramatically different from that previously suggested.

Just as all this seemed clear, a new orthodoxy – emanating from the ANC government itself – began to assert that Africanness did exist after all, with distinct, traditional African values (such as '*ubuntu*') and African culture, replete with African dance, dress and thought. Even more confusing, the new elite, to prove its Africanness, delighted in dressing up in garb loosely borrowed from West Africa – which had no history or tradition of any kind in South Africa where, alas, it belonged to the realms of pantomime fancy dress. Similarly, the Africanist government of Thabo Mbeki had within it several women who retained their maiden names in double-barrelled form – though, of course, this ran clean contrary to patriarchal African tradition. Seldom has the invention of tradition been a busier occupation than in post-1994 South Africa. Before one's very eyes many assertive individuals – a whole new elite – reinvented themselves, proudly parading in new dress and new names. The historian, regarding this spectacle, may blush but may also safely ignore it.

One result of recent research is that one must start much further back than historians have been wont to do. For South Africa has, at every stage, been at the forefront of the development of life on earth. In its first billion years the earth was probably still too hot for life to develop but in the silicon-rich chert layers of South Africa's greenstone belts we can find traces of blue-green algae, the earliest form of life anywhere on earth, dating back 3.5 billion years. It is even possible that these life-forms spread outwards from this area.

The key geological evidence for the birth of the continents 3.5 billion years ago is also to be found in South Africa's Komati valley. The movement of tectonic plates gradually produced further continental drift, with the result that Africa became part of the super-continent of Gondwanaland, encompassing with it present-day Antarctica, South America, Australia and the Indian pensinsula. But it would appear that South Africa was also the crucial theatre for the development of more complex forms of life, for its Karoo basin not only has the earliest fossils of mammals found on earth, dating back

240 million years, but the evidence is that such mammals – the ancestors of the dinosaurs – were found in abundance in South Africa at a time when there is no trace of them elsewhere. Thus the possibility clearly exists that the first animals – and early dinosaurs – spread out to conquer Gondwanaland, occupying about half the world's land area, from South Africa. If so, any possibility that humans could eventually ripple out along the same paths was prevented when, some 180 million years ago, Gondwanaland split into pieces – the split occurring right down what is now South Africa's east coast – and further tectonic movement carried the other continents away.

For at least the next 172 million years the earth, including South Africa, belonged to the dinosaurs and their successors. In the last few decades, however, the discoveries of paleo-anthropologists have extended the history of humankind from several hundred thousand to several million years – and once again it seems that the first hominids and, later, contemporary man originally emerged in south and east Africa, which are thus the cradle of humanity – and perhaps of life itself.

The paleo-anthropological evidence suggests that 6 to 8 million years ago the earliest hominids branched off from a broader family of primates which also included African forest apes, the gorillas and chimpanzees. The hominids differed from the apes in that they ventured out of the tropical forest into the open eastern and southern savannah grasslands and woodlands where, for some reason, they developed the ability to walk upright, a revolutionary growth in capacity which changed their whole way of life and may have later resulted in the invention of tools and language.

The first skull of such a hominid was discovered in 1924 near Taung in South Africa. The paleo-anthropologist Raymond Dart named it Australopithecus, describing it as the 'missing link' between apes and humans – though this discovery gained full acceptance only in the 1950s. Since then the remains of dozens of early hominids have been found in East and South Africa, the earliest of them (in East Africa) dating back over 6 million years. The earliest hominid remains found in South Africa, in the Sterkfontein cave, date back 3.3 million years. The 'Little Foot', as this recent find was dubbed, is the oldest nearly complete skeleton ever discovered.

At first it was thought that humans evolved directly from Australopithecus by a single line of descent, but it gradually emerged that there were many branches of these upright-walking hominids, some of whom had to be discarded as possible human ancestors for the simple reason that they lived at the same time as the earliest humans. In 1959 in the East African Olduvai gorge Louis and Mary Leakey discovered the remains of the earliest man so far found, *Homo Habilis*, who emerged more than 2.5 million years ago. Later remains of *Homo Habilis* were also found in Swartkrantz, Sterkfontein, Drimolen and Kromdal in South Africa. It is now believed that the ancestors of humankind evolved either from the South African man-ape, *Australopithecus Africanus* (a minority view first suggested by Dart) or from another South African branch of Australopithecus, *Praeanthropus Afarensis* or 'Lucy' (the majority view), or from yet another, earlier and still undiscovered branch of Australopithecus.

*Homo Habilis*'s ability to make crude stone tools marked the beginning of the early Stone Age. The emergence of *Homo Erectus*, a more advanced humanoid with a bigger brain, brought about the first technological revolution with tools, starting with axes, made to a preconceived shape. *Homo Erectus*, the first 'social' human with the ability to co-ordinate activities such as hunting and gathering with others like himself, developed symbolic rituals and, perhaps as far back as 2 million years ago, learnt to use language to communicate with others. About 1.8 million years ago these hominids left Africa and colonised much of Eurasia for they had achieved the crucial feat of taming fire and were thus able to countenance colder climes. Thus began the great epic of hominid travel.

Until recently it was thought that the first *Homo Sapiens* – the Neanderthal – emerged in Africa some time between 200,000 and 150,000 years ago, and migrated to Europe about 100,000 years ago. However, recent DNA studies of Neanderthal bones show that while they did indeed emerge in Africa, this took place 500,000 years ago. It had also been thought that Neanderthals were the direct ancestors of modern humans but this theory, like so many other theories about the origins of man, has been thrown into doubt by the new data pouring out from areas of science such as genetics which had not previously made contributions to this field of knowledge. One odd result is that whereas our stock of knowledge about, say, William the Conqueror or Ivan the Terrible is fairly fixed, our knowledge of these immeasurably more distant predecessors has been expanding rapidly. On the one hand it turns out that the Neanderthal's brain was actually bigger than that of a modern human, though he used little of this capacity. On the other hand, it emerges that modern man – *Homo Sapiens Sapiens* – has been around much longer than we thought, coexisting with Neanderthals for some time.

DNA studies show that *Homo Sapiens Sapiens* emerged about 300,000 years ago. The earliest traces of the new technology associated with modern humans – dating back over 195,000 years – have been found in the Border cave in northern KwaZulu-Natal. By about 150,000 years ago these, our ancestors, had the same anatomy as we do and by 80,000 years ago had developed sophisticated stone and bone tools. However, before then, about 100,000 years ago, they had moved up through Africa and had crossed the Red Sea into the Levant where they stayed for some 40,000 years. Finally, about 60,000 years ago, they moved on into Europe and 20,000 years later spread all over Europe and into Asia so that by 30,000 years ago they had replaced all other hominid species. About 10,000 BCE (Before the Common Era, the term which has replaced the old 'Before Christ' but effectively amounts to the same thing) they fanned out to inhabit all major areas of the world. The saga of these successive great migrations, all of them inevitably crossing the isthmus of Suez, lies at the root of all human history. It is tempting to believe that the myth of Moses leading his people out of Africa, through the desert and across that same isthmus, is a distant human memory of that great saga.

The replacement of other species by *Homo Sapiens Sapiens* took only about 10,000 years. Why and how this happened is not at all clear. There is no evidence of major massacres in Europe and Asia 30,000–40,000 years ago, so perhaps the earlier hominids were simply squeezed out by the growing numbers and superior technology of *Homo Sapiens Sapiens*. Interbreeding would have been unlikely for Neanderthals and *Homo Sapiens Sapiens* were different species. Yet red-haired people today carry a particular genetic trace which is older than the genetic tree of modern humans: could this be a sign of Neanderthal ancestry and thus of interbreeding? Then again, the study of the genetic roots of a village population in Middle England shows that today's population bears evidence of genetic mutations which arose 200,000 to 400,000 years ago, mutations which connect them to Asia rather than Africa. Equally, DNA tests of Australian Aborigines reveal differences from the DNA of other groups which clearly took a very long time to develop and which may thus be inconsistent with African ancestry. The problem is that the data connecting *Homo Erectus* to modern man is incomplete and inconclusive but, overwhelmingly, the evidence supports the 'Out of Africa' theory.

What the DNA studies do not confirm is the notion of several wholly different human races which, in effect, underlay colonial (mis)treatment of technologically less advanced peoples in the Third

World. For the genetic structure of all modern humans is remarkably similar and the number of genes responsible for different racial features is minimal. Genetic studies suggest that all Africans and non-Africans probably descended from a common ancestor only about 52,000 years ago. Moreover, researchers have found more genetic differences within the African population than among all non-Africans, which strongly suggests both that Africa's population had more time to develop these variations (and is thus older) and that only a narrow subset of this population crossed the isthmus of Suez, providing the common ancestors for the rest of the human race. According to this theory the ancestors of contemporary humanity emerged in Africa, some of them moving about 52,000 years ago into Europe and Asia where, it would seem, their numbers began to increase rapidly from about 38,000 years ago. This rapid population increase would doubtless help explain the disappearance of other hominids by 30,000 BCE.

Further research is likely to resolve the remaining contradictions before long. Soon we should be able to analyse the complete genetic tree of humankind and many riddles in this sphere will disappear. But from what we already know it seems clear that globalisation started much earlier than had been commonly thought, and that this movement's impetus came from the south, in a direction exactly opposite to the one so widely denounced today.

The contemporary South African population began to appear in the subcontinent some 40,000 years ago. It seems that there is a direct link between the original late Stone Age population which then inhabited South Africa and the Khoisan, the name now substituted for both Bushmen and Hottentots, terms which have come to be considered as derogatory. Khoisan is a combined word indicating two closely related languages – and population groups – the Khoi and the San. Even this is not unproblematic for while Khoi is a self-name, San is merely what the Khoi called the group which the later white settlers called Bushmen, a name some still prefer.

In their anxiety to avoid accusations of racism, historians and anthropologists today claim that the terms Khoi, San and Khoisan are purely linguistic and do not denote cultures at all. However, traces of 'cultural' and even 'biological' approaches to San and Khoi speakers abound in the academic literature. To begin with, despite the disclaimer that the Khoisan are being treated as merely a linguistic group, they are said to have come from the same 'gene pool' as the Negroid population of the continent. The quest for a more precise answer to the question of when Khoisan speakers first appeared in South Africa immediately leads to the production of cultural and even physical evidence from paleo-anthropology and archaeology. This evidence seems to prove that there was a direct link between the late Stone Age inhabitants of South Africa and Khoisan speakers. Both the archaeological data, i.e. their tool-making technology and San rock art which date back as far as 27,000 years, confirm this view.

But how can one speak of a language group which comes from the same gene pool as a racial group and which can only be described and attributed to material evidence? In fact, this confusion is merely a testament to the suffocating political correctness which has enveloped history and the social sciences in recent years, particularly in South Africa. On the one hand historians and anthropologists are desperately keen to avoid accusations of falling into the trap of apartheid racial definitions – hence the insistence that they are studying not 'tribes' but merely language groups. On the other hand they are at pains to stress the ancient roots of South Africa's black population both in order to refute the apartheid myth of recent settlement and also to bolster black self-respect by emphasising that African culture is probably the world's oldest. Hence the nonsensical readiness to use physical, cultural and even genetic evidence to prove the existence of a language group. Such motivations may be high-minded but the result is a complete failure of logic.

But let us return to the San rock art. Both paintings and engravings are found in South Africa, the former mainly in the more mountainous areas, the engravings mostly on the central plateau – and they are very different. The paintings depict humans involved in various activities while the engravings depict mainly animals and geometric figures. The paintings are also far older: the oldest known painting (found in Namibia) dates back 27,000 years while the earliest known engraving is 10,000 years old. For a group which, before the last half of the first millennium BCE, was associated only with hunting and foraging this art is an incredible achievement. In terms of its aesthetic, philosophical and even historiographical interest, San rock art is the equal of palaeo-lithic rock art anywhere else in the world, whether in France or at Tassili-n-Ajjer and Fezzan in the Sahara. The extraordinary thing about both paintings and engravings is that while they are variously described as realist, surrealist and impressionist, they all also seem strikingly modern.

We don't know whether the San enjoyed the beauty of their art – for in their eyes it was not an exercise in aesthetics but a symbolic representation of their rituals and philosophy. The paintings were all executed by shamans and reflected their memories of the trances and hallucinations they underwent in order, as they believed, to connect their communities with the natural and supernatural universe (a notion carried on down the ages in the form of oracles and fates speaking through semi-conscious seers in a seance). The rock art expert, David Lewis-Williams, has decoded the sacral meaning of these paintings and shown that the San vision of the universe was far more complicated than many had associated with such early stages of humankind's intellectual and spiritual development.

These San paintings presented a clear account of the San world and of many events in their history. The San, living in small groups which came together in time of need but then dispersed again, were hunter-gatherers, supplementing their hunting and fishing by gathering roots, nuts and shellfish. They did not have chiefs: the shamans were the main authority in San society but even they did not enjoy political power. Inevitably, given that the San lived in a dry, hot climate, rainmaking ceremonies – one of the shaman's main duties – were the subject of many paintings. But before even that the San had to eat, so the most common motif is the hunting of animals, particularly eland, the most commonly depicted objects. But there are also scenes of burial, trance dancing and rituals associated with war.

San art may have been symbolic but it was also realistic, not just in the gory details of the hunt and in its illustration of the growing power of the shamans but in the depiction of San relations with other groups as they arrived in San territory: indeed, painting style changed in order to depict this fateful reality. The scenes of war showed not only who fought whom but were not squeamish about showing the dreadful fact of the San's inability to stem the tide of the advancing Bantu. Many paintings, with an almost pathetic commitment to the cruel truth, depicted the San defeated or retreating from bigger and darker attackers armed with spears and shields, the San themselves having only bows and arrows.

Some time after 500 BCE the practice of sheep herding emerged in southern Africa, probably on the territory of today's Botswana, and by the first century CE pastoralism had reached the Cape. The archaeological data shows that these early herdsmen – like the San – still used late Stone Age tools even though their new pastoral economy was clearly more advanced.

This new economy, based on breeding sheep and later cattle, is commonly associated with the spread of Khoi languages (this, again, despite the 'linguistic disclaimer'). These tongues were closely related to some San languages and are thought to have originated in what is today Botswana where Khoi speakers first took to herding – and developed a vocabulary to describe it. From Botswana the Khoi spread to the east of the Drakensberg and to the western part of South Africa where their descendants were found by white settlers centuries later. In the eastern part of the country the majority were later absorbed or driven away by Bantu speakers – as were many San who had settled there before them. Coexistence and then collision with the Bantu resulted in the prominence of the click sounds characteristic of Khoisan languages in the major contemporary South African Bantu languages, Xhosa and Zulu. Similarly, many of these languages use the Khoi vocabulary for all cattle-based pursuits.

Unlike the San the Khoi lived in large groups, moving about together with their cattle. These groups consisted of several clans and could include alien client groups whom they had absorbed (e.g., San or early Bantu speakers). The Khoi were the first unequal society in South Africa for some groups accumulated more cattle (and thus wealth) than others. This inequality inevitably produced a social hierarchy and a stronger chieftaincy – indeed, each group was held together by the authority of a leadership based on (cattle) wealth and seniority. The bottom line was simply that during a drought survival lay in becoming a client of the biggest cattle owner, who could keep you alive through his greater supplies of milk and meat. Both power and wealth were inherited but if a leader lost his cattle his group dispersed to join luckier neighbours. Equally, if the group became too big – with the fruits of clientage spread correspondingly thin – this too might be a reason for splitting.

Despite the introduction of herding, there was no rigid distinction between the San and the Khoi. They spoke related languages, both groups hunted and foraged, and some San adopted herding and were absorbed by the Khoi or just 'became' Khoi, living the Khoi way of life and speaking the Khoi language, perhaps intermarrying with the Khoi and thus gradually changing their identity to Khoi as well. This gradual integration seems to have been voluntary, for there was still enough land, game and pasture for both groups to live separately had they wanted to.

The advent of a settled agriculture in South Africa is usually associated with the inward spread of Bantu speakers and of early Iron Age culture, although this process may have been much less straightforward than is often suggested. Originally Bantu speakers spread from today's Cameroon around 1500 BCE, perhaps as a result of advancing desertification on the edge of the Sahara. They spread in two different streams, one south down the Atlantic coast, the other right across the continent to East Africa, reaching the Great Lakes region about 1000 BCE – where they developed ironworking some two centuries later. It was this eastern branch that finally reached South Africa: the western branch, migrating down only as far as Namibia.

The picture becomes more complicated with the further migration of the eastern Bantu to the south. The archaeological data shows a trail of Iron Age tools and pottery usually associated with the eastern Bantu spreading southwards from present-day Tanzania in three streams: to today's Zambia; to present-day Zimbabwe via Malawi; and to what is now KwaZulu-Natal through Mozambique. This migration appears to have been remarkably rapid, with the iron-using people who left East Africa in the second century CE reaching northern South Africa by the end of the third century. By the fourth century they were found throughout central and eastern South Africa. The linguistic data also indicates a rapid expansion but it shows that Bantu languages spread from Tanzania to the Zambezi in a single stream, and that this expansion took place before the emergence of iron tools. The archaeological data is also inconsistent with some finds in Zambia revealing the usage of pottery generally associated both with Bantu speakers and Iron Age implements in sites together with Stone Age tools.

This clearly confirms the now universally accepted view that cultures, technologies, languages and people can move or develop separately, and quite often did. There were no 'tribes' which possessed their own – unique, characteristic and unchanging – culture and language. A language could spread faster than any particular cultural trait, or might even move in different directions from such traits, which could only mean that there was no single stable group of people to whom a particular set of cultural and linguistic traits could be attributed. The European mind tends to work in terms of national stereotypes but none of these stereotypes applied historically – even in the Roman era or during the Asian migrations into Europe. The picture was similar in Africa. But the contradictions and inconsistencies in the data mean that our picture of early Iron Age South Africa is still not entirely clear. Nonetheless, despite occasional inconsistencies between the arch-aeological and linguistic data, the correspondence between them is strong enough to support the conventional view of a direct link between early Iron Age cultures and the contemporary Bantu-speaking popu-lation. Had Iron Age people spoken a non-Bantu tongue it would have left traces in later Bantu languages, just as the Khoisan languages did – but there are no such traces.

These early Iron Age South Africans were agriculturalists. Although they kept some cattle and supplemented their diet by hunting and foraging, the archaeological evidence shows that they relied primarily on agriculture. Accordingly they needed good soil and good rainfall, and for this reason they mostly occupied South Africa's fertile eastern seaboard. They mined or smelted iron, and produced iron tools and a distinctive type of pottery. They seem to have been less interested in symbolism than the San but the clay figures of animals commonly found at the sites of their settlements suggest some form of symbolic and perhaps religious belief.

We know little about the social organisation of these early farmers. Agriculture requires a settled way of life, in turn making for more complex social arrangements – and agriculture can certainly sustain bigger communities than herding. The archaeological data confirms this: the early Iron Age not only saw an increase in the number of settlements but a steady growth in their population.

Given that these new Bantu iron-using settlements were technologically superior to the Khoisan population already there their relationship was problematic, though the fact that their numbers were sparse doubtless made coexistence easier. We know from San rock paintings that there were fights, which the Bantu tended to win, but the two groups also exchanged food and artefacts with one another and there was at least a degree of cohabitation. The Bantu clearly had better weapons, tools, technology and organisation, both in peace and war. But they needed the Khoi because they were richer in cattle and knew cattle herding better, just as they needed the San because of their rainmaking skills, their knowledge of charms and poisons, and their hunting and tracking abilities. Perhaps most important, the Bantu needed the Khoisan in order to legitimise their occupation of the land, for the Khoisan were the original 'owners'. Thus many Khoisan continued to live among the Bantu and gradually more and more of them were absorbed into these Bantu Iron Age communities as clients and partners. This process would in practice have consisted of polygamous Bantu men choosing Khoisan wives, a process which would have seen Khoisan mothers teaching their children some of their own language, which is doubtless how Bantu languages came to incorporate Khoisan click sounds and various Khoisan words.

This happy coexistence did not last. The Bantu must have soon noticed the benefits of the Khoisan pastoral economy. Once you had enough cattle there was an easy supply of milk and meat with far less hard work than was required in raising crops. So the Bantu began to accumulate cattle too. By the end of the early Iron Age, in the last centuries of the first millennium, cattle had begun to play an increasingly important role in their whole economy and way of life, and though many continued with agriculture as well, by the beginning of the late Iron Age some of these Bantu had let agriculture slip to the point where they too were predominantly pastoralist.

The rise of Bantu pastoralism made life much more difficult for those Khoisan groups which had not yet been assimilated – particularly the San element among them – for there was now outright competition for cattle, pastures and hunting grounds. Without doubt many of the San rock paintings showing the San fighting and losing to their stronger neighbours derive from this period. Apartheid ideologues took comfort in this notion of black vs black conflict which tended to make the later conflicts between white farmers, Bantu and Khoisan part of a more 'natural' larger picture – 'we may have subjugated the Bantu but that's nothing compared with the way they exterminated the Bushmen'. This in turn led later politically correct historians to reject the perfectly clear evidence of conflict between the two groups in the name of 'deconstructing the apartheid myth'. This is just as silly as it was for apartheid apologists to overlook the equally clear archaeological evidence of coexistence and co-operation between Khoisan and Bantu. In fact, the heightened competition between Khoisan and Bantu drove more Khoisan into becoming clients of Bantu farmers while others found refuge higher up in the Drakensberg. Those in the really difficult situation were the remaining Khoisan who neither retreated to the mountains nor became clients. Some did hang on somehow – the archaeological data shows that Iron Age Bantu and Stone Age Khoisan communities continued to coexist during the late Iron Age era and there were still Khoisan groups to the east of the Drakensberg in the eighteenth and nineteenth centuries, well after the arrival of the white farmers. After that, however, these Stone Age settlements disappeared: contrary to the old apartheid version, it seems to have been the arrival of the whites which dealt them their final *coup de grâce*.

The growth of Bantu pastoralism in the last centuries of the first millennium was followed by a major shift in the whole pattern of settlement and economy throughout the eastern side of the African continent, including South Africa, as better and more sophisticated tools appeared, allowing a considerable technological leap forward at the beginning of the new millennium. This move to late Iron Age technology ushered in a period of striking and rapid change.

For the new technology had a multiplier effect. It enabled stone to be cut and thus saw the widespread use of stone as a building material for the first time. A new type of pottery appeared. More striking still, the benefits of iron tools were now so obvious that a large-scale mining industry was born with a proliferation of mining sites. Inevitably specialisation of skills followed, opening up trading possibilities so that soon long-distance trade emerged for the first time.

For a while these late Stone Age settlements coexisted with early Iron Age settlements but from about 1400 BCE these late Iron Age settlers began to move further west and to far higher altitudes than the early Iron Age settlements had ever done, spreading into the highveld of present-day Gauteng and the Free State. Although early Iron Age settlements continued – some well into the colonial era – late Iron Age sites proliferated and began to dominate the eastern part of South Africa.

Today's South African Bantu speakers are clearly the direct descendants of this late Iron Age population but the nature of the human link between early Iron Age and late Iron Age cultures is less clear. The differences between the two groups became so marked that it is tempting to hypothesise that they resulted from some large new migratory movement – but there is no evidence for this. It seems more likely that these differences developed locally, perhaps as a result of the accumulation of cattle wealth and the concomitant growth of the human population.

By this time the fertile lowlands and river valleys had already been occupied by early Iron Age settlements so these new late Iron Age communities sought pastures on the higher grounds of the highveld. Timber was scarce there – which doubtless acted as a spur to building in stone. Similarly, the less lush highveld made it impossible to sustain large villages and encouraged dispersion into smaller settlements. Finally, the new style of ceramics is attributed by some to a shift of pottery making from men to women. Of this there is no direct proof but analogues exist in other societies in Africa and such a notion makes sense: with the move to the highveld men's time would be needed far more for cattle herding. This would certainly fit in with the great drive towards specialisation visible in every area of late Stone Age life. This specialisation of functions changed the shape of communities so that they became far more diverse than hitherto. The fact that we get much of our information from early European observers who viewed African society as static should not fool us into believing that it actually was.

This specialisation and diversity both required and thrived on the development of trade. Naturally, there had always been some exchange of goods between local communities but the difference now was that some goods were bought not because local communities could not produce such goods for themselves but because they found it more profitable to specialise in some other area and then exchange their produce. Trade grew rapidly, connecting late Iron Age communities not only with one another but with the outside world. And trade brought the growth of the state: the first Swahili city-states had grown up on the East African coast from the middle of the eighth century, acting as intermediaries for trade right across the Indian Ocean, connecting the East African interior with countries as distant as Oman, India and China. Similarly, the first South African state, Mapungubwe, had emerged before the end of the tenth century.

A prominent feature of this late Iron Age economy was mining. The basic technology of iron casting could obviously be applied to other metals, so not only iron but copper, tin and gold were mined by late Iron Age communities in South Africa. The extent of mining was staggering: Iron Age mines were counted not in the dozens or scores but in the hundreds. Later, white settlers would claim that they had provided the know-how for mining, Africans the labour – but actually many thousands of tons of rock containing iron and copper were excavated long before the whites ever arrived. The biggest mining areas were at Phalaborwa and around Messina. Gold and copper were mined to be sold down to the coast while iron and tin were mined mainly for local consumption.

The unsolved mystery about the mines is that the ancient mine shafts, especially copper mine shafts, were very narrow, leading some to suggest that women and children were used as miners – but there is no evidence for this. Perhaps the miners were the diminutive descendants of the Khoisan population, which continued to be assimilated into Bantu groups right into the late Iron Age.

South Africa's late Iron Age societies were complex and rather rigid, with a hierarchy based on a division of labour and power between both the sexes and age groups. Cattle played a central social role as both the main symbol and the main measurement of wealth, and it was no accident that all tasks connected with cattle (herding, protecting, cleaning, milking, slaughtering, processing the skins, etc.) were performed by men. Young boys herded sheep and cattle, unmarried men protected the herds and rustled the neighbours' cattle, married men participated in the many conflicts and wars fought over cattle or grazing while older men used their ownership of cattle as the basis of their prestige and power. Small specialised groups of men were also responsible for the key economic activity of mining.

Age groups were strictly defined, with each new generation given its own name which it bore throughout the lives of its members. History was measured in terms such as 'this happened when [generation name] were warriors ...' Complicated and dangerous initiation rites accompanied the transition from childhood to adulthood, showing the great seriousness and importance attached to becoming a full member of the group.

The occupations of women, who maintained the household and engaged in foraging and other agricultural activities, were also defined by age and they too underwent initiation. Women were perceived as a different kind of wealth not only because they were the most important part of every household's labour force but because the more children they had the stronger and more powerful their husbands were. They were thus interchangeable with cattle in the form of bride wealth, the price in cattle a man had to pay for his bride to her family. This also served the purpose of tying together the polygamous and patrilineal family structure with an economic bond.

Households were usually shared by extended families or lineages made up of the descendants of a single male ancestor, with the young men leaving over time to form new lineages. When several lineages claimed a more distant common ancestry they constituted a clan – which might be either exogamous or endogamous. Several clans together could develop into a territorial unit or chiefdom, a development which usually occurred through one of the clans gaining sufficient wealth to overpower their neighbours militarily or, at least, politically.

This social organisation was a powerful mechanism for maintaining order within a community and thus of strengthening its survival chances but it was brutally unequal. Its whole thrust was aimed at maintaining the power of older men at the expense of women and younger men, of chiefs at the expense of commoners, and of richer lineages and clans at the expense of poorer ones.

South Africa's first polity, Mapungubwe – a large settlement at the northernmost tip of South Africa, close to the intersection of modern-day Botswana, Zimbabwe and South Africa, emerged at the beginning of the late Iron Age and lasted into the twelfth century. Mapungubwe was the first 'big state' in the African interior, mentioned by an Arab author in 916, but never achieved the fame of Great Zimbabwe, which it clearly preceded. Though first discovered in 1933, few South Africans, even today, have heard of this dramatic proof of the antiquity of their civilisation. Partly this was because, unlike Zimbabwe, it left no dramatic ruins behind but it was also because such a discovery stood in sharp contradiction to apartheid ideology and to white colonial prejudice in general. The discovery, when it was not ignored, was simply disbelieved.

Mapungubwe started as an ordinary settlement but, from the ninth century, one particular household began to grow in importance, gradually developing into a large ruler's court on top of a hill. Between 3,000 and 5,000 commoners lived on this plateau, exercising the usual agricultural and artisanal professions but in a state of clientage to the ruling family. By the beginning of the eleventh century Mapungubwe's control had been extended over a number of subordinate settlements as well but what truly distinguished it from other settlements was not so much its size as the fact that – as with city-states elsewhere in Africa and with early states in the world at large – its rise derived from trade.

This trade was organised and controlled by the elite, and it was from this source that the elite derived its wealth and power, for trade brought far greater wealth than either agriculture or animal husbandry could possibly produce. Mapungubwe and later Great Zimbabwe, which existed from the twelfth to the fifteenth centuries, traded with the Swahili city-states on the Mozambican coast, supplying them with gold, copper and ivory from the interior. In exchange they gained a variety of goods including beads and pottery from as far away as India and China. The wealth thus produced was enough to support court officials and an elite beyond that, to pull weaker vassal settlements into a state of clientage and then to exact tribute from them, further extending the empire of Mapungubwe.

Archaeologists have discovered a great deal of pottery and many copper and iron artefacts in Mapungubwe, together with a number of gold objects such as beads, pieces of gold foil and fragments of coiled wire. But the main finds came from the graves of three rulers on top of the hill: a sceptre, a golden bowl, a golden rhinoceros and fragments of other rhinos. Gold was not mined in Mapungubwe or near it so this was either the fruit of trade or, as seems more probable, the rulers had established control over gold mines to the north of the Limpopo, then exporting gold objects on to the coast. It seems likely that the golden objects found in the rulers' graves were symbols of their majesty and power, rather as with similar gold objects found with mummified pharaohs in Egypt. Both the sceptre and the golden rhino have been proclaimed as national treasures in South Africa and the highest national honour is now the Order of Mapungubwe. Despite this – and rather sadly – not one South African in 10,000 has heard of Mapungubwe today.

It would have helped if we knew more – the name of its rulers, for example, or if it had left some ruins. As it was, Mapungubwe declined, leaving no visible trace. Some ascribe this to a change of climate but the reality of the time was the growing power of the far stronger state of Great Zimbabwe, which was to replicate the achievement of Mapungubwe, albeit on a far greater scale. Perhaps Mapungubwe's rulers moved north of the Limpopo: almost certainly many of its population did move to the new growing centre to the north and the early glory that was Mapungubwe melted away, a tale of Ozymandias, leaving only a golden bowl, a sceptre and a golden rhino.

# II
# THE MOVING FRONTIER
◎ ◎ ◎

Tracing a direct link between South Africa's late Iron Age inhabitants and today's Bantu-speaking communities is difficult because, crucially, no written script existed and oral tradition, our main source for setting the history of today's black South Africans into the framework of the past, seldom goes back more than a few centuries. Imagine if European history lacked written sources between, say, 1100 and 1700. We would still be able to locate the continent's modern nations as (roughly) the descendants of its earlier inhabitants but we would have missed the Renaissance, the Reformation, endless wars of religion and much else besides, including the formation of numerous states. Without doubt the missing history of those centuries in Africa would also have included great turmoil, wars and migrations. One cannot stress enough that, contrary to what both apartheid apologists and African nationalists now assume, African society in that era was not stuck in an immobile and changeless tradition.

It is easy to see how this mistake was made. When whites first encountered African societies they saw that their technological and educational development was far behind that of Europe; that, so to speak, African development had apparently stalled in the late Iron Age (though, of course, technically we still all live in the late Iron Age), with some groups at an even earlier stage. Unaware that Africa had made the greatest contribution of all to human development – the evolution of man himself – the settlers and colonial anthropologists alike concluded that this backwardness was somehow 'natural' to Africans, from which it was an easy step to conclude that it was better that they were kept that way. Thus, from the earliest days of colonialism, blacks were discouraged from developing skills which would make them competitive with whites. This prohibition required increasingly tough legislation and brute force to make it work, to keep Africans 'in their (traditional) place'; proof, if such were needed, of how absurd it was to imagine Africans for ever subject to changeless tradition. And yet – such is the power of that original colonial perspective – no sooner had African nationalists come to power than they too often adopted the notion of an unchanging African set of traditions, now viewed through the rosy glow of a lost golden age before the whites.

But both are wrong. No culture or tradition exists outside history: they change and develop just as languages do. So while it is perfectly sensible to talk of Zulus or Englishmen in 1850 or 2000, one has to assume in both cases that the meaning of what it was to be a Zulu or an Englishman at those two dates was actually quite different.

If we go back as far as oral tradition allows – that is, several generations – we can discern five groups of Bantu speakers living in what is today South Africa, though these groups were very unequal in size and influence: the Venda, the Sotho-Tswana, the Nguni, the Thonga and the Lemba. All these groups were Iron Age communities whose economy was based both on agriculture and cattle herding, with cattle as the principal form of wealth that bought everything else – prestige, wives and a clientele of dependants. Cattle also played an important part in most ceremonies and rituals, and its supreme importance was recognised by the fact that while most agricultural work was allocated to women, cattle were looked after exclusively by men. All of these societies depended on a staple diet of sorghum and millet, supplemented by pumpkins and gourds, beer made out of grain and the leaves of wild plants collected by their women. Increasingly, however, this diet was revolutionised by the decision of the Portuguese to import and plant maize in Mozambique. Maize rapidly spread right across southern Africa, becoming the principal staple that it is today.

The Venda, who inhabited the fertile Soutpansberg mountains, were linguistically close to the Shona of contemporary Zimbabwe, and their oral tradition tells of a flight from the north, from the Rozvi – a group who had risen to power in south-western Zimbabwe in the seventeenth century. However, both archaeological and linguistic research show that there was a core Venda population in this area (where they still are today) from very early times, merely incorporating Shona migrants over the centuries. Their way of life was, however, closer to that of the neighbouring Sotho and they borrowed and developed some of the distinct style of the Lemba, the neighbours – and often the subordinates – of the Venda.

For centuries the Venda devoted much energy to mining copper at Musina and iron ore to the south of Soutpansberg, with the Lemba doing most of the metal work. A great deal of this production was exported to the East African coast, first to Sofala and then, after Sofala's eclipse during the eighteenth century, to Inhambane and Delagoa Bay. A Venda polity, Thovela, emerged by the beginning of the century, its ruling family living in stone-walled enclosures similar to those of the Shona. But in the second half of the eighteenth century a group of Shona immigrants calling themselves the Singo conquered the Vendas' territory and founded a new ruling dynasty. They may have been an offshoot of the Rozvi's Changamire dynasty which dominated Zimbabwe from the seventeenth century on, for they built a polity modelled on that of Changamire and received tribute from the entire Venda population. But the Singo were gradually absorbed in the same way earlier Shona migrants had been, adopting Venda language and customs. At the beginning of the nineteenth century, however, the Singo quarrelled and in the ensuing war their polity broke into two independent halves.

Of all South Africa's people none have more confused historical roots than the Lemba who live in scattered groups among the Shona, the Venda and the Pedi, speaking the languages of the surrounding peoples but seldom intermarrying with them. Not only do they remain separate but they have recognisably distinct features and, not-withstanding the mirth such assertions provoke, they claim Jewish origins and observe such Jewish customs as male circumcision and abstention from pork. Some historians believed that they must have got this idea from Moslem traders from the coast but recent DNA studies seem to confirm that the Lemba may indeed be genetically connected with the Jews. Moreover, rather like the Jews of Eastern Europe the Lemba depended not on agriculture but on manufacturing and trading, forming almost a separate caste of skilled iron, copper and gold smelters who would travel long distances in order to exchange their produce. Similarly, Lemba women made and traded a distinctive pottery, much in demand among their neighbours.

To the south of the Venda lies a vast area bordered by the Limpopo river, the Drakensberg mountains and the Kalahari desert, inhabited by a group speaking the closely related Tswana and Sotho languages. Taken together the peoples of this group might be the numerically dominant group in southern Africa today were it not for the fact that the southern Sotho are divided between the Free State province and Lesotho, and the Tswana (or western Sotho) between South Africa and

Botswana. Only the northern Sotho live almost entirely inside South Africa. Archaeological evidence suggests that their ancestors may have lived in what is today Gauteng ever since the original Bantu migration around 1000 CE. It is not clear when the present Tswana-Sotho lineages emerged, though the Fokeng were clearly the oldest lineage, so that all Sotho and Tswana trace their ancestry either from this lineage or the later 'founding lineages', the Kwena, the Kgatla and the Rolong, all of which had emerged by the sixteenth century and developed into separate political entities during the seventeenth and early eighteenth centuries.

As early as 1661 the Dutch at the Cape heard about a people who were recognisably the Tswana. Since there was no direct link between the Cape and the interior at that date this information could only have come from traders plying the Indian Ocean coast. For already the Tswana were active traders, their trade routes running in three directions: eastwards to Delagoa Bay, north-west into the Okavango valley and central Namibia, and later south to the Kora on the Orange river. They sold furs, copper, iron and tin decorations and tools, tobacco and, perhaps most important, ivory, and in exchange they bought beads, buttons, cloth and livestock. Some Tswana lineages specialised – the Tlhaping and Hurutshe, for example, competed over trade in metals while the Hurutshe also grew and exchanged tobacco. The ivory trade was a particularly lucrative business and there was a lot of competition around it but at least equally important was the trade in ivory and copper with Quelimane from 1760 on. The Tswana traded through a chain of partners, all of whom they knew, right down the trading route as far as the Tsonga on the east coast – a distance of over 1000 kilometres.

During the seventeenth and early eighteenth centuries the growth and territorial expansion of the Sotho-Tswana communities resulted in multiple fissures, with many new lineages splitting away from the four founding lines. The Fokeng fragmented into several groups which, however, all kept the original name. The Kwena also fragmented and split. Some fragments kept the founder's name but some founded new lineages such as the Ngwaketse and the Ngwato. The Rolong, who had risen to prominence in the seventeenth century, became even more powerful under their ruler Tau in the early eighteenth century – before losing some of their population to the new chiefdom of Tlhaping, which had become independent by the end of the eighteenth century. The Rolong themselves split into four chiefdoms: no centralised power lasted long among the Sotho-Tswana.

But despite these fissures the population was simultaneously concentrating into large settlements, particularly in the western part of the Sotho-Tswana country. The South African section of the Tswana, made up of the Rolong, the Hurutshe and the Tlhaping, lived in large stone-built towns of 10,000–25,000 people. One or two such settlements, together with their surrounding agricultural and grazing areas, could house a whole community. Some settlements – the best-known examples being the Rolong's Dithakong and Taung, built in the seventeenth and eighteenth centuries – had stone walls around them for, of course, the process of fissure was often not achieved peacefully.

Historians have argued about the reasons for these apparently contradictory processes of fission and population concentration in Tswana societies. It may be that population growth and land shortage were the reason for both processes. For while there was plenty of land in absolute terms, a great deal of it was unusable either because it lacked water or was infested with tsetse flies. Others have argued that the scarcity of water and the variety of soils required strict co-ordination of agricultural activity and thus concentrated settlement – though undoubtedly these larger settlements gave an extra degree of protection.

Historians sometimes refer to the Sotho-Tswana communities as constituting polities or even states but these terms are used loosely and the situation within the Tswana communities was in any case fluid. A 'chief' – kgosi in Tswana, nkosi in Zulu – could be an authority at different levels with varying powers. In the seventeenth and eighteenth centuries the administrative structure of these communities was based on kinship, which suggests that chiefdom would be a better term than polity.

The smallest unit of Tswana society was an extended family household. Several such households, all descended from a common male ancestor and situated close to one another in a settlement, formed a lineage in which the chief authority was the senior male descendant of the common ancestor. Several lineages either formed a distinct ward within a town or a separate settlement of their own. Several units would be grouped together under a kgosi who represented supreme power within them. These clusters or chiefdoms constituted the political, social and economic basis of Tswana society. It was only in the late eighteenth and early nineteenth centuries that new structures emerged which included families that were not kin and in which there was a distinct social stratification of the population – signs that they were turning into true polities.

The Tswana economy, though based on herding and agriculture, depended heavily on trade. Although there was only one mine in all the Tswana territory, some Tswana chiefdoms – the Rolong and Hurutshe in particular – developed iron smelting on a considerable scale. Each cluster of units under a *kgosi* traded with other chiefdoms and with the Indian Ocean coast in cattle, skins, metal work and, from the middle of the eighteenth century, in ivory. The Rolong, who dominated the area to the south of the Molopo river, controlled the trade between present-day Namibia and the Orange river while the Hurutshe controlled the trade between the southern Kalahari and what is today Gauteng, as well as operating a trade network connected to the Tsonga on the east coast.

The Sotho-Tswana groups seem always to have been dogged by quarrels – sometimes with outsiders like the Kora but most particularly with one another. The eighteenth and early nineteenth centuries saw the intensification of such civil strife, perhaps as a result of competition for the control of the lucrative – and continually growing – trade with the east coast, with a particular demand for the ivory the Tswana could supply aplenty from the vast elephant herds which roamed their territory – as, in Botswana, they still do today. It is possible, too, that the growth of the nearby Oorlam and Bastaard-Griqua communities at the turn of the nineteenth century and the growth of trade with the Cape produced further occasions for conflict.

The Sotho-Tswana were, then as now, scattered across a vast territory and had to adjust to a variety of different environments – which explains why the three branches of the Sotho-Tswana developed differently, politically and socially, and in the end developed different dialects of their common language.

The southern Sotho, comprising the Fokeng, the Kwena, the Tlokwa, the Taung, the Sia, the Phuthing and the Kgoloko lineages, occupied a higher, more mountainous terrain than the Tswana, with soils and pastures of poorer quality. Pastures often had to be a long way from the villages and separate cattle posts established, some of which developed into new villages over time. By the beginning of the nineteenth century, however, this process had run its course: the surplus grazing land had all been taken and, uncomfortably, population density grew. Thus, unlike the Tswana, the southern Sotho lived in mere villages of fifty to a hundred inhabitants, though a few settlements were larger. These scattered southern Sotho settlements were inevitably more independent. Trade was both far less and more localised than among the Tswana and, as a result, there was far less of an economic gap between them and the Khoisan with whom, accordingly, they frequently intermarried – with the result that the Sotho language incorporated Khoisan click sounds.

The northern Sotho, comprising the Pedi, Pulana, Kutswe, Pai, Roka, Koni, Tau and Lobedu lineages, were the most linguistically and culturally diverse group among the Tswana–Sotho speakers – yet they were the first to create a centralised polity.

In the mid-seventeenth century the Maroteng, who were to form the nucleus of the Pedi polity, moved from their area near today's Pretoria and settled in the Steelpoort river valley. By the later eighteenth century this strong and wealthy Maroteng chiefdom began to expand its power. For the Maroteng displayed an unusual skill in metalwork which they turned to good account by acquiring more cattle which, together with metal hoes, they were able to use as bride payments, attracting more wives and becoming more populous. As their power grew the Maroteng fought a series of wars of expansion, bringing more and more of their neighbours under their paramountcy. The resulting Pedi polity which the Maroteng founded in the late eighteenth century consisted of several chiefdoms which continued to enjoy a relative autonomy even after their military defeat. The loyalty of the chiefs was ensured by making them take Maroteng women as their main wives, thus gradually making the ruling group more homogeneous – and meanwhile these chiefs had to fight for the Maroteng whenever required.

The population of the chiefdoms which constituted the Pedi polity lived in settlements numbering anywhere between fifty and 5,000 people. Such settlements were run by the *kgoro* – elders – in fact all adult males, whose meetings, also called *kgoro*, were presided over by a *kgosi* (chief), who listened to the debate and then pronounced his verdict. Paramount chiefs, who possessed supreme judicial power, also regulated land relations, oversaw the bonding of the society through marriage and through the creation of clienteles, and were held responsible for the well-being of the whole society.

This bonding process, together with a relatively strong chieftaincy, gave the Pedi a clear military advantage. They reached the peak of their power in the early nineteenth century when, during the reign of paramount chief Thulare, their military expeditions reached the Vaal river in the south and what is today Rustenburg in the west. To the north the Pedi were attracted by the rainmaking abilities of the Lobedu 'rain queens' who ruled the Lobedu from the beginning of the nineteenth century and they moved to incorporate the Lobedu chiefdom – where the Pedi language became increasingly widespread.

The power of the Pedi polity, led by its Maroteng chiefs, was enhanced by trade for the Pedi were ideally placed to exchange metal goods from the Phalaborwa region. By the end of the eighteenth century they were part of the trade route between Delagoa Bay and the central and western highveld. Their counterparts on the coast were the Tsonga to whom they sold cattle, skins and ivory, buying European and Asian fabrics and beads in return – which they then exchanged for the produce of areas further to the west. Maroteng tradition claims that during Thulare's reign they established direct contact with Delagoa Bay.

Some non-Sotho-speaking groups lived among the Sotho and were collectively called the 'trans-Vaal Ndebele'. Their origins are unclear though oral tradition places them on the highveld as early as the sixteenth and seventeenth centuries, and they may actually have been there long before the Sotho. These trans-Vaal Ndebele occupied the steep (and easily defensible) hilltops of the middle and upper Limpopo valley. Sotho-Tswana speakers called them Matabele, perhaps from '*go tebela*' – 'to strike or knock about with a fist' – for among the surrounding population their image was that of brigands and mercenaries. They certainly rustled as well as traded cattle, though some developed more sophisticated skills. The Laka, for example, produced iron, copper and tin, the Malete became rainmakers, while others turned to mining and iron smithing. By the nineteenth century some of these trans-Vaal Ndebele were still speaking their own language though others had become completely integrated into Sotho-Tswana society and spoke its language. Solving the riddle of the origins of the trans-Vaal Ndebele is important: the answer could help us to understand where the Nguni (to whom they may be related) came from before settling on the east coast, and how long they have been there.

Until the second half of the eighteenth century the hinterland of the coastal area around Delagoa Bay was occupied by the Tsonga (or Thonga or Shangaan), intrepid traders who spoke a Bantu language quite different from either the Sotho or Nguni languages. For centuries they traded with the Swahili speakers and Arabs, then with the Portuguese, selling iron, copper, ivory and later slaves from the interior and buying beads, fabrics, crockery, brassware, guns and other Asian and European commodities. In order to reach their suppliers in the interior the Tsonga sometimes used intermediaries such as the Pedi but they also travelled great distances themselves. Goods from Delagoa Bay have been found as far south as the Mzimvubu river and one European witness even encountered Tsonga traders deep in the Eastern

Cape. The first known Tsonga group to control the trade were the Thembe but by the end of the eighteenth century it had been taken over by the Mabhudu, who had emerged as the main force on the Makatini flats between the Lebombo mountains and the Indian Ocean in what is today KwaZulu-Natal.

The origins of the Nguni, the Tsongas' neighbours down the east coast, are unclear, but by the sixteenth century, when they were first mentioned by shipwrecked European travellers, they were already well established there – indeed, some accounts place them there in the tenth century. Nguni is not a self-name; it is used simply as a convenient linguistic classification. The subdivision of the Nguni into two groups, the northern and the southern – ancestors of what are now South Africa's dominant groups, the Zulu and Xhosa – also had little meaning before the beginning of the eighteenth century. Even today the Zulu and Xhosa languages remain so close that a member of one group can always understand a member of the other.

Until the late eighteenth century the Nguni lived in relatively small, decentralised communities. After that, perhaps because of the growth of the Delagoa Bay trade, this started to change as several groups began to expand in size and power – among the Tsonga, the Thembe and Mabhudu, followed by the Ngwane, Ndwandwe and Mthethwa among the northern Nguni.

The Ngwane, the most northerly of the Nguni groups, were ruled by the Dlamini lineage who, according to oral tradition, had lived in the coastal area around Delagoa Bay for a long time before they came under pressure from the Thembe in the late eighteenth century. As a result during the reign of King Dlamini III they migrated southwards and settled in what is now southern Swaziland, conquering the Sotho speakers they found there – though in the process the Ngwane borrowed much Sotho vocabulary and many Sotho customs, even adopting the Sotho practice of endogamy (cross-cousin marriage) as opposed to the normal Nguni practice of exogamy.

The Ndwandwe occupied the territory to the south of the Phongolo river. During the late eighteenth century, under their ruler Yaka and then under his son Zwide, they subjugated the neighbouring lineages between the Phongolo and the Black Mfolozi river.

The Qwabe, the southernmost of the north Nguni groups, were just one of several independent lineages in their area in the sixteenth and seventeenth centuries. But in the early eighteenth century, under their ruler Kuzwayo, the Qwabe gained control of the Ngoye hills between the Mhlathuze and Thukela rivers, forced the rival Cele and Thuli to move south of the Thukela and then continued to extend their control west of the Ngoye hills.

The Mthethwa occupied the area north-east of the Qwabe, between the Mhlatuzi and the Mfolozi rivers. Already endowed with particularly good land, they also managed to establish control over the lower Mfolozi crossing points, thus gaining much profit from local trade, making them the dominant group in the area by the mid eighteenth century. At the end of the eighteenth century there occurred an event which was to be of crucial significance in South African history. In 1790 Jobe, the ruler of the Mthethwa, sent his senior son Dingiswayo into exile so that upon Jobe's death the succession went to another son, Mawewe. Oral tradition has it that Dingiswayo returned, riding a horse and carrying a gun to chase away Mawewe and establish himself as the new ruler. He built an army in which one of his clients, Shaka, served prior to becoming the most powerful chief that South Africa was ever to see.

By the late eighteenth century the southern Nguni comprised the Xhosa, the Thembu, the Mpondo, the Mpondomise, the Xesibe and the Bomvana. Little is known about the origins of these groups though it seems clear that the first four of them moved from or through the territory of today's KwaZulu-Natal before the seventeenth century to what is now the Eastern Cape.

The Thembu who occupied the hinterland area between the high Mbashe and Great Kei rivers, are said to have a particularly old lineage but it is difficult to date their arrival in the southern Nguni area. One of their early rulers, Nxego, was buried on the Mbashe river in the first half of the seventeenth century, suggesting that the Thembu had arrived there some time before this. Indeed, it seems possible that survivors from a Portuguese ship wrecked off the coast in 1593 may have encountered them at the mouth of the Mbashe. However, from the mid eighteenth century on the Thembu came under pressure from the Xhosa – that is, saw their cattle stolen and their people pressed into labour by Xhosa raiders.

The Xhosa had been the earliest southern Nguni to migrate to their present area and were the southernmost group of these southern Nguni. The Xhosa claim descent from a (possibly mythical) common ancestor, Xhosa, who was said to have ruled in the 1530s, but the true origins of the Xhosa are unknown. Historians agree only that the process of centralisation among the Xhosa began somewhere between the late sixteenth and late seventeenth centuries when the ruler Tshawe made his lineage the dominant one.

As whites expanded into the Eastern Cape the first southern Nguni they encountered were the Xhosa and they then applied this term to all southern Nguni. This was misleading for they were a heterogeneous group with different histories, varied widely in customs (some practised circumcision, others did not) and spoke different dialects: indeed, the Mpondo dialect was closer to that of the northern Nguni than to their southern neighbours.

Like the northern Nguni, the southern Nguni gave an even greater importance to cattle than other Bantu groups. They supplemented their diet with coastal produce such as sugar, pumpkins, bananas – and smoked dagga (marijuana), for probably the best marijuana in the world grows easily in the Eastern Cape. Although the Nguni did not mine any metals the northern Nguni were able to obtain what they required by selling their agricultural produce, particularly dagga, to other Bantu groups to the north or, in the case of the southern Nguni, to whites to their west. The climate also meant that Nguni living habits were different. Most Sotho-Tswana had built large thatched round huts of mud, the low parts of which were often faced with stone for protection from rain. Their cattle enclosures were also stone-walled and the huts were decorated with ornaments drawn in coloured clay. The floors were polished with earth and cow dung. Living along the warmer coastal belt, the Nguni were far less elaborate: they built smaller and lower huts, dome-shaped and made of grass.

For centuries the Nguni had been in close contact with the Khoi. The Nguni languages bore a deep Khoi influence, particularly those of the southern Nguni and especially the Khosa: of fifty-five Xhosa consonants twenty-one are traceable to Khoi languages. Even the self-name of the Xhosa derives from the Khoi term 'angry men'; another rendition is that Xhosa means 'to destroy'. During the eighteenth century the Xhosa actively absorbed the Khoi both as clients and by intermarriage – though some Khoi groups opposed the Xhosa and opted instead to co-operate with the new force emerging from the west, the whites. Nguni relations with the San were also diverse but intermarriage was rare. Nguni trade with the San consisted of cattle and dagga being exchanged for ivory. The relations of the Xhosa with the San were particularly complex: there was a great deal of trade; some San paid tribute to Xhosa chiefs and lived among the Xhosa (at least one Xhosa clan was said to be partly San in origin); and some Xhosa joined San groups – but there was also evidence of Xhosa brutality towards the San.

From about 1715 to 1775 the Xhosa were ruled by Phalo. Little is

known about him or his predecessors but it was during his reign that
the dominant Tshawe lineage split. Phalo's sons, Gcaleka and Rharhabe,
fought over the succession, a war ending in Rharhabe's defeat and
capture. Upon his release he moved across the Kei river, taking the
elderly Phalo with him. Both Phalo and Gcaleka died in the 1770s and
Gcaleka's successor, Khawuta, who ruled from 1778 to 1794, turned
out to be a weak ruler under whom the power of the Gcaleka–Xhosa
started to decline. Rharhabe, on the other hand, built up his power to
the west of the Kei, defeating the neighbouring Khoi and San groups,
and then fought both with Khawuta and with the Thembu. In 1782
both he and his heir, Mlawu, were killed in battle. The next successor,
Mlawu's son, Ngqika, was still a small boy so power was vested in
Ndlambe, Mlawu's brother.

For twelve years Ndlambe continued to strengthen the Rharhabe
Xhosa chiefdom to the west of the Kei, defeating and outmanoeuvring
his local opponents – the smaller Xhosa chiefdom of Dange and the
mixed Xhosa-Khoi chiefdom of Gqunukhwebe. In 1795 came the
inevitable clash with the now adult Ngqika. But Ngqika proved a
talented leader, first defeating Ndlambe – who was captured and held
prisoner in Ngqika's household – and then gained the support of the
Dange and made the Gqunukhwebe pay him tribute. But in 1800
Ndlambe managed to escape from captivity and reorganised his support
to the west of Rharhabe. Having been defeated once by Ngqika,
Ndlambe knew that if he lost again there would be no third chance so
he sought alliance with the growing power of the whites. This fateful
move opened the way to a very different drama with powerful new
players: the era of colonial conquest was now to begin.

# III
# THROUGH A
# PERMEABLE HEDGE

@ @ @

The first Europeans to arrive on South African shores were the Portuguese. In 1488 three ships led by Bartolemeu Dias sailed round the Cape in an attempt to find a sea route to India. This was just one further step in the long quest to find an easier way to bring the gold, spices and silks of the East to Europe. Crucially, maritime technology was developing fast: with their new types of ships, the caravels and carracks, and new navigation technology such as the astrolabe, the cross-staff and the magnetic compass, the Portuguese could circumvent their old enemy, the Moslem Moors. With Europe's technological advantage now increasing with every year it was merely a matter of time before South Africa became one of the early fruits of colonial endeavour.

Dias missed the Cape on his outward journey and landed in Mossel Bay. He then sailed further east but turned back once he had ascertained that the newly discovered land was now unfolding steadily northwards on his port bow for this was the final proof that a sea route to India existed. Hugging the shore on his return journey, Dias was thus the first European to gaze upon Africa's southernmost point.

Only a decade later, following Dias's route, Vasco da Gama's four vessels sailed directly to the Cape, rounded it, sailed across the Indian Ocean and landed in Calcutta. But already much had changed. Columbus's discovery of the Americas in 1492 had led to a formal division of the world between Portugal and Spain. By the Treaty of Tordesillas (1494), the Pope sought to pre-empt any rivalry between these two Catholic powers by drawing a line from pole to pole at a distance 1175 miles west of the Azores, giving Spain all territories (whether discovered or not) to the west of the line and ascribing to Portugal everything to the east. Thus Vasco da Gama had been sent to India in an attempt to explore Portugal's new domains. His voyage was far longer and more dangerous than that of Columbus and its results entirely comparable in historic importance with those of his famous contemporary. For da Gama's voyage not only launched the Portuguese colonial empire but was a major step in the globalisation of the world, tying together several of its most distant corners into a new commercial whole.

At first South Africa seemed to have been left behind in this development. Da Gama's voyage resulted in the establishment of several trading posts in Angola, Mozambique and East Africa all the way to Goa (the eastern empire's administrative centre and the seat of its viceroys) and Macao. In less than two decades spices, gold, precious stones and silks were shipped to Lisbon along this network. South Africa had little to offer: the adverse winds and currents at the Cape made landing difficult for outgoing ships, and although fresh water was available there, meat was difficult to procure and wine, fruit and vegetables impossible. Moreover, the local population was generally viewed as unfriendly, to say the least.

Both Dias and da Gama had encountered the local inhabitants whom they described as light-skinned cattle breeders – clearly the Khoi. Da Gama and his successors were amazed to discover how skilful these people were with their cattle: they not only rode their beasts but trained them for war and controlled them by whistling. Dias's meeting with the Khoi had speedily deteriorated into a furious exchange of stones and arrows. Da Gama fared better at first: the Khoi provided his men with meat and offered flute music with dancing, a favour returned with a trumpet concert. However, a quarrel broke out and da Gama's men ended by discharging a cannon at those they had been serenading shortly before. Further trouble followed. In 1503 Antonio de Saldanha landed in the bay that has since borne his name but could not even get fresh water before his men were ambushed by the Khoi. In 1510 Admiral Francisco de Almeida seems to have tried to take some cattle from the Khoi who responded by riding their cattle into battle against him, killing him and fifty of his men.

This resolute opposition discouraged the Europeans from further contact, especially since South Africa seemed unlikely to become a good source of slaves. This was not because the Khoi could protect themselves better than other victims of the slave trade; on the contrary, what protected them was their weakness rather than their strength. Elsewhere in Africa the slavers were able to find powerful and efficacious chiefs or even states perfectly willing to deliver large numbers of their neighbours and countrymen into slavery for the right price. But such centralised and well-organised intermediaries did not exist anywhere near the Cape and without that there was no way of achieving a steady and sustainable supply of slaves from the interior. So, although a smattering of slaves were captured and borne off to the sugar plantations of Madeira and Latin America, for most of the sixteenth century South Africa was largely left alone.

From the early seventeenth century on, however, the ships of several European nations, particularly those of the rising powers, Britain and Holland, began to visit South Africa more often. The Dutch and British East India Companies, both established early in the seventeenth century, had brought about a steep rise in the volume of trade as well as a century-long rivalry. At first the Dutch had the upper hand. The Dutch company, with its head office in Batavia (present-day Djakarta) took over the Portuguese trading posts and established new forts and trading stations all over the Indian Ocean and en route to its Asian empire. However, it shared the access to Table Bay with the British, and for several decades the Cape was used as a transit landfall and post office where the crews of outgoing ships left letters to be collected by those on their return trip.

Favourable reports about the Cape from passing ships and ship-wrecked sailors led to two unsuccessful attempts by the British to settle convicts at Table Bay early in the seventeenth century, spurring the Dutch to take the initiative, and on 6 April 1652 three ships carrying settlers and led by a Company employee, Jan van Riebeeck, docked at Table Bay – the event which until 1994 was celebrated as the foundation of South Africa.

The need for a settled community was obvious. The settlers could provide passing ships with the fruit and vegetables necessary to combat scurvy and with meat and water on an easier and more regular basis than the Khoi were ever likely to do. They could also look after sick sailors left behind with them who could be put aboard their ships in good health on the return voyage. Today, perceptions of the event that inaugurated white settlement in South Africa are dramatically polarised. Many whites still see Van Riebeeck's arrival as the beginning of a fundamentally benign process which left South Africa as the most modern state on the continent. Many African nationalists say that 1652 simply marks the beginning of colonial oppression: in any case, they argue, blacks can hardly see this as a foundation event since their forefathers 'were here long before Van Riebeeck arrived'. The fact that Van Riebeeck longed to leave South Africa – and soon did so – hardly makes the argument easier. This argument is, of course, pointless and has more to say about contemporary attitudes than about history.

Before the new settlers could begin supplying ships with food they had to depend on initial rations from those ships and on a very uneven supply of meat from the Khoi. The local Khoi had to be invited, induced and sometimes forced to barter their goods – particularly cattle – for tobacco, guns and gunpowder. Relations between black and white quickly deteriorated into 'the first Hottentot war' (1658–60), as the settlers called it, 'Hottentot' being their name for the Khoi. The colonists numbered only a few dozen but the Khoi were divided and often fought among themselves. By the end of 1660 they had to recognise that they had lost the Liesbeek lands to the colony (today's Cape Town and southern suburbs). Van Riebeeck ordered that the colony's boundary be demarcated by a fence and a hedge of bitter almonds planted from Salt river mouth to the slopes of Table mountain behind Wynberg. This was to remain the only properly demarcated boundary until the end of the eighteenth century.

The hedge was, of course, merely symbolic and neither the Khoi nor the Dutch made any effort to stay on 'their' side of it. Sex alone made that unlikely. In 1660 the colony had only forty-six free adults and fourteen children. Even twelve years later there were only sixty-four free men or, with the garrison, 370 – but there were very few marriageable women. Extramarital relations with Khoi women were correspondingly common. Van Riebeeck, however, recommended official marriages, and in 1656 the first mixed marriage between a white colonist, one Van Meerhof, and Eva, a Khoi woman, took place, though many more Khoi women lived in concubinage with settlers in Cape Town – 'De Kaap', as it was called.

At first few colonists settled at the Cape. The initial arrivals had had to endure considerable hardship and the settlement's future was anyway unclear. The only incentive for immigration lay in land for private farming but the Company allowed only a handful of its officials to establish such farms. Even twenty-five years later there were only three dozen privately owned farms. The year 1689 saw the biggest influx of new settlers, when about 180 Huguenot refugees arrived from France. However, after a clash between free burghers and the local administration early in the eighteenth century the Company made no attempt to attract new settlers for another half-century. Even by the end of the Company's rule in 1795 the colony had only about 15,000 free burghers.

The new Governor, Simon van der Stel, had already founded Stellenbosch where he gave the settlers freehold land but the Huguenots' arrival lent crucial impetus. They settled in the Berg river valley at Drakenstein and what is now Franschoek, and by the end of the seventeenth century, together with Dutch and German colonists, they had spread to Paarl, Wagenmakers' Vallei and the Land van Waveren. The colony's boundary expanded continuously thereafter.

The nomadic pattern of the Khoi's economy created the impression that there was ample land, unoccupied and unused, in the Cape. The Khoi may have seen it differently but they were in no position to oppose, let alone prevent, the occupation of the land by those wielding superior weaponry. From 1652 till 1701 the Company distributed freehold plots of up to 135 acres in size and by the end of the seventeenth century all the land on the Cape peninsula was allocated. In 1702 the Company introduced a new system which allowed it to distribute much bigger farms, averaging 6,000 acres, 'on loan' – a status involving a yearly payment of a nominal sum. If a farm proved a success the 'loan' could be converted into freehold ownership; if it were a failure it could simply be abandoned. By 1750 more than 100 million acres were thus claimed.

Ironically, the Company's decision to allocate such huge farms may have derived from its wish not to allow more free burgers to settle in the Cape lest, gaining in numbers, they would want to get rid of the Company's rule. This tenure system meant that the new farmers could not cultivate their land themselves but would have to be landlords with large numbers of tenants, workers or slaves. Thus even with a much higher level of production the number of free burghers would remain relatively small.

In the seventeenth and early eighteenth centuries the colony was ruled by the Governor-General of the Indies and by the Company's governing body in Amsterdam, but from the late seventeenth century on, the Cape had its own Governor and a Political Council, representing the merchants and burghers, which acted as a regulatory and judicial body.

Until the early eighteenth century the colony's economy was organised around its initial *raison d'être*, the supply of the passing ships. The Company had a monopoly on these supplies and on virtually all economic activity in the colony, and it issued leases for the production and sale of spirits, wine, tobacco, oil, vinegar, grain and meat. Some of the leases were dropped by the early eighteenth century but all requests by the burghers to sell grain and wine independently were rejected.

However, private farming and trade were still lucrative – so much so that even governors, let alone lower officials of the Company, moved into private farming and trade. Two successive Governors, the father and son, Simon and Willem Adrian van der Stel, who governed the Cape in the late seventeenth and early eighteenth centuries, transferred particularly huge estates into their own hands, provoking much indignation among the free burghers and farmers. Adrian van der Stel's attempt to allocate lucrative meat supply contracts to his friends proved the last straw and a movement of protest was started by the free burghers, Henning Huising and Adam Tas. A petition was sent to Amsterdam in 1705 and the Company dismissed van der Stel and confiscated his estate.

The settlers, who shared common economic and political interests, were thus further united by their common reaction to the governors' policies. Despite their varying origins, by the early eighteenth century they began to develop a degree of homogeneity on the basis of the Dutch language and the Dutch Reformed Church. And thus, slowly – as the masterful de Kiewet, a great South African historian, puts it – the Boer race was formed during 'the long quietude of the eighteenth century'. Contrary to Verwoerdian myth, this was a race formed with continuous admixtures of Khoi, mixed-race and other partners. Indeed, for the early burghers it must have been obvious, given the paucity of white women, that it could not be otherwise. Moreover, the Company pledged early on 'to Christianise' the Khoi and so Khoi children were admitted to the school together with white children and some slave children.

Such 'liberties' were soon to stop. As the number of white women increased, so the pressure for segregation grew – a pattern seen everywhere in Africa, for white women could be relied on to oppose à l'outrance unfair competition from black and mixed-race concubines. Moreover, continued agricultural expansion meant a growing demand for labour, which could hardly be met if Khoi, slave and mixed-race children were all brought up as whites. But while the general segregationist trend became obvious early in the colony's existence, the policy was not always consistent. Thus, while as early as 1685 Commander van Rheede prohibited marriages between Europeans and 'free blacks' (usually liberated slaves), even if they were Christian, church records show that such marriages made up a whole 10 per cent of all European marriages to the end of the eighteenth century. And official policy veered back too: as late as 1752 Governor Ryk Tulbagh proclaimed that 'free blacks' should enjoy the same rights as free burghers. But as the white community grew, so did the power of its social taboos. By the time Company rule ended in 1795 it was already firmly established that the mixed-race children of whites and 'free blacks' were excluded from white society.

In the first decades of the colony's existence the Khoi were not readily available for agricultural work. One possibility would be to import slaves but this was an unattractive option for Company officials: it meant having to invest in procuring them and again to house them when they arrived, together with all the attendant problems of having to regulate the slave trade, deal with runaways and so on. So the Company decided instead to subcontract its own labourers, or *knechts*, to the farmers. These were Company employees – some of them freed slaves – despatched to South Africa and loaned to farmers on contracts, though there were also free knechts who worked for higher salaries without contracts. Between 1658 and 1707 there were 424 free knechts in the colony, constituting more than a quarter of all free adult men. From the Company's point of view the system was simplicity itself; no capital investment was required and it could even make a profit out of hiring them out.

From the point of view of the burghers and farmers the system was a great deal less satisfactory. Whether free or contracted, knecht wages were relatively high and the knechts didn't really want to be workers: whenever they could they opted to become landowners themselves. Thus, this form of labour was used in earnest only in the seventeenth century. Thereafter the declining number of knechts were mostly employed as overseers.

What the burghers wanted was slaves. Slaves were cheaper, they reproduced themselves, and they could be hired out or hired in for a much lower remuneration than knechts would require. In other words the country was 'condemned to slave labour', as the historian Eric Walker put it, the moment it introduced large land grants to free burghers in the absence of readily available labour.

According to Robert Shell, the premier historian of South African slavery, the first slaves arrived in 1658–9. By 1717 there were already 8,589 slaves in the colony – more than the number of settlers. In 1783 the slave population stood at 14,561; in 1807 (when the slave trade was abolished) at 31,558; in 1834, the year of slave emancipation, at 36,278. It should be noted that all statistics about the slave population have to be treated with caution because of the intricacies of the legal status of some categories of slaves and because not all of them were registered.

The first slaves to be brought to the Cape were from West and Central Africa but the Company naturally looked east so by the first half of the eighteenth century the majority of slaves were imported from India and Ceylon (now Sri Lanka) and after 1750 the majority came from the Indonesian archipelago and Madagascar. After Holland was defeated in the Anglo-Dutch war of 1780–4 the Company's trade rapidly declined, and most slaves thereafter were brought by the British and the French from Madagascar, the Mascarene Islands and Mozambique, this last reflecting the increased role of Portuguese slavers in the trade.

One of the most important sources of slaves was, of course, slave society itself. According to Shell, by the mid eighteenth century 30 per cent of all the Cape's slaves were born there. By the 1780s this figure had risen to 50 per cent and by the 1830s to 75 per cent. Not only did slave owners encourage slave women to have children but they often fathered these children themselves, sometimes living with their female slaves as husband and wife. Even in that case the owner gained another slave – for any child of a slave woman remained a slave (just as a child of a free woman and a male slave was free). Indeed Creole (mixed-race) slaves were particularly valued because they were generally better educated and less prone to rebel or 'misbehave' in other ways.

South Africa's slave-owning past fails to trouble or even mark the memory of contemporary South Africa in the way that it still scars the consciousness of the USA or the West Indies. This is so for an ironic set of reasons. White liberals tended to be English speakers, heavily influenced by the conventional British view, which was that slavery was always a relatively small phenomenon in South Africa, was anyway sharply inhibited by the abolition of the slave trade in 1807, only twelve years after Britain took over the Cape, then ended altogether by the abolition of slavery throughout the British Empire in 1833. This did not deal with the fact that slavery was an integral part of Cape life for 180 years and that slaves often outnumbered freemen.

Second, the descendants of the slaves melded into what is now the Cape Coloured community which under white rule was relatively privileged compared with the black majority, and which has, since the advent of democracy, tended to vote with most whites and Asians against the ANC. This is not a community given to remembering its slave roots, particularly since it is so polyglot that few individuals would be able to vouch with any certainty that they were the descendants of slave ancestors. Moreover, given the subsequent upward mobility of the Coloured community, probably few would wish to make such a claim.

But African nationalists also have little to say about the era of slavery. There is a tendency – frequently expressed by President Mbeki – to treat the whole period since 1652 as a simple and undifferentiated history of white oppression. There is little room for real history in such a conception. Moreover, today's African nationalist elite is mainly drawn from groups which had no experience of being enslaved by the whites. Instead, African nationalist indignation is too preoccupied with the more recent wrongs of the twentieth century to spend any time worrying about the far greater oppression a group like the Khoi suffered centuries before.

In fact, the Company tried hard not to enslave the local black population. It wanted to maintain the goodwill of the Khoi and thus early on issued a statute forbidding the enslavement of the local peoples. Accordingly, those Khoi who decided to offer their labour to the burghers and farmers did so on a free and occasional basis. This remained the pattern despite the smallpox epidemic of 1713 which killed many Khoi and scared others away, causing a perceptible shortage of labour in the colony.

Khoi women were usually the first thus to offer their labour. They came without their menfolk and settled in their own huts. Some of these women formed relationships with the household slaves and had children by them. In that case, while the mother remained free the children were obliged to stay and work for their mothers' employers, often until they reached the age of twenty-five – unless their mothers opted to return to their Khoi kin straight after giving birth. This practice – which allowed the de facto enserfment of Khoi children and thus of their mothers – was commonplace long before it was made law in 1775. Other ways of enserfing the Khoi were far cruder. In the frontier areas the settlers would simply capture both Khoi and San and force them to stay on their farms. This practice was, however, dramatically ratcheted up by the abolition of the slave trade in 1807. As the price of slaves rose, Khoi and San labour became particularly valuable.

The Company was itself the biggest importer – and a large employer – of slaves. Ninety per cent of the Company's slaves worked in Cape Town and lived in one huge building, the Lodge – which by 1770 had about a thousand residents. Although the majority of these slaves were agricultural and menial labourers, some were artisans and some even worked as supervisors. Local Company officials were forbidden to own slaves but it was hard to control what happened in Cape Town from Amsterdam or Batavia and in practice many local officials were large slave owners. A few slaves were owned by free blacks but the majority of slaves were, of course, owned by the farmers and burghers, and since it was virtually impossible to regulate the treatment of slaves on far-flung farmsteads and plantations these slaves often had reason to envy those who lived in the Lodge where their treatment was strictly regulated and reasonably humane: they were well fed and their children were baptised and educated at a special school – with those who gained the age of twenty-five given their freedom.

The Cape slave population was a motley ragbag of ethnic and linguistic groups but slave owners had no difficulty in making distinctions between them. Skills – and thus slave prices – were attributed to slaves predominantly on the basis of origin. Indonesian women, for example, had the reputation of being particularly good seamstresses. They were correspondingly expensive and never used for fieldwork. African women slaves who, in America, were to do back-breaking work in the fields under a baking sun, were regarded as domestic workers in the Cape and lived a much gentler life indoors. Slaves from Mozambique were viewed as willing workers who could be used for just about anything, including brutally hard work in the fields. Malays were said to be better at any kind of work which required 'imagination and genius'. But at the apex of slave society stood the Creoles, a small but privileged category. Within the Company Lodge the Creoles acted as slave supervisors and many of the skilled artisan slaves were also Creoles. Inevitably they carried the highest prices, followed by slaves from Indonesia, Africa, India and Madagascar. In some categories women were more expensive than men, perhaps because slave owners had an eye for their sexual services as well.

This stereotyping of slaves by ethnic origin sat easily with the fact that the Company elite and most of the burghers and farmers were – or passed for – white while the 'primitive' Khoisan were black. That is to say, the racial hierarchisation of the social order had already come to seem natural by the end of the eighteenth century. This was true despite the fact that the perception of race itself often rested on some very rough and ready stereotyping, for the reality was that there had already been and still was a considerable amount of racial interbreeding. Both in the Lodge and in slave-owning households the slave population was mixed: it was thought that it was better to have slaves of different origin both for security and efficiency reasons. The result was a racially very mixed society – not only among its 'Coloured' component (a terminology already well entrenched by the beginning of the nineteenth century) but also among its 'whites'. For as Shell points out, 'nearly all Creole slaves in the Lodge were half-breed of European descent' and that, when manumitted, such former slaves 'stood a reasonable chance of passing for "whites"'. Shell is not alone in making the point that Afrikaans is a Creole language, from which fact it derives much of its idiomatic verve and power. Shell goes further, suggesting that even 'the Afrikaner identity, or at least its soul, the Afrikaans language' derives from the 'syncretistic, domestic Creole culture of the Cape's slave population'. Not the least remarkable feature of twentieth-century Afrikaner nationalism was to be its fierce denial of these Creole roots. Indeed, in Verwoerd's heyday South African stamps were franked with the slogan 'Die Wonder Van Afrikaans': by an immense act of bad faith white Afrikanerdom simply claimed Afrikaans as its own creation.

What made this historical sleight of hand possible was South Africa's expansion of scale. Modern South Africans look back to the world of the Cape Colony as their common inheritance, the first instalment of the far larger country – just as Americans living thousands of miles from Plymouth Rock recognise their entire country's infancy in the early dramas of the thirteen colonies. (For South Africans Cape Town is the 'mother city', just as Boston is for Americans.) And yet, just as New England was hardly typical of the whole USA, so the Creolised society of the Cape was atypical of the wider South Africa. The expansion of South Africa saw the incorporation of large populations of Nguni, Sotho-Tswana and other peoples – and at the same time from 1867 on huge new waves of white settlers and Indians poured in, transforming the country's demography, with the resulting national society far less Creolised than the Cape had been. In that new, more racially distinct world it was far easier for the racial formulae both of the National Party and, later, of the ANC to find acceptance.

The employment of notions of 'race' in the highly Creolised society of the eighteenth-century Cape was always somewhat artificial. Neville Alexander is surely right to suggest that the term 'caste' might usefully be substituted for 'race' throughout South African history – for by the end of the eighteenth century the Cape's 'races' could hardly be said to be based on blood, and in many cases 'race' was a malleable category – it was often convenient to classify pretty Coloured girls as white, for example. There is much historical debate about how a strictly racially divided (or caste-divided) society could have emerged in a situation of such considerable Creolisation and whether the situation might have been different if more white labour had been used in the place of slave labour or if the plots of land allocated to white farmers had been smaller, not requiring so much imported labour, or if the Company had allocated such properties to non-whites. But these are mere hypotheticals. Instead, we have the strange paradox that under the Company's rule the Cape was turned into both a racially mixed *and* a racially divided society.

For several decades after its foundation the territory of the colony was limited by the natural border, the Cape Fold mountains. The valleys and plains stretching the fifty miles from Cape Town to these mountains were well settled already by the beginning of the eighteenth century. Originally these mountains were inhabited by Khoi and San beyond the Company's rule but they soon began to be joined by refugees from white rule as Khoi communities, displaced from the Cape and unwilling to be submerged within the colonial order, began to retreat further into the interior. The forceful subjugation of the Khoi continued as colonial rule expanded: in 1739 colonial commandos suppressed the last vestiges of Khoi resistance in the area south of Namaqualand and west of Roggevelt. This created a further wave of refugees. Thus the result of colonial expansion was to send successive waves of Khoi and San flying deeper into the interior.

They were joined by the *drosters*, a mixed bag of runaway slaves, ships' deserters and others fleeing the Company's service – though at first the Khoi were reluctant to welcome them, not only because they were armed and desperate but because they were often pursued by colonial commandos who carried out punitive raids if the Khoi didn't hand them back. Several decades passed before a common interest in survival in the face of this colonial imposition brought the *drosters* and the Khoi closer together.

The early eighteenth century brought a new and far more threatening wave as cattle-farming colonists themselves began to penetrate the mountains. These were the trekboers, thus called to distinguish them from the crop boers, farmers who stayed and grew their crops within the borders of the colony. Sometimes the trekboers were those who had simply been squeezed out of grazing land by the colony's fast growing farming population, for the settlers' families were large and the Roman-Dutch law of inheritance, which divided land equally among all heirs, created an expansionist dynamic of its own, often forcing those who wished to farm to seek new land further afield. But some were doubtless just attracted by the ease with which they could get title deeds in the new territory, or by the desire to escape from the Company's strict control.

By 1720 the trekboers had crossed the Berg and Breede rivers. The 1739 victory over the Khoi opened the passage through the mountains and over the next few years they began to move into the Little Karoo. By the mid eighteenth century they had moved into the plains below the Roggeveld and Nuweveld mountains of the Great Karoo and by the 1770s they had already settled the area of the Camdeboo mountains and begun to move beyond Sneeuberg and Bruintjes Hoogte (near the present-day towns of Graaff-Reinet and Cradock). As in America, the frontier moved continuously as the Company sought to maintain at least some degree of control over the trekboers. In 1743 the eastern frontier was set at the Great Brak river and a new magistracy was created at Swellendam. In 1785 the border was moved to the upper Fish and Bushman's rivers, and a new magistracy created in Graaff-Reinet, with a further magistracy proclaimed at Uitenhage in 1803.

The Company was attempting a hopeless task, for the trekboers' links to the colony became increasingly tenuous. Their roving households (consisting of family members and slaves) were almost self-sufficient for while they relied mainly on cattle farming and hunting they grew some food crops as well. Depending on the weather or the season, they moved their cattle continuously – something they'd learnt from the Khoi – often covering great distances in search of better pastures. Periodically they returned to the Cape bringing hides, meat and ostrich eggs for sale in order to buy gunpowder and other goods which they couldn't make themselves. Such trips were, however, kept to a minimum for they involved unsafe passage over long journeys for little profit.

As the trekboers moved into the interior they frequently sited their farms close to the kraals of the independent Khoi and San they found there for, as in the Cape, they were determined to compel the Khoi to supply them with labour. To this end they often seized not only Khoi cattle but their women and children as hostages. There was little to prevent the trekboers from such brutal practices: the Khoisan could not stand up to them and the Company was too far away. These seizures of women and children devastated Khoisan communities even more than military defeat had. For a while the struggle was intense: by the 1770s commandos were mounted almost continuously throughout the frontier area, crushing resistance, catching the *drosters* and forcing the Khoi into labour servitude. Although a few kraals of independent Khoi remained scattered among the trekboer farms of the Karoo until the late eighteenth century, most surviving Khoi were working on the farms.

For a while the eastern frontier Khoi acted as middlemen between the farmers and the Xhosa, but soon the trekboers made their own contacts with Xhosa communities. Some of the Khoi thus squeezed out were forced into farm work but others got together with runaway slaves to create raiding bands which briefly dominated the area between the Sundays and Great Fish rivers. This inevitably brought down the settlers' wrath upon their heads and the Khoi remnants were remorselessly ground between the settlers and the Xhosa. Some of the Khoi were absorbed by the Xhosa but by 1780 the Khoi in the Cape had simply ceased to exist as an independent group.

The strongest resistance to settler encroachment came from the San inhabiting the Nuweveld mountains to the north of the Great Karoo. They raided the settlers' farms for livestock, sometimes killing the Khoi herdsmen, and by the 1770s large groups of them had combined with runaway farm workers to dominate the territory between Beaufort West and Graaff-Reinet. Settler reprisals were predictably ferocious with commandos of hundreds of farmers and 'loyal' Khoi sent to retaliate. During a single such raid in 1774 some 500 San were killed and 250 more taken prisoner. Since even this did not stop the cattle raids the settlers responded by a policy of virtual extermination.

These desperate last-ditch sagas of resistance were merely chapters in the forced assimilation of the Khoi. In the early eighteenth century some Khoi, retreating from the advancing trekboers, reached the confluence of the Vaal and Harts rivers and linked up with other Khoi already living there to form a group known as the Kora. Several Kora groups then united under Jan Bloem, a German deserter from the Company's service, and fought against the Tswana clans, whose cattle they raided. Paradoxically, some of these cattle were then traded with the colony for guns and ammunition. After Bloem's death his son, also Jan Bloem, inherited his power and played a prominent role in trans-Orangia, the area between the Orange and Vaal rivers.

By the beginning of the eighteenth century the descendants of the Khoi, mixed with slaves – many of them of white parentage – began to emerge as a separate population group called Basters or Bastaards. As late as the eighteenth century it was not uncommon for Basters to own farms in the colony but the growth of the settler farming population and the resulting competition for land saw them either absorbed into the farm labour force or just squeezed out. By the mid eighteenth century this squeezing out process had begun to produce a determined movement of Basters out of the colony, further into the interior. Initially their main area of settlement was Khamiesberg between the

Olifants and Buffalo rivers which they settled as independent farmers but by the 1780s they had begun to feel the pressure of advancing trekboers again and so migrated further north to Namaqualand, inhabited by the Khoi Nama, and to the north-east, to the middle Orange river and the area of the confluence of the Orange and the Vaal, close to where the Kora lived. Word had, of course, travelled back to the colony of the way the Basters had chosen freedom outside the colony and from the late 1770s on large numbers of Khoi and Basters began to leave the colony to join them. This movement provoked fears of a labour shortage in the Cape and led to a ruling of 1774 virtually obliging the Basters and Khoi to serve in the commandos and to the 1775 law allowing farmers to bind children of mixed parentage to stay in their service – but this merely provoked further out-migration.

The intrepid trekker was to become the founding and iconic figure of white South Africa, just as the equally intrepid frontiersman was of WASP America – and in both cases the myth had a power which spread far wider than its original constituency. Even today as one drives across South Africa's magnificent highway system through narrow passes and up vast inclines it is impossible not to stop and wonder at the hardiness and enterprise of those early trekkers. In particular, of course, Afrikaner nationalism was to fasten on the Great Trek of 1838 as its foundation myth.

Far less attention has been paid to the outward waves of movement by the remnants of the Khoi and those of mixed race which preceded the Great Trek by several generations. In fact, both these movements should be placed alongside the continuous outward movement of the trekboers, a series of spreading demographic ripples. The effect is to reduce the apparent significance of the reasons why this or that group left and to focus instead on the centrifugal dynamic set in motion by the spreading settlement of the Cape, a dynamic in which all problems, ambitions and conflicts could be overcome by outward movement. Sadly, nobody in South Africa today celebrates the intrepid Khoi and mixed-race trekkers who turned their back on Dutch rule to brave the perils and hardships of the interior long before the Boers of the Great Trek turned their back on British rule. Only in present-day Namibia, where some of these earliest trekkers ended up, is there any recognition of their pioneering role.

Yet they were a force to be reckoned with. Indeed, by the later eighteenth century the Basters had become the dominant force on the Orange river frontier. They formed the core of the so-called Oorlams who settled among the Nama and incorporated many 'free blacks' and

Khoi. The Oorlams were skilful riders and good shots who raided the length and depth of Namaqualand and southern Namibia, shifting their support back and forth between the white farmers and the Khoi and thus managed to maintain their independence. The Basters inevitably bore Dutch names and were the first group to call themselves Afrikaners. The first group of Basters to settle in the mid-Orange river area was led by the Kok and Barends families but a following group led by Klaas Afrikaner and his son, Jager Afrikaner, pushed these first arrivals further east towards the confluence of the Orange and Vaal rivers. The missionaries of the London Missionary Society, who began their work among these Basters at the end of the eighteenth century, felt an inevitable Christian revulsion at their name and got them to change it to Griquas (after Grigriqua, one of the Khoi groups). The missionaries also helped them to found their capital, Griquatown, and to introduce a proper system of government early in the nineteenth century. Jager Afrikaner built a large following among the Khoisan and established a state which raided the colony and the surrounding populace on both sides of the Orange river. He in turn was to father Jonker Afrikaner, celebrated today as the man who founded Windhoek and who was in a sense the father of Namibia.

By the mid nineteenth century the Khoi had been almost completely integrated into various other groups. Those who stayed within the colony were lumped together with liberated slaves and a small population of 'free blacks' to become part of the Cape Coloureds, a newly acquired – indeed, imposed – identity. Those who migrated to the north and north-east developed their own new identities based on the Dutch language and generally European lifestyle. Nonetheless, despite their mixed ancestry these groups – the Griquas, Basters, Oorlams – are today classified (along with some Cape Coloureds) as subgroups of the Nama, a group scattered across southern Africa but with its core in Namibia. But they are to a large extent forgotten people, uncelebrated even by many of their Coloured descendants. For South African history has been dominated by the twin perspectives of Afrikaner and African nationalism, and the Khoi fit comfortably into neither.

# IV

# THE DIFFICULT BIRTH
# OF AFRICAN POLITIES

@ @ @

The early nineteenth century was a period of unprecedented turmoil, suffering and change throughout southern Africa, with large demographic movements sending one group after another cannoning into its neighbours and, amidst this confusion, the rise of several major African polities. The revolutionary changes thus effected were until recently explained simply as the result of the rise and expansion of the mighty Zulu state in what is today KwaZulu-Natal. This in turn was commonly ascribed to the talents of just one man, the Zulu leader Shaka. Shaka, the argument went, was both a military genius and a bloodthirsty psychopath: nothing could stand against his Zulu impis and Shaka was so immensely ruthless that people fled not just from his advancing armies but from his mere reputation. Flee they certainly did – some as far north as present-day Tanzania, fighting and scattering the locals on their way. Thus at the same time that the Cape colony had developed its own centrifugal dynamic in the western parts of South Africa, so an even stronger centrifuge arose in the eastern region of the country. This Shaka-centred process was termed the 'mfecane', a Xhosa term associated with weakness and hunger (the Sotho term is 'difaquane').

More recent research has thrown much of this framework into doubt, so that even the term mfecane is rejected by some. Nobody doubts that the formation and expansion of the Zulu polity under Shaka had large and disruptive results but it is asking too much of the notion of 'the great man of history' to attribute everything to Shaka. The first question has to be why the Zulu polity arose at that point – and when one has elucidated the reasons for this one is doubtless looking at factors which continued to drive events during and after the *mfecane*: already the notion of Shaka and the Zulus as the first cause of all these migrations and clashes has been lost.

Almost certainly one such factor was the intensification in the late eighteenth century of trade to and from the Portuguese settlement at Delagoa Bay (today's Maputo). Originally the trade was mainly in ivory but from about 1820 on there was a sharp increase in the slave trade too. The rich ivory trade was itself destabilising – creating sources of wealth outside the subsistence economy and causing conflicts over who was to control that trade – though this was as nothing compared with the disruption caused throughout the region by the slave trade.

The rise, in the late eighteenth century, of the Thembe chiefdom (a sub-group of the Tsonga) and, much further away, of the Pedi polity were both related to the Delagoa Bay trade, as were the rise and expansion of several other chiefdoms in what is today northern KwaZulu-Natal, in the area between Delagoa Bay and the Mfolozi river. By the end of the eighteenth century one such group, the Mabhudu, living to the east of the Phongolo river, had established control over access from the south to Delagoa Bay, thus curbing the power of the Thembe, while other groups – the Ndwandwe, the Ngwane and the Mthethwa – all struggled to secure access to this lucrative trade. Their rivalry came to a head early in the nineteenth century when Dingiswayo, chief of the Mthethwa, made an alliance with the Mabhudu. Then, in about 1817, the Ndwandwe, under their chief Zwide, attacked two Ngwane groups, the first led by Chief Matiwane, the second by Chief Sobhuza – this latter group later becoming known as the Swazi. These conflicts set in motion a long chain of events which ultimately had repercussions far beyond this area.

While the Delagoa Bay trade was doubtless the key factor behind the irruption of state formation in south-east Africa, this trade had been going on for centuries without resulting in major changes in the interior – so the question is why these changes should have suddenly begun in the late eighteenth century.

The answer seems to lie in a combination of demographic pressures and a series of droughts and cattle diseases. South-east Africa experienced major droughts in 1800–1803, 1812 and again in 1816–18, and cattle epidemics in 1816 and 1818. The growing population meant that a drought or loss of cattle produced a major food crisis. Rather as the endemic insecurity of life in Dark Age Europe had led to the rise of kings and barons, so the same Hobbesian logic meant that food crises brought desperate populations under the control of those leaders strong enough to chart a way through the crisis – usually by an ability to rustle cattle successfully or find well-watered land.

And such leadership was now available because the wealth of the Delagoa trade had provided the economic basis for the rise of the new elite who controlled the trade. But the trade also created a Darwinian struggle between the groups who sought to control it or at least have access to it, a struggle sharpened by the fact that the ivory trade led to the depletion of the elephant herds, making everyone more determined to control this rich but shrinking resource. Naturally, those who came out on top in such struggles were the notables that people turned to for protection and food when crisis struck. For an able leader such a crisis was also an opportunity, for the more followers he had, the stronger the leader – and the greater the chance of his and their survival. These factors lay behind the turmoil of the early nineteenth century not only among the Sotho-Tswana on the highveld but down on the coast among the Nguni living between the Phongolo and Thukela rivers.

The Delagoa trade played a major role in shaping African society, but the ever-moving Cape frontier was a far more powerful source of tension and social pressure throughout south-eastern Africa.

As we have seen, by the end of the eighteenth century several groups of Khoi and ex-slaves had fled from the Cape and settled in the area of the confluence of the Orange and the Vaal rivers. These were the Kora (or Korana), the Basters (later renamed Griquas) and the Bergenaar (who split from the Griquas in 1821). From the outset these groups were the focus of attention for various and often conflicting interests from the Cape. Missionaries proselytised among them and used them as a platform for penetrating further into the interior. Company officials at the Cape hoped to use them as virtual marcher lords to secure their northern borders. And Cape traders saw them as suppliers of ivory, skins, ostrich feathers, cattle and slaves. Since these latter objectives were bound to provoke conflict with the neighbouring Sotho and Tswana, Cape officials and traders supplied them with arms with which to raid and pillage their neighbours.

These raids started around 1800 and continued for more than three decades. Towards the end of this period – and despite the proscription of the slave trade in 1807 – the Bergenaar (especially) and the Kora began to raid the Sotho and Khoi for slaves as well. Most of the Griquas – those under Adam Waterboer at Griquatown and those led by Cornelius and Adam Kok – refused to have anything to do with slave trading but, alas, the trade was too lucrative for the same to be said of all Griquas, despite the fact that they had themselves fled the horrors of slavery in the Cape. Some Griqua groups – those led by Barend Barends, for example – remained true to their roots and not only gave refuge to slave runaways from the Cape but refused to have anything to do with the blandishments of Cape officials.

This incessant raiding had devastating effects – but the situation was immeasurably worsened by drought. Something like 70 per cent of South Africa's rain falls on the lush coastal belt of what is today KwaZulu-Natal so that not much remains of the rain clouds as they pass west of the Drakensberg, where the Sotho and Tswana live. There the flat pastures of what is today the Free State soon give way to the sands of the Kalahari desert. Human depredations led to further deterioration: the Tswana, particularly the Tlhaping, cleared forests for their huge settlements, which in turn led to the drying up of springs and rivers.

The droughts of 1800–1803, 1816–18 and 1824–6 were so severe that complete destabilisation followed, with famine, migration and violent clashes over food and pasture. Under such conditions communities broke down into a desperate, demoralised rabble willing to do almost anything in order to survive – including selling their freedom to a strong chief or slaver. Many ended up as slaves or free labourers in the Cape: when the famine was over and slavery abolished, many Sotho who had fled to the Cape or been sold there trekked back home in the 1830s and 1840s.

An even greater drama was building among the northern Nguni clans who populated what is today KwaZulu-Natal. There the high rainfall and abundant pasture led to growth in the numbers of both people and cattle, and consequent pressure of one group upon another. Already by the late eighteenth century the Mthethwa and the Quabe had emerged as clear winners in this process. Under pressure from the Quabe, the Thuli were pushed across the Thukela and forced their way into the Mngeni river valley, settling in the area between present-day Durban and Pietermaritzburg. One result of the myriad collisions thus occasioned between various groups was the expansion of the Mpondo who dominated the lower Mzimvubu valley by the 1820s. Another was the dislocation of the Cele who also moved across the Thukela and eventually established control over the territory between the Thukela and Mdloti rivers. Ultimately, the Thuli, the Cele and many other of these Nguni groups were to be subsumed as clans within the Zulu nation (where one still finds these names today).

But the epicentre of events remained the area between the Phongolo and the Mfolozi rivers. After an attack by the Ndwandwe, the Ngwane under their chief Matiwane left their territory and, about 1821, moved westwards, attacking and utterly vanquishing the Hlubi. Some of the Hlubi submitted to Matiwane, but others moved south, becoming the first component of what became known as the Mfengu or, as the whites called them, the Fingoes. Another group, under Mpangazitha, crossed the Drakensberg and fled into the highveld. But the next year the victorious Ngwane followed suit and settled on the upper Thukela where they established themselves as the area's dominant chiefdom.

The effect of these collisions had not yet spent itself. The fleeing Hlubi under Mpangazitha attacked the Sotho-speaking Tlokwa, who fled, raiding their neighbours for crops and cattle with such success that they incorporated thousands of people from broken communities and, under their chief Sekonyela, became a formidable force. This in turn led to a twenty-year war between the Tlokwa and the Sotho polity of the great Chief Moshoeshoe, ending only with Moshoeshoe's victory in 1853 and the incorporation of the Tlokwa into the Sotho nation.

Meanwhile Matiwane's pursuing Ngwane had caught the fleeing Hlubi and completed their destruction. Their chief Mpangazitha was defeated and killed, and the Hlubi remnants dispersed. Some of them attached themselves to the Ngwane, some to the Ndebele and some to the growing Sotho polity of Moshoeshoe. The victorious Ngwane now began to attack other groups at will and only met their match in 1827 when they fell victim to the rising power of the Zulus – invited in by Mpangazitha's sons, vowing revenge for their father's death. Thereafter the Ngwane were gradually ground into fragments by the surrounding Xhosa, Sotho and Zulu, the *coup de grâce* being delivered by the Zulu ruler, Dingane.

For by this time the Zulus, originally just a subordinate clan within the Mthethwa group, had begun their decisive rise to power. Already, as we have seen, the turmoil which lay behind that ascension had seen groups colliding bloodily with one another all the way to the edges of the Kalahari: but there the Tswana and Sotho were also being weakened by struggles of their own.

## The long agony of the Sotho and the Tswana

By the later eighteenth century internal struggles among the Tswana had intensified, with other clans bitterly contesting Hurutshe superiority. What usually settled these terrible wars was inviting in a more powerful outsider. In this case the Fokeng ultimately sought help from the Pedi. The end result was a considerable strengthening of the Pedi grip on the interior, increasing their control of the trade routes, and the weakening of the Fokeng who, after 1810, had become easy prey for any intruder. Meanwhile the Ngwaketse had also emerged as major players as they attempted to break the monopoly control of the Tlhaping and Kora over the trade routes east and south from their territory. Under their chief Makaba and from their stronghold in the Kanye hills they attacked the Kwena who were consolidating north-east of the present-day town of Brits. The Ngwaketse had, indeed, become a formidable power. Around 1800 they beat off an attack by both the Kora and the Griquas under Jan Bloem, then in 1808 defeated and incorporated a group of the Kgatla, previously tributaries of the Hurutshe, and then defeated the Hurutshe themselves and killed their chief. Their continued raids forced the Hurutshe to forge an alliance with the Tlhaping, the Kwena, other Kgatla remnants and some of the Kora.

In 1815 this Hurutshe coalition enlisted the support of Coenraad de Buys, one of the first trekboers to move into their area, and by 1818 he had helped them to regain some of their hold over their vassal groups. Seeing this, the Ngwaketse won him over and their combined army then attacked and defeated the Hurutshe.

These wars were a desperate struggle for survival. The losers did not stand to be enslaved, colonised or discriminated against but simply to disappear, either through starvation from loss of cattle and crops or through absorption – usually, in effect, a mixture of both as men died and women were taken as extra wives by the winners. This could easily happen even to groups once regarded as strong.

There was one other alternative, the amalgamation of the defeated into a ravening, starving horde. This happened to the Tswana and Sotho groups raided by the Hlubi and thrown out of the upper Thukela by the Ngwane. The Phuthing and Hlakwana in particular, stripped of their cattle by the Ngwane, moved north and west, plundering others on their way. Their route was a desperate search for food and water for they had already been stripped of their cattle and crops by others. They were little more than a rabble and had no warlike intent, resembling more a plague of locusts, looting the land as they went and beating back those who tried to resist them by their sheer numbers. By 1823 they had become a horde of up to 50,000, for their numbers grew continually as those other Tswana and Sotho groups (the Rolong, the Hurutshe and the Tlhaping among them) whose crops they plundered had little option but to join them. This was no warrior force: many were weak and dying. In June 1823 this pitiful horde – men, women and children – converged near the Tlhaping settlement of Dithakong.

Dithakong was huge: even after their chief had ordered several thousand of its inhabitants to move to Kuruman where a mission had been opened in 1820, there were still up to 10,000 people left. The Tlhaping had left the town before the onslaught, retreating to Kuruman where they spread the news of the advance of what they called the 'Mantatees' – the terrible hordes bringing devastation and death. Robert Moffat, the Kuruman missionary, recruited the Griquas to help protect the mission and the Tlhaping. On 26 June 1823 the Tlhaping returned to Dithakong with the Griquas and three Europeans – Robert Moffat, George Thompson, a visiting Cape Town businessman, and John Melville, a visiting Cape colony official. Both the Griquas and the Europeans were mounted and had firearms. In several hours the battle was over. The invaders burnt the town but suffered a crushing defeat. Many were killed and the Tlhaping captured a thousand of their cattle. Some of the Mantatee women and children were taken by the Griqua as labourers or slaves, while others were sent as labourers to the Cape – some doubtless ending as slaves as well (although Moffat tried to prevent this). Even this would have represented a sort of mercy, for the only other fate available was death.

The battle of Dithakong was unique only because of the participation in it of Europeans (who recorded it in detail) – and perhaps because of the numbers of people involved. But other Tswana, Sotho and Khoi settlements on the eastern highveld suffered a similar fate. The logic of the situation was by now quite clear and when the (Tswana-speaking) Taung, under their chief Moletsane, had been forced into nomadism by Hlubi and Ngwane raids, they managed to keep most of their cattle and carefully organised themselves for their new role as raiders, knowing everything now depended on that. Nonetheless, and doubtless like most of those forced to live this nightmare, they dreamt only of returning to their old home once times improved. In such a situation almost everything could depend on good leadership and the Taung were lucky in having in Moletsane one of the most resourceful Sotho leaders, who launched successful raids on many of his neighbours before being thrown back by the Rolong in the battle of the Molopo river in 1824. They lived to fight another day, however, clashing with the Griquas and Ndebele before suffering a severe defeat at the latter's hands in 1829, after which they wisely sought refuge with the missionaries in Philippolis. The cost of these reverses was that many Taung ended up as migrant labourers in the Cape – though a good number did eventually make it back to their now deserted home territory.

The word 'Mantatee' comes down to us, symbolising this terrible age. It derives from descriptions of another ravening horde, the Tlokwa, under their female leader, MaNthatisi. By the 1830s this word had come to denote any group of displaced or wandering marauders, particularly those of non-Tswana origin and most particularly those coming from the east. Such ethnic connotations lost their sense, however, for such groups attracted all manner of refugees, local ruffians and, of course, the victims of the horde itself. All such people, if they reached the Cape, were called the Mantatees, the word coming simply to mean refugees who fled troubled areas. Thus the offenders and their victims became one – as, indeed, they were.

## The rise of the Zulu nation

Meanwhile, the struggle for supremacy at the epicentre – the area between the Phongolo and Mfolozi rivers – was reaching its peak. In 1818 the Mthethwa launched an attack against the Ndwandwe but were defeated; their chief, Dingiswayo, was captured and killed. Ndwandwe supremacy was now contested only by the Qwabe and the growing Zulu chiefdom which dominated the area between the White Mfolozi and the Thukela rivers. This chiefdom, led by Shaka kaSenzangakhona, had been part of the Mthethwa confederation and now came into its own after the death of Dingiswayo. The Ndwandwe launched several attacks on the Zulus – which they barely withstood. Shaka realised that survival depended on building a broader coalition: he managed to defeat the Nyuswa and turn them into tributaries, forced the Qwabe to submit and the Mkhize submitted without a fight. To avoid the same fate the Chunu migrated south of the Thukela while the Hlubi were defeated by the Ngwane and disintegrated, Zulu power expanding into the old Hlubi area of the Mzinyathi to fill the vacuum.

These developments turned the Zulu chiefdom into the major power in a huge area between the Mfolozi, the Thukela and the Mzinyathi. Its great rivals were the Ngwane in the upper Thukela and the Ndwandwe under the leadership of Zwide – and a showdown was inevitable. The first Ndwandwe attack on the Zulus was thrown back and then in 1819 Shaka's armies beat Zwide's Ndwandwe at Gqokoli Hill and again on the Mhlatuze river. With this the Ndwandwe chiefdom simply collapsed into divided remnants, with some moving off to what later became Swaziland and others to seek safety with the Portuguese at Delagoa Bay. Zulus moved into all the territory the Ndwandwe vacated and set military settlements between the Black Mfolozi and the Mkhuze rivers.

During the conflict with the Ndwandwe, Zwide's grandson, Mzi-likazi, a member of the Khumalo clan, went over to serve Shaka as one of his military commanders. But Shaka was not one to take things on trust and when, after a successful cattle raid two years later in 1821, Mzilikazi failed to hand over the cattle Shaka demanded, Shaka's fury was such that Mzilikazi had to flee for his life. Mzilikazi led his followers across the Drakensberg. His small band of refugees turned out to be formidable for they adopted much of the superior military organisation and tactics they had learnt from Shaka. Adopting the name Ndebele, they built themselves into a major power by raiding the local communities, dispersing and killing some and absorbing the rest – just as Shaka had done. By 1832 the Ndebele had created a powerful polity occupying virtually the whole of what later became the Transvaal. Their raids greatly worsened the plight of the Sotho and Tswana, forcing them to flee westwards towards the Kalahari desert.

Mzilikazi was taking no chances. He exercised close control over the large settlements comprising the core Ndebele population, situated at the centre of the polity. This was surrounded by an extensive belt of pasture, containing only cattle and their herdsmen. On the outskirts were the client semi-autonomous communities and chieftainships that had either been conquered or accepted Ndebele supremacy and paid tribute to them. These were surrounded by a wide cleared area which functioned as a march.

In 1827 the Ndebele moved to the Magaliesberg mountains (to the west of present-day Johannesburg) from which they raided the hapless Tswana. On the other hand the Ndebele ascendancy on the highveld did at least see an end to the plague of unpredictable marauding gangs – ruthlessly put down by the Ndebele who would not tolerate rival raiders. The Ndebele raids not only chased away the Fokeng but led the Taung and various Rolong communities to give up owning cattle (and return to agriculture) simply so as not to be a target. The Ndebele duly turned their attention to others – their devastating raids on the Ngwaketse in 1828 and 1830 drove the survivors all the way into the desert while the Hurutshe – already tributaries to the Ndebele – had to send their youth to work as servants for the Ndebele and were forced to cultivate Ndebele fields rather than their own. Even the formidable Kora were not safe from Ndebele raids and the mere danger of being raided caused more and more Tswana groups to forsake fertile areas and move further towards the desert.

No one, acting alone, could stand against the Ndebele so several coalitions were mounted against them. The first of these, formed under the Kora brigand Jan Bloem, was defeated by the Ndebele in 1829 but other coalition attempts followed. The biggest coalition – some 1,300 fighters – assembled in 1830–1 by the Griqua captain, Barend Barends, included Griquas from Griquatown, Campbell and Philippolis, together with elements of the Kora, Tlhaping and Rolong. The coalition had initial success but ended in disaster when in a surprise night attack the Ndebele killed some 400 Griquas and scores of Kora and Tswana. Often resistance was mere desperation, as when the Rolong community of Khunwana killed the Ndebele representatives who had come to take their children as tribute. This merely provoked a devastating Ndebele attack against the Rolong the next year (1833), in the course of which the Ndebele moved their capital still further west, to the Marico river valley. The whole region between the Mashowing and the Setlagoli rivers was filled with the starving remnants of the Hurutshe, the Ngwaketse and the Rolong. Even today mention of Zulu warriors causes many Sotho and Tswana to recoil for the folk memory of the ferocity of the Ndebele – a Zulu offshoot in many eyes – remains strong.

The Ndebele stayed in the Marico valley for another five years but increasingly they came under pressure from the advancing Boers, as well as from the Griquas and Zulus. In 1837 they migrated north of the Limpopo river, re-creating their state in what is today Matabeleland in Zimbabwe.

Meanwhile, having secured his northern border, Shaka systematically expanded his sway southwards by establishing client polities which he encouraged to expand under his authority and with his assistance. Gradually all these client clans – the Sithole, Cele, Mkhize and others – began to be counted as part of a single Zulu entity. By the early 1820s the Zulu state thus dominated an area all the way down the coast to present-day Durban.

## The ripples spread: the Eastern Cape

The Mzimkhulu valley is, to this day, an ethnically confused area with the Mzimkhulu district a Xhosa-speaking island in the midst of KwaZulu-Natal, while the Mount Currie district further south is part of KwaZulu-Natal in the midst of what is today the Eastern Cape. The rise of Zulu power and the complex ethnic collisions which followed soon turned this area too into a battleground as refugee waves, fleeing from Shaka, broke against the resistance of the Xhosa, the Thembu and other local clans, supported as necessary by the British. The latter were disgusted as they saw the victors bearing away many cattle, women and children from the vanquished, though the fate of those thus forcibly incorporated into the conquering groups may not have been as bad as that of many others who ended up as slaves or labourers in the Cape. All the remnants of these desperate, broken refugees were collectively called the Fingo or Mfengu.

The Fingo arrived in southern Nguni territory at different times and in small groups, though by 1835 some 50,000 of them had attached themselves to local communities, some as clients paying tribute, others offering their services in return for the use of land or cattle, others simply marrying an Nguni. Their status remained inferior and they looked increasingly to the colonial power in the Cape as their best bet in life. Locals left destitute as a result of internal clashes or wars with the colony often also adopted their identity, for many in African society were used to gravitating in Hobbesian fashion towards any power able to offer protection in these troubled times. Hundreds of them were employed as labourers on Eastern Cape farms or fought as colonial soldiers, some managing to acquire cattle and land in the Eastern Cape from the colonial authorities, to whom they were invariably known as 'the loyal Fingoes'. Paradoxically, it was the Fingo, the outcasts and downtrodden of the era when independent African rule was being crushed in the Eastern Cape, who benefited most from their suffering in the long run. For they were the first to adhere to the new European religion and its values, the first to embrace white ways and education – and thus the first to become an *évolué* class who could take up the challenges of the new era and lead the way for their brethren.

Although the stories of cannibalism in South Africa at this time were, historians now say, somewhat exaggerated, they are a measure of the terrible suffering and devastation this era brought to the country's eastern half. Similarly, the turmoil in the hinterland led to the rise of the slave trade from Delagoa Bay. And, for the Hobbesian reasons we have seen, the biggest and most powerful African polities in this part of the continent also emerged in this period. Differing in strength, size, social organisation and ethno-linguistic composition (none was, in fact, mono-ethnic) what they had in common was the necessity of growth for the sheer sake of survival.

Strongest of all these polities was the Zulu state founded by Shaka. Shaka was born before his mother, Nandi, was married to his father, Senzangakhona, and was thus an illegitimate child. Nandi and her children were first driven out of the Zulu chiefdom by Senzangakhona's household and then from her own Langeni clan by her relatives, an experience which seems to have left Shaka passionately loyal to his mother but paranoid and psychopathic. As a young man he served in Dingiswayo's army and when Senzangakhona died in 1816, Dingiswayo supported Shaka's claim to the chieftaincy. Shaka had the legitimate heir killed: nobody thereafter dared object to his leadership.

Shaka was a talented warrior who revolutionised existing methods of warfare and weapons. Before Shaka, hostilities typically began with two armies standing in opposite lines, throwing spears at one another. Shaka, realising that this literally meant throwing your weapon away, pioneered the use of the assegai, a short stabbing spear used over and over again, like the short Roman broadsword. His warriors used their shields not just for protection but as a weapon, thrust into the enemy's face, and they discarded sandals, fighting barefoot to add extra speed and agility. All these innovations he made obligatory. He also devised new battle tactics, usually encircling the enemy from the flanks before driving right through the centre to finish it off.

Shaka had a genius for organisation. Following Dingiswayo's example, he changed the existing circumcision rituals to incorporate them into the new system of *amabutho* – age regiments. Both males and females were organised separately into such regiments, each going through a complete life cycle. A male regiment would pass as a unit from an early age when small boys helped elder regiments to look after their cattle, to a circumcision stage, to warriors, to married warriors and thence to seniors. The life cycle of female regiments was less complicated, rotating around marriage and childbearing and, unlike the men, not requiring girls to leave home for lengthy periods of time.

Each *ubutho* was led and controlled by an *induna*, a military commander and Shaka's trusted friend or relative. The *amabutho*, though conceived primarily for military purposes, were used to inculcate a legendary discipline which was then available for other purposes as well. For about twenty years young men were taken out of their kinship-based homesteads, the main productive unit of Nguni communities, and made to serve the state. This weakened the kinship system and hugely strengthened Shaka's central authority. Young men from the many conquered communities were also put into regiments under Zulu *indunas*. The chiefs of these communities who had survived the conquest were usually allowed to retain legal judicial power over their territories but were, crucially, allowed no power over the regiments.

This greatly enhanced the efficiency of Shaka's army – as also the concentration of power in Shaka's hands and the centralisation of the Zulu state.

Shaka ruled with an iron fist. He managed to suppress or keep at bay all opposition and his orders were the law of the country. These were not always within the limits of logic or reason, particularly in the last years of his rule. When his mother died in 1827 Shaka announced conditions of mourning which included planting no crops next year and using no milk, thus condemning the whole country to starvation. Childbirth was also prohibited and women found to be pregnant within a year of Nandi's death were to be killed together with their husbands. In fact, the mourning lasted for three months – but even in this time thousands were put to death.

Shaka's bloody but successful military campaigns, his iron grip on conquered communities, his leadership prowess and vision, as well as his limitless cruelty towards his opponents, helped create a state which, by the time of his death, stretched all the way from Delagoa Bay to the Mzimkhulu. In recent time we have seen a concerted attempt by Africanist historiography to airbrush away Shaka's faults, concentrating instead on his unique power and 'greatness', rather in the way some Russian nationalists still hero-worship Stalin. The comparison is apt for Shaka ruled through terror and murdered large numbers of his own subjects, let alone his enemies. When Shaka was killed by his two brothers and a trusted servant in 1828, people were afraid to come up to his body to perform the customary rituals.

The Zulu state was inherited by one of Shaka's assassins, his half-brother Dingane who, having denounced Shaka's excesses, soon embarked on a similar course, suppressing opponents and murdering potential rivals within his family. However, despite a disastrous reverse at Blood River at the hands of the advancing Boers, he largely maintained the power of the new state until 1840 when he was defeated by an alliance of his half-brother and the Boers. Dingane fled and was killed by the Swazi.

His successor, Mpande, despite the reputation he seemed actively to cultivate as a lazy, sex-driven sybarite, was a clever and effective leader who managed to avoid direct confrontation with the encroaching whites and kept his territory and army intact. He attacked the Pedi and Swazi but otherwise seldom engaged Zulu military power in battle: by now its fearsome reputation awed all he dealt with, the whites included. He ruthlessly eliminated all remaining rivals within his family but otherwise relaxed the regime of terror established by his predecessors and often took the advice of his council. This did not save him, however, when rivalry began between his two elder sons. In 1856 one of them, Cetshwayo, defeated and killed his main opponent – whom Mpande had supported – as well as his other five brothers, and assumed control of the army and the state. Thereafter, until his death in 1872, Mpande remained a merely titular ruler.

## The Swazi and Pedi states

The two other major African states in South Africa in the nineteenth century both emerged as a response to Zulu power and both gave refuge in mountain areas to escapees from war and terror. One of these, founded by Sobhuza's Ngwane at the eastern edge of contemporary South Africa, is today's Swaziland. Sobhuza, having led his people to safety, ruled until 1838 and was followed by his son Mswati, who ruled until 1865. The other, a southern Sotho state, today's Lesotho, grew under Moshoeshoe – an outstanding statesman and leader. Moshoeshoe established himself in Thaba Bosiu, an inaccessible mountain fortress, offering perfect protection even from a stronger enemy. Both Sotho and Nguni refugees from the ravaged territories all around flocked to this safe haven to seek Moshoeshoe's protection, which was invariably granted. Moshoeshoe built his state not by terror but by binding his new subjects to him by negotiations, hospitality, a network of marriages, the loan of cattle and so on, gradually installing his relatives as chiefs throughout his country. Though he led successful military campaigns these were mostly of a defensive nature and he established himself as a major regional power with consummate skill and diplomacy. Typically, he positively welcomed Christian missionaries into his country while carefully avoiding getting baptised himself.

The Pedi (northern Sotho) state which had emerged in the eighteenth century, earlier than any other African state in the region, survived the time of troubles and strengthened its position under Sekwati who ruled from 1824 till 1860. Sekwati withstood clashes with the Ndwandwe, with an advancing Boer column and even with Zulu raiders, and managed to extend his power from the Soutpansberg mountains to the Vaal river, restoring order, if not peace, in this large territory. Sekwati's state was based on his paramountcy over more than a hundred separate units, each headed by its own semi-independent chief. These chiefs controlled their own age-group regiments but were tied to Sekwati's lineage by marriage: none could retain power if not married into Sekwati's family. Inevitably the northern Sotho consolidated around this unchallenged Pedi centre.

Like Moshoeshoe, Sekwati handled his neighbours with diplomatic skill, making peace with Mpande and establishing friendly ties with the Boers and even with the Cape colony. This latter development, together with the fact that the Pedi had a historic involvement in long-distance trade – and were thus used to finding sources of income outside their borders – resulted in the early development of migrancy in Pedi society. Long before they came under colonial rule with its pressures to provide labour, many Pedi voluntarily sought outside employment – some as far away as the Cape.

The legacy of this terrible time of troubles in southern Africa was very asymmetrical. While it brought enormous suffering and hardship to the entire population of the region, the Tswana and northern Nguni clans bore the brunt, some disappearing altogether as independent units, some barely surviving. Other northern Nguni, such as the Zulu, the Swazi and the Ndebele, as well as the southern and northern Sotho, strengthened their positions, creating or significantly expanding their states by incorporating many people of 'alien' origin. Thus at the end of this period a myriad of small groups had coalesced into fewer but larger ethnic groups. These larger groups now all revolved around nascent states – clearly the condition of their survival.

The exception was the Xhosa. Whereas most northern Nguni in what is now South Africa had become amalgamated into a single Zulu nation well before 1850, it took very much longer for a similar process of consolidation among the southern Nguni to coalesce around the Xhosa – and even today the process is not complete. Why was this so? Some historians have argued that the southern Nguni marriage system fermented rivalry between the children of the chiefs' senior wives, thus preventing the emergence of anything like the centralising Zulu monarchy. Others have dwelt upon the scarcity of fertile land in the Eastern Cape and the burden imposed by a higher population density, further swollen by refugees from war-torn and hunger-stricken areas. But the greatest difference of all was simply the proximity of the Cape colony whose political, military and economic influence permeated the southern Nguni long before it affected the other major Bantu groups. The paradox of this greater proximity lay in the dialectic of conflict and change which resulted from it. For while on the one hand it meant that the southern Nguni – the future Xhosa – bore the brunt of colonial expansion, suffering endless frontier wars, the greater colonial penetration of Xhosa society ultimately produced a better educated Xhosa elite which was to inherit the political kingdom of South Africa.

Something of the same dialectic also holds true for the other groups to survive successfully the traumas of the early nineteenth century. The Lesotho (encompassing the southern Sotho), Botswana (the Tswana) and Swaziland (the Ngwane) were all to become British protectorates, protecting them from the harshness of white rule in South Africa itself, while the Zulu, for a lengthy period under Shepstone, were to achieve a sort of internal protectorate status within South Africa. In all these cases the resulting encapsulation had the effect of protecting the structures of African society from the full impact of colonialism, which was why the institution of monarchy or paramount chieftaincy survived.

Whether this was beneficial or not is a moot point, for the effect was comparable to the 'blessing of empire' on medieval Spain and Portugal: on the one hand the inflow of silver from Latin America enriched these countries, on the other hand it protected their monarchies from the need for change and thus froze traditional social structures. In the end this was a doubtful blessing, for these societies were thus unable to evolve in the way the rest of Europe did and by the twentieth century both had become reactionary backwaters. It is hard today not to look at the stagnant, indeed semi-collapsed, state of Lesotho, the outrageous denials of democracy in Swaziland or the selfish and backward Zulu monarchy and conclude that something very similar has happened in southern Africa. From this point of view it is difficult not to believe that those African societies to feel the full brunt of colonialism may in the end have been major beneficiaries from the greater modernisation resulting from it.

Certainly, the experience of colonialism and white rule was to be Janus-faced, bringing great deprivation and yet great benefits. No easy calculus is possible, particularly since, contrary to Africanist mythology, there was no golden age of traditional African society before the fall. The truth is that life was nasty, brutish and short even before the advent of colonialism. However, the apparent neatness of this dialectic between colonial oppression and greater material progress has one important exception: the Tswana of today's Botswana were able to avoid white rule and full colonialism, to preserve their traditional social structures – and yet also to achieve a striking modernisation and a higher GDP per capita than even South Africa itself. This is both a painful illustration of the significance of successful leadership and a warning against any form of simple determinism in the way people construct and write history.

# V

# THE LONG CENTURY
# OF CONQUEST

### ◉ ◉ ◉

Unlike most African countries South Africa had no simple 'pre-colonial' period that ended in a clearly defined colonial conquest. Moreover, for a long time there was no sharp division between the coloniser and the colonised, the victors and the vanquished – instead, the South African frontier was, like the American frontier, a continuously moving reality with a large penumbra of uncertainty in which shifting alliances and desperate compromises were the norm. There were far more actors of a variety of racial hues and political identities involved in this process than anywhere else on the continent. The influence – ultimately the dominance – of settler colonialism spread gradually, unevenly and in a far more complicated fashion than is allowed for in the mono-dimensional vision of African nationalism today, which asserts that the whole period since 1652 is a simple, undifferentiated history of racial oppression.

In fact, the extension of colonial (or 'white') rule involved not only brutality but compromise and sometimes retreat. There was frequently opposition to the extension of this rule not only by the colonised but by many of the colonisers, and there were endless instances of co-operation between the colonisers and the colonised. But in two senses the struggle was simple. Its final outcome was never in doubt thanks to the overwhelming military superiority of the colonisers – though the concrete form which subjugation took depended on many other factors, including the personalities of the leaders on both sides. Second, at no point was there any doubt that what the struggle was all about was survival and the control of the means of production, which for many years meant simply the land.

Thus colonisation was not a big bang, not a single act. It developed as an ever-growing and many-sided factor – through traders, missionaries and soldiers as well as colonial officials – until, by the turn of the twentieth century, it had become overwhelming and omnipotent, no longer one factor among others but the context within which everything else subsisted.

## Frontier wars and the coming of the British

The southern Nguni bore the brunt of the first engagement with the colony, fighting its forces in nine frontier wars that were to last for a century from 1778 to 1878, the so-called 'kaffir wars', the colonists using the Arabic word '*kaffir*' (unbeliever) as a generic term first for the Xhosa and the related southern Nguni, and later for all Bantu.

But during these wars the colony's identity had changed. In 1795 the British, with the agreement of the House of Orange, took over the Cape from the Netherlands which had been defeated by the French. The British were careful to maintain good relations with the local Dutch, particularly in view of the perennial clashes with the Xhosa and a massive Khoi uprising in 1799. In 1803, by the Treaty of Amiens, the Cape was returned to the Netherlands. But in 1805 war in Europe resumed and in 1806 the British sent a large force to the Cape which easily defeated the small Dutch garrison. Doubtless the southern Nguni did not immediately register the fact but the consequences for them were enormous: behind the European settlers there now stood not a corrupt company and a small European state but the world's strongest empire and large new reserves of manpower.

As we have seen (at the end of chapter II), the succession conflict within the Rharhabe Xhosa – between Ngqika and his uncle Ndlambe – was the first in which Europeans took a hand. By the end of the eighteenth century Ngqika had taken Ndlambe prisoner and enjoyed considerable power and influence, including the support of some Boer adventurers. Ndlambe, however, escaped to the Cape and began to consolidate forces against Ngqika west of the Fish river. Meanwhile, to the east of Ngqika's territory the Gcaleka under their chief Hintsa also began to rebuild their power. Ngqika sought the Cape's help and in the fourth frontier war of 1811–12 colonial troops drove Ndlambe beyond the Fish and Ngqika, now the colony's ally and agent, was rewarded with the status of Paramount Chief of the Xhosa – a title to which Hintsa had a far better claim. None of these leaders could prevent the cattle rustling by the Xhosa which was the repeated *casus belli* of the frontier wars. The problem was endemic: the more the colony pushed into Xhosa territory, the more the desperate Xhosa would seek to compensate themselves with cattle. Ever since the 1770s colonial officials had attempted to regulate land, labour and trade relations between their subjects and the Xhosa. In 1778 a frontier along the Fish river was proclaimed – which, it was ludicrously announced, could not be crossed either by colonists or the Xhosa. In 1797 an only slightly more realistic proposal allowed frontier crossing provided 'passports' were obtained. In fact, the only regulation that mattered was that backed by armed force.

In 1818 Ndlambe, supported by Hintsa, challenged Ngqika again – and this time he won. A year later he attacked Grahamstown but was defeated in the fifth frontier war. Ngqika participated in the colonial counter-attack – as a result of which some 23,000 cattle were captured from Ndlambe and Hintsa. The colonial forces, having used Ngqika, then betrayed him, forcing him to hand over 4,000 square miles of his own land between the Fish and the Keiskamma rivers, now called the 'Ceded Territory'. It was hardly by chance that Ngqika ended his days as an alcoholic. Ndlambe naturally fared no better: together with his 20,000 people and the Gqunukwebe he was forcibly moved out of the Zuurveld, which was thus opened up for white occupation. Despite this object lesson in divide and rule, the divisions within the southern Nguni continued.

The British authorities now invited British settlers to occupy the Zuurveld – the idea being to create a buffer zone between the colony and the southern Nguni. This project failed – indeed, conflicts with the Xhosa intensified as these settlers too encroached upon their land. But these 1820 settlers, as the 4,000 English immigrants who settled the new district of Albany were called, were to have a major political influence as they progressively demanded and got the same liberties and rights they were used to back home. It was largely under their pressure that executive and legislative councils were created in 1834. Ultimately, in 1853, the colony was granted representative government on a qualified male franchise. Only those who earned £50 a year or had property of not less than £25 could vote – with race not mentioned at all. The Boer farmers supported this liberal legislation, hoping that the enfranchisement of their coloured workers would strengthen the position of non-English speakers vis-à-vis the growing English-speaking population.

Other changes brought by British rule had been far less acceptable to Boer farmers as well as to urban Dutch speakers. The British tried to introduce the English language into every public sphere including the schools and courts. The old Dutch judicial and local government systems were replaced with municipal boards and jury trials. But the Boers were also infuriated and insulted at the continual efforts both by British missionaries and colonial officials to regulate their relations with their slaves and indentured labourers, for all their multiple ordinances and regulations carried the implication that the Boers could not be trusted to act in a civilised fashion towards those in their care. First the slave trade (in 1807) and then slavery (in 1833) were abolished throughout the British Empire. All slaves were to be liberated after four years – and so they were, at least on paper, though there was, of course, no way of knowing or controlling what went on on outlying farms. The fact that compensation for slave owners was payable only in London was an insult on top of injury to the farmers.

Even slaves and Khoi labourers were not unambiguously happy about all these innovations, for the British introduced tighter control not only of the farmers but also of their labourers, instituting measures against Khoi 'vagrancy' and attempting to control their movement. Freed slaves would find themselves without land or any guarantee of a job while the Master and Servant Ordinance (1841) stipulated that a breach of contract was a criminal act.

The Dutch settlers regarded these developments as aimed directly against their interests, their particular hostility being reserved for the policy of anglicisation and for interfering liberal missionaries personified by Dr John Philip of the London Missionary Society. Their earliest and best-remembered reaction was the Slagtersnek rebellion of 1815. This started with an attempt to arrest a Boer farmer who, charged with maltreatment of a Coloured servant, refused to appear in court and then resisted arrest. He was shot dead by a detachment of Coloured soldiers. His brother, having enlisted Ngqika's support, raised a rebellion against the British. This was quickly defeated and its leaders sentenced to death by public hanging. The first time the rope broke, an event which often occasioned a pardon, but this was not granted: so they were hanged again. This became the first in a long list of Afrikaner grievances against the British.

## The continuing dynamic of expansion

European influence began to be felt right across eastern South Africa long before formal colonisation, as adventurers, traders and missionaries roamed far ahead of the colonial advance, many of them establishing relations with local chiefs and exercising considerable personal influence. One such person, John Dunn, an adventurer and trader who settled in Zululand, became a personal friend of Cetshwayo and married into several prominent Zulu families, himself acquiring chiefly status. Similarly Eugene Casalis of the Paris Evangelical Missionary Society established his mission at the foot of Thaba Bosiu and developed an influential relationship with Moshoeshoe, who acquired a taste for such European goods as horses, guns and blankets. Later he began wearing European clothes and even denounced such important Sotho customs as youth initiation and witch-hunting. Missionaries worked among many African groups for decades before colonisation – particularly successfully among the Griqua, Sotho, Tswana and Pedi.

But although the missionaries sometimes had a degree of political influence they were far from deserving the vehement dislike they have been rewarded with both by Afrikaner and African nationalists; by the former because of their image of meddlesome liberals, by the latter because of their image as ideological harbingers of colonialism. Today one often hears the quip that 'when missionaries arrived they had the Bible and Africans had the land, but fairly soon the Africans had the Bible and the whites had the land'. This not only omits from memory the enormous contribution made by missionary education, and the many brave churchmen, from Philip to Colenso to Huddlestone, who fought for African rights, but fails to note that the missionary tradition lies at the source of much radical politics in South Africa. The white liberals and communists who preached and fought against apartheid, bravely bearing witness for their principles and seeking to spread their gospels of enlightenment among the masses, were all recognisably heirs to this missionary tradition: Helen Suzman and Bram Fischer alike trod in the footsteps of Dr Philip.

The traders and adventurers who penetrated the interior ahead of the advance of colonialism had a far greater influence. Most notably, they founded Port Natal (Durban) in 1824 as a small trading station. Several traders and hunters, the best known of whom was Henry Fynn, managed to establish good relations with the Zulu kings. Both Shaka and Dingane ceded huge tracts of the future Natal to them, clearly without understanding the deals they were making. Initially this hardly mattered, for these enterprising whites were far too few to make good their claim and depended entirely on the goodwill of the local people. Had Shaka decided to do away with them they would not have lasted a day and would have left little trace in history.

## The Great Trek

The situation changed dramatically as thousands of Boers trekked out of the Cape colony, moving northwards and eastwards to create their own independent states. In 1834 the Cape Boers sent reconnaissance parties to Natal, the Soutpansberg and South-West Africa. Over the next three years trekker groups of various size, wagon after wagon, men, women and children, mostly from the eastern part of the colony, crossed the border out of the colony and moved, each by its own route, in a north-easterly direction. The trekkers were a various bunch, some well off, some fleeing from debts, with every kind of purpose and vision among them, united only by their determination to get away from the colony for good.

The Trek was often interpreted as a protest against the liberation of slaves. This sentiment may have existed but in none of their official or unofficial documents did any of the trekkers express the wish to preserve slavery in general or even to keep their own former slaves. Among the trekkers there were many former slave owners who travelled with their ex-slaves, now working for them as free labourers. They were free to leave – but didn't. These black voortrekkers were far more numerous than most paintings of the Trek depict: when trekkers in Natal were attacked by the Zulu it is recorded that some 500 trekkers were killed, 'of whom nearly 300 were white'.

It is more plausible to see the Great Trek as a broader protest by Boers against the fact that the Cape – their Cape – was no longer ruled by people like themselves but by foreigners determined to impose their own new order, an order within which the Boers felt pervasively uncomfortable. But there was also no doubt that many were simply land hungry. The Trek was to become the primary symbol of Afrikaner resistance to the encroachment by alien forces against their nationhood and language; indeed, it became the perceived starting point of Afrikanerdom itself. The leaders of the Trek became icons of Afrikaner nationalism, their names living on in place names all over South Africa: Louis Trichardt, Andries Pretorius, Hans van Rensburg, Hendrik Potgieter, Gerrit Maritz and Piet Retief. The decision by the ANC government after 1994 to rename many of these towns was seen by many Afrikaners as an attempt to obliterate the proudest feats in their history.

The trekker groups moved independently of one another but in September 1836 converged near Thaba 'Nchu to co-ordinate their plans. They could not agree on the direction of their next move for their leaders were divided by rivalry and distrust. And leadership was crucial: in mounting steep escarpments or venturing into hostile territory the quality of leadership was a life-and-death matter for the whole wagon train. The continuously fissiparous nature of Boer leadership must be understood against that background as well as that of their rough-and-ready frontiersman democracy. In the apartheid period National Party leaders treated Afrikaner unity behind a single leader as both essential and natural but history shows that it was anything but natural.

In December 1836 the trekkers elected their first Burgersraadt (citizens' council) and six months later at Winburg they proclaimed their first independent state, the Free Province of New Holland, with Piet Retief elected as 'overseer'. The new state didn't last – the Boers frequently founded states which didn't last, for they just moved on – but already the shape of things to come was clear. Freed of British colonial constraints, the Boers were to establish distinctively Afrikaner republics. These were strangely mixed systems, vehemently maintained democracies based on universal male suffrage among Boers only, and using the semi-military governance structures appropriate to a dangerous trek through hostile territory. Nonetheless, it is worth noting that one of the nine articles of this first trekboer constitution declared the ill-treatment of servants or forcible bringing into servitude of black children to be a crime.

The Boer leaders then moved off in different directions – but everywhere they were determined to procure land by any means necessary, an objective which inevitably provoked conflict with the local population. The first serious clash occurred between Hendrik Potgieter's wagon train, moving north across the Vaal river, and Mzilikazi's Ndebele. Even before the Thaba 'Nchu meeting the Ndebele had attacked the Boers, taking them for Griquas, but had been beaten off. After the Thaba 'Nchu meeting Potgieter returned to the fray – but luckily the Ndebele, some of the toughest opponents the Boers were to meet, soon moved away to south-west Zimbabwe.

Despite their small numbers, the Boers' military superiority was not in doubt. They had firearms and horses, which their opponents lacked, were generally better organised and knew something about tactics. They also invented a key defensive tactic: when attacked they drew their wagons into a circle and then used relays of loaded rifles to maintain a withering fire from within it. As the battle of Blood River was to show, this defensive tactic of forming a laager could be deployed to deadly effect.

## The struggle for Natal

Retief, followed by Maritz, moved eastwards through what they described as a totally empty land, reaching Port Natal in October 1837. Retief was sure that Dingane had already heard of Mzilikazi's defeat and decided in February 1838 to demand land from him in person in exchange for the return of the Zulu cattle stolen by the Tlokwa which Retief had recovered. Inexplicably, Dingane signed a paper granting all the land between the Tugela, the Umzimvubu river and the Drakensberg to the Boers. Then, for no apparent reason – we still only have conflicting theories and no certainty – when Retief returned with the promised cattle Dingane ordered his warriors to murder him and his men. They were all impaled through the anus with a sharpened stake and had to watch as each in turn had his skull beaten in. Dingane's warriors then fell upon a virtually undefended wagon train and killed – often in horrible ways – forty-one Boers, fifty-six Boer women, 185 Boer children and 250 of their black servants. This massacre at Weenen (Weeping) was to sit in the Afrikaner mind for over a century as the epitome of 'black barbarism' and, more to the point, the sort of fate Afrikaners might meet if they relented in their stern struggle for survival.

This brought Andries Pretorius to Zululand. Starting from the Eastern Cape later than the other voortrekkers, he had already earned a formidable military reputation. He and his commando ventured deep into Zulu territory and at the confluence of the Nkome river they formed a laager, tempting the Zulus to battle. The Boers commemorated their overwhelming victory as the battle of Blood River (16 December 1838), seeing it as the result of a compact between God and the Afrikaner nation (3,000 Zulu were killed and no Boers). The Boers soon retreated from Zululand over the Thukela into Natal while Dingane prepared to attack the Swazi. However, Dingane's brother, Mpande, heard that Dingane also had designs on his life and together with thousands of his followers he too fled to Natal where he made alliance with the Boers. In 1840 the allies marched on Zululand. Meanwhile Dingane's war with the Swazis went badly and ultimately he was caught and killed by them. Mpande was declared the new Zulu king by the Boers who returned from their raid with 36,000 cattle and 1,000 Zulu orphans whom they indentured as servants.

The first independent Boer state, the Republic of Natalia, was born out of these victories – again a popular but racially and gender-limited democracy: Natalia was ruled by a Volksraad (People's Council), elected by white adult males of the Dutch Reformed faith. The republic's president was no more than a chairman of the Council, and the Commandant-General (usually Andries Pretorius), who presided over the War Council, was not even allowed a vote on the Council – which in turn could be overruled by a public meeting of all Boers.

The British had been watching developments and were alarmed both by the way the Boers' vigorous treatment of black peoples was impacting on the Eastern Cape (they had received a bitter complaint from Faku, the Mpondo leader, about Zulu refugees being driven on to his land) and by the signs that the new republic might become a viable and independent commercial entity – an American ship had just called at Port Natal. So a British force under Captain Thomas Smith was sent to occupy Port Natal in May 1842 – a move to which trekkers replied by a siege of the town. Dick King – Natal's Paul Revere – rode the 600 miles to Grahamstown and summoned reinforcements who duly secured Natal for the British. The Volksraad submitted and in 1845 the formal annexation of Natal took place.

In essence the new colony inherited the land grant made to the Boers, which meant that the key divide lay along the Thukela. North of that the writ of the Zulu kings continued to run, south of it that of the British Crown. Immediately the colony found itself deluged by returning refugees who had fled from Shaka, a flow to which was added a steady stream of Zulus wishing to escape the king's rule. By the mid 1850s there were a quarter of a million of these 'Natal kaffirs' and the authorities only choked off the refugee flow by requiring (in 1856) every newcomer to work three years for a European employer before being allowed to settle. Meanwhile, some 5,000 British settlers were encouraged to settle in Natal, transforming the colony's political and social climate, much as they had in the Cape.

African affairs in Natal were managed by Theophilus Shepstone, the Secretary for Native Affairs, often considered as the father of indirect rule and racial segregation in Natal. This latter-day demonisation of Shepstone misses the point. He had indeed been a member of the 1846 land commission set up to delineate the boundaries and allocate land to black and white, and it is also true that he promoted the institution of chieftancy and helped keep the majority of the African population under a colonial version of customary law. But at the time these measures were perceived as protective of the Africans and they earned Shepstone the hatred of many settlers who accused him of creating reservations where Africans 'stagnated' rather than being 'developed' by becoming labourers on European farms. The policy was equivocal. Protection meant segregation and control; indeed, with the development of casual labour it was Shepstone who introduced influx control to the colony.

The incompatibility of this sort of protection with the colonial order, which turned chiefly powers and the tribal order into a mockery, was proved beyond doubt when a Hlubi chief, Langalibalele, was tried by a court consisting of colonial officials, including the Governor and Shepstone himself, and six chiefs. The 'guilty' verdict was confirmed by the Cape parliament and Langalibalele was sent into exile on Robben Island. In the end the verdict was found invalid by the British government and Langalibalele was returned to Natal.

The legislature of colonial Natal was based on a non-discriminatory franchise with blacks admitted to the electoral roll if they possessed a fixed property of £50 or if they paid at least £10 a year in rent. However, with the continued influx of Africans into the colony the outnumbered whites quickly found this to be far too liberal, so by 1865 further stringent qualifications for inclusion on the voters' roll were enacted.

Thus within a few years of its founding Natal had acquired three of its most lasting characteristics, each of them laced with irony. First, although the site of the original Boer republic, it was soon to become culturally the most English of all South Africa's provinces, long celebrated as 'the last outpost of the British Empire'. Second, this was always an extremely precarious status for nowhere else in southern Africa were a few thousand whites so vastly outnumbered by the surrounding blacks. Moreover, Natal's whites were pervasively aware that despite Dingane's defeat the might of the Zulu kingdom was still largely intact, constituting the most powerful black obstacle to white rule anywhere in the subcontinent. The resultant fears of Natal's whites – later the most determined white opponents of Afrikaner nationalist rule – led them to become pioneers of residential segregation, influx control, an exaggerated attempt to preserve traditional chiefly structures and all the other building blocks of apartheid.

But perhaps the greatest irony was on the black side. South of the Thukela lived those Zulus who wished to be free of the power of the Zulu kings and who were willing to live in a white-ruled state to secure that freedom. North of the Thukela lived those Zulus still under royal sway. The Zulu state put up with Shepstone's suzerainty through the long middle years of the nineteenth century, only to launch itself into all-out opposition to British rule in 1879, inflicting the most severe defeat imperial arms ever suffered at the hands of Africans. Yet a hundred years later it was the descendants of the loyalist Zulus who had sided with the British who backed the radical ANC, while the descendants of those who had fought the British were to support Chief Buthelezi's (more conservative) Inkatha movement. Thus the irony that the ANC, who would have loved to appropriate as their own the dramatic resistance of Cetshwayo to white rule, were unable to do so because this heritage belonged firmly in the Inkatha camp.

## The rise of the Boer republics

Voortrekkers on the highveld had seen Natalia as the centre of an emerging common voortrekker statehood in which all Boers would be linked as one. There was, at this stage, no idea of separate Boer republics and Pretorius, perhaps the pre-eminent leader, commuted between trekker settlements, trying to hold them all together. In 1841 an Adjunct Council was created in the new settlement of Potchefstroom, though merely as a branch of the Natal Volksraad. This council rejected Natal's capitulation to the British in 1842 and continued as an independent body but two years later a new Boer republic was created north of the Vaal with its constitution reflecting the same mix of populist democratic sentiment tempered by the military imperatives of ensuring survival.

But once again the British Crown, which the trekkers had worked so diligently to escape, followed hard on their heels. In February 1848 Harry Smith, the Governor of Natal, announced the annexation of Trans-Orangia, including not only the voortrekker territories but also the Sotho state, Adam Kok's Griqua, Sekhonyela's Tlokwa and Moro-ka's Rolong. Pretorius refused to accept this and in July issued an ultimatum to Smith, moving his troops to meet him in southern Trans-Orangia. Smith, together with a Griqua force, defeated Pretorius at Boomplaats and proclaimed the Orange River Sovereignty with its capital in Bloemfontein.

This represented a major crisis for the trekkers who gathered at

Magaliesberg in February 1849 to create a United Volksraad and to consider what to do. But personal rivalries together with a deep-seated distaste for placing authority into any one set of hands meant that instead of choosing a single commandant the Boers elected four. Of these, however, Pretorius soon emerged as the most resolute and energetic opponent of the British.

As it happened the British had overreached themselves. Moshoeshoe, having moved against the Tlokwa, Rolong and Kora, now also fell to blows with Sovereignty farmers over land. When he defeated a Sovereignty government force and made an alliance with Pretorius the British bluff was called – for they had no appetite for the much larger military adventure clearly required to maintain their position. Instead, they concluded that the occupation had been premature. In January 1852 they met Pretorius at Sand River and agreed to recognise the voortrekkers' right to full independence beyond the Vaal, repudiating all their previous treaties with 'the Coloured nations' to the north of the Vaal. In February 1854 the new Boer republic of the Orange Free State was proclaimed.

What became the Transvaal was acquired gradually over a period of decades. In the time-honoured tradition of *broedertwis* (brothers' quarrel) there was much animosity between its different Boer communities and the united Volksraad that was supposed to move from one location to another was extremely inefficient. Only on 12 September 1859 did the united Volksraad meet in Pretoria for the first time and found a new state, the South African Republic. The constitutions of both republics were based on white male suffrage, further limited in the SAR to the adherents of the Nederduitsh Hervormde Kerk. Both were to be led by an elected president, assisted by an executive council. The OFS constitution also completely outlawed black land ownership. There were to be Boer farmers and black farm labourers. These, the essential lines of Free State society, are still visible today.

Marthinus Pretorius, the son of Andries Pretorius and the first President of the South African Republic, tried to revive the dream of a single united Boer republic by accepting the presidency of the OFS in 1860. The British objected and the Volksraad backed down. It was a dream not finally fulfilled until Verwoerd declared South Africa a republic in 1961 – still visibly a Boer republic based on a whites-only franchise.

In both Boer republics the main source of wealth was land. Indeed, that is what they were for – the Boers trekking to find and possess land. For a white, acquiring land in the Transvaal was simplicity itself: he just had to find a piece of vacant land and register his claim. Africans, on the other hand, were forbidden to own land as individuals and although by 1900 there were three times as many Africans as whites in the Transvaal, only 1.2 per cent of the land had been made available for African chiefdoms or locations. The Boers could not conceive that land would come to seem quite secondary to the precious mineral resources found in both republics. Yet, with the characteristic irony of South African history, this soon occurred, changing everything.

The rise of the Boer republics was to transform southern Africa: Afrikaner nationalism was still trying to fulfil their inherent promise three and four generations later. But the trek and the emergence of the new republics had sealed the fate of the surrounding African peoples. For whatever their relations with the British or the Boers, there was simply no room for independent chiefdoms between these two white powers.

## Frontier wars again

Throughout this period the Cape colony was seldom really at peace with its neighbours. In 1828, having defeated the Ngwane with the help of the Xhosa, Thembu and Mpondo, the colony decided to create a buffer settlement of friendly Khoi on the Kat river. To accomplish this they had to evict Maqoma, brother of Sandile, Ngqika's successor, even though he had never fought against the colony.

In December 1834 the Rharhabe Xhosa attacked the colony, virtually besieging Grahamstown and Fort Beaufort. The surrounding farms lost tens of thousands of cattle. Hintsa, the chief of the Gcaleka and the paramount chief of the Xhosa, had supported the invasion while the Mfengu sided with the colony. This produced a determined British riposte. By April 1835 the Xhosa had been driven back and when British troops invaded Gcaleka territory Hintsa tried to negotiate a peace. He was promised security at the British camp but was then imprisoned and a ransom demanded for his release. He tried to escape and was brutally killed, British soldiers cutting off his ears and trying to dig out his teeth with bayonets as souvenirs.

The colony's only solution to the continuing problem was either to insert clumps of settlers – like the Khoi or the 1820 settlers – as 'buffers' or progressively to evict the Xhosa from more and more land. The Cape Governor, Benjamin D'Urban, now tried the latter, annexing the territory between the Keiskamma and Kei rivers, and demanded that the defeated chiefs remove their people from this area – but Lord Glenelg, the British Colonial Secretary, cancelled the plan, returned the border to the Fish river and decreed that no whites or Khoi be allowed to settle east of the Fish. D'Urban countered by extracting some 17,000 friendly Mfengu from the jurisdiction of the Gcaleka, and settling them and their 20,000 cattle at Fort Peddie, thus creating another buffer settlement – a move hardly calculated to make the Mfengu popular with the Xhosa.

Glenelg was determined to stabilise the situation and in 1836–7 got the colony to sign treaties with the Rharhabe, Gqunukwebe, Thembu and Mfengu, defining the boundaries between them and the colony, and stipulating the application of customary law (or what the colonial authorities considered to be customary law) in their territories. To make this stick, colony representatives were appointed as diplomatic agents to the chiefs with the task of negotiating the peaceful resolution of conflicts, while the army patrolled the borders on the colony's side.

The Glenelg system worked until the severe drought of 1842 caused great loss of cattle among both the eastern frontier settlers and the Xhosa. Cross-border rustling increased and the system of treaties had to be abandoned in 1844. Farmers were again allowed to try to recover stolen cattle beyond the border and to demand compensation when they failed to do so. In 1846 the seventh frontier war began – the so-called 'War of the Axe', after the incident, involving the killing of a farmer, which started it. Once again cattle exactions from the Xhosa provoked an initially successful Xhosa invasion of the colony but after a few months the Xhosa had to return home to cultivate their fields or face starvation. By 1847 it was all over. Sandile, the Ngqika chief, was deposed and all the territory between the Keiskamma and the Cape was annexed to the Crown as British Kaffraria, to be ruled through magistrates with chiefs becoming, in effect, colonial officials in the Crown's service. The former 'Ceded Territory' was now renamed Victoria and was settled by white farmers and the Mfengu.

This drastic act of confiscation provoked an inevitable rebellion. In 1850 the Ngqika, supported not only by some Thembu and Ndlambe but even by the Kat river Khoi, rose in revolt which was, equally inevitably, put down. But the uprising led the British to change their policy yet again: Sandile was restored, the status of other chiefs recognised and the Xhosa were allowed to stay in the territory to the west of the Kei river. This was accompanied by the now customary population shuffle. 'Friendly chiefs' were moved to the frontier to strengthen it; the Khoi were evicted from the Kat river valley and white farmers settled in their place; the Thembu were moved to make way for the Khoi – and British Kaffraria was designated for white settlement.

The greatest disaster to befall the Xhosa, however, was self-inflicted. A young Gcaleka girl, Nongqawuse, prophesied that if the Xhosa killed their cattle and destroyed their crops their ancestors would rise from the dead, driving the whites into the sea, and replace the slaughtered cattle many times over. The Gcaleka chief, Sarhili, called on his people to comply and in 1857 a massive cattle killing took place. The result was a devastating famine in which tens of thousands died and even more fled into the colony to seek employment. The population of the future Ciskei fell by two thirds and the number of migrant workers from the Ciskei increased tenfold to around 350,000 people. This event lived on in apartheid era history books as 'the national suicide of the Xhosa', an all too revealing phrase, since banished as politically incorrect. The British government prosecuted fourteen chiefs for 'conspiracy' following this disaster and went ahead with the settlement of white farmers in Kaffraria. They were unwilling, however, to allow settlement beyond the Kei, so that the southern Nguni were left with considerable autonomy in the so-called Transkei just as the northern Nguni were within Zululand – a fact which still profoundly marks South Africa, for these are the two areas in which traditional chieftaincy retains legitimacy to this day.

In 1877 the last frontier war irrupted. A Gcaleka was killed in the house of a Mfengu headman; Sarhili's Gcaleka attacked the Mfengu; the colony sided with the loyal Mfengu – which meant fighting and suppressing Sandile's Ngqika who had supported the Gcaleka. In 1878, after a bloody campaign which cost more lives than all the three previous wars, the land of both the Ngqika and the Gcaleka was confiscated and their chiefdoms divided to diminish the power of the chiefs. The Cape's annexation of the Transkei in 1879 produced an inevitable uprising there but by 1881 this had been suppressed with the help of the Mfengu and Bhaca. The territories of the Thembu, the Bomvana and the Gcaleka were then annexed to the Cape in 1885.

The Cape's incorporation of the Mpondo took another decade. In 1878, against the will of the Mpondo chief, Mqikela, the British acquired Port St Johns. Mqikela, advised and supported by white traders, responded by imposing a tax on the trade caravans passing through from the Cape. Moreover, he attempted to create an alternative to Port St Johns by opening a new trading outpost, Port Grosvenor. Unwilling to tolerate such a challenge, the British declared a protectorate over the Pondoland coast in 1885 and, although Mqikela rejected it outright, internal dissensions within the Mpondo forced him to agree to cede part of his territory. The Cape made sure that their ally, Sigcau, succeeded to the chieftaincy on Mqikela's death and then incorporated Pondoland into the Cape in 1894 as part of the Transkei.

## The war against the Zulus

Given that the Zulu state was by far the strongest in southern Africa, it is amazing how much Zulu territory was alienated to the whites without a fight, first by Dingane's inexplicable generosity (which, his behaviour towards Retief suggests, he regretted later), then by Mpande's dependence on the support of the whites and his willingness to co-operate with them. However, both the British and the Boers were uncomfortably aware that Zulu military might was still intact and there was always a sense that the completion of white control of the region would require a showdown with the Zulus sooner or later. Sure enough, in 1856, with Mpande still in power, a war of succession broke out between Cetshwayo and Mbuyazi. When Cetshwayo won, thousands of Mbuyazi's followers fled to Natal, soon followed by many of Mpande's supporters as Cetshwayo made his bid for the throne. Shepstone managed to get Cetshwayo to accept Mpande as king, though only at the price of Cetshwayo being formally proclaimed as Mpande's heir. Thenceforward, until Mpande's death in 1872, Cetshwayo accumulated more and more power, enhanced by purchases of firearms through his friend John Dunn.

Both Mpande and Cetshwayo repeatedly complained to the Natal government about Boer encroachment on their land. The fact that these complaints were generally ignored saw Cetshwayo become distrustful of British good faith. Hardly had Cetshwayo ascended the throne than he expelled most of the missionaries from Zululand. Then, when Shepstone supported the British annexation of the Transvaal in 1877, Cetshwayo's trust in him evaporated completely: rightly so, for the combination of labour shortages on Natal's sugar plantations and the expansionist ambitions of Transvaal's farmers, who cast their eyes on the Mpholozi-Pongolo area, both produced pressures which could not be met while the power of the Zulu state remained intact.

So when, in 1878, a party of Zulu warriors crossed the Thukela into Natal to kidnap and kill two runaway wives of a Zulu chief the Natal authorities blew the incident up into a major *casus belli*. Sir Bartle

Frere, the new British High Commissioner, demanded not only that Cetshwayo pay compensation but that he also disband his army and accept a British Resident who would be the final arbiter of war and peace. This ultimatum, reflecting Frere's brief to consolidate British territories in southern Africa in a confederation, was a quite deliberate attempt to provoke war.

The ultimatum was rejected and British forces invaded Zululand. On 22 January 1879 an 800-strong British unit was surrounded and wiped out by the Zulu army in a battle at the foot of Isandlwana mountain. Just as the Zulus had shaken the Boers, so now they delivered an enormous shock to British self-confidence and prestige. Indeed, the award of eleven Victoria Crosses for the defence of Rorke's Drift, which followed shortly thereafter, was motivated largely by the need to raise the morale of a stunned British public. The British then moved up heavy artillery to shell Cetshwayo's grass hut capital, Ulundi, and this was declared a triumphant victory. Cetshwayo was captured and sent to Cape Town while further Zulu resistance was stilled by the promise that they would keep their land.

The British then sought to destroy the very fabric of the Zulu state. Not only was the monarchy suppressed altogether but the country was divided into thirteen chiefdoms, none of whose chiefs had any right to have an army or maintain the Zulu military system of age regiments. The subdivision of Zulu territory was presented as a return to the pre-Shaka situation but in reality the new system of power had little in common with any idea of 'traditionality'. The powers of the newly established chiefs were defined by the British and a British Resident was placed permanently in Zululand. The territories ruled by the new chiefs bore no relation to the pre-Shaka dispensation and even some lineages and clans directly connected to Shaka were placed under chiefs in no way connected to them. Moreover, the new chiefs were appointed simply on account of their loyalty to the British – the outstanding example being John Dunn, who had switched to the British side during the war, a piece of treachery for which he was rewarded with the largest chiefdom, later known as the Reserve. On orders from the British, Dunn and the other new chiefs stripped Cetshwayo's clan, the Usuthu, of cattle and firearms.

Cetshwayo and his supporters fought for the restoration of the monarchy. In 1882 a deputation of Cetshwayo's Usuthu supporters – a crowd of about 2,000 people – gathered in Pietermaritzburg and demanded the restoration of the monarchy. Cetshwayo petitioned the British authorities from Cape Town and in 1882, thanks to the assistance of Bishop Colenso, managed to visit London to present his case. He was allowed to return to Zululand in 1883 and restored as a ruler of the central part of his former kingdom – which left Dunn's Reserve and the territory of another appointed chief, Zibhebhu of the Mandlakazi clan, intact. Only six months later Cetshwayo clashed with Zibhebhu, suffered a complete defeat and fled. He died – was perhaps poisoned – in February 1884.

Cetshwayo's young son, Dinuzulu, was pronounced king, but the British decided to support Zibhebhu as a strong leader whom they could rely on. Dinuzulu accordingly appealed to the Boers, and their combined Usuthu-Boer force attacked the Mandlakazi – who had to flee to the Reserve to seek British protection. Dinuzulu rewarded the Boers with some 4,000 square miles of his land. The British negotiated the borders of this new territory with the Boers – not with the Zulus – and yet another independent Boer state, the New Republic, was born, comprising over a third of Zululand, including much of its core pasture and several sacred areas and chiefly homesteads. In 1887 the British annexed the remainder of Zululand and the New Republic was incorporated into the Transvaal.

Soon after this the Mandlakazi were allowed to return to Zululand, only to be attacked and defeated by Dinuzulu. The British, regarding this as a challenge to their authority, attacked and defeated Dinuzulu, who attempted to find refuge with the Boers but, on the advice of Colenso's daughter, Harriet, submitted to the British. In 1889 he was exiled to St Helena.

With Zulu independence crushed, disasters followed thick and fast. In 1889 Zulu crops were struck by drought, in 1894–5 locusts destroyed their grain, in 1897 85 per cent of their cattle were killed by rinderpest. The same year the British transferred Zululand to Natal and allowed Dinuzulu to return home. A few years later the British sold off 2.6 million acres (40 per cent) of what remained of Zululand, hugely enriching the white sugar barons.

The crushing of Nguni independence was an inexorable process. Although there were many twists and turns, the end result was never in doubt. What lives in the popular imagination, however, is the formidable Zulu resistance to the Boers and the dramatic Zulu victory at Isandlwana; the Xhosa (as Zulus are still wont to remind them) never came remotely near such feats of arms. But in some ways this symbolism conceals more than it reveals.

While there is not much point trying to divide Nguni leaders into those who resisted and those who collaborated with colonialism – too many did both – it should be noted that the experience of the southern Nguni was very different from that of their northern cousins. The southern Nguni were frozen in an attitude of defiance through endless wars over the course of a century, whereas the Zulu monarchy was left intact until 1879, then quite suddenly crushed before being reinstated as a shadow of its former self in the twentieth century. When in 1990 the era of democratic politics dawned, opinion surveys showed a virtual Xhosa unanimity behind the ANC but the large majority of Zulus north of the Thukela arrayed behind the Inkatha leader, Mangosuthu Buthelezi. It is difficult not to trace this Xhosa militancy on the one hand to their long drawn-out resistance to colonial encroachment and the more accommodationist stance of traditional Zulu voters to the fact that until 1879 the Zulu state had reached a modus vivendi with the advancing power of the whites – and that some care went into re-creating at least the forms of that accommodation in the twentieth century too.

## The sad overwhelming of the Kora and the Griquas

By the 1850s the territory along the Orange river, particularly to the north, was dominated by the Griqua, the Kora, the Tlhaping and the Rolong. The Kora dominated the lower Orange but they had lost their earlier dominance of the triangle between the Orange and the Vaal as the whites acquired their land and settled in the area. Some Kora retreated north of the Vaal; those who stayed did so as farm workers for the whites. Even then the Kora remained a force to the west of the Orange-Vaal confluence. What finally broke Kora power was the drought of 1868. Losing many of their cattle, the Kora turned to rustling the colony's cattle. The Cape set up a border police and then in 1869 a full-scale war broke out, putting an end to Kora cattle raids. The south bank of the Orange was designated for white settlement and the north bank left to the Kora with two of their leaders, Klaas Lukas and Klaas Pofadder, recognised as rulers. Many Kora, however, decided to stay on the south bank and in 1879 the government began to evict them in order to settle white farmers there. As a result many joined the uprising in Griqualand West in 1878. Inevitably the colony won and the Kora lost their remaining land, subsequently renamed Gordonia.

The Griqua under Adam Kok II had founded Philippolis as far back as 1826 when the Griqua had expelled the San from the area and occupied it themselves. With the onset of the Great Trek the Boers began to acquire Griqua land so in 1843 the Cape offered them protection and by 1845 the borders of their territory were drawn. Their land was divided into alienable and inalienable sections – although some of the inalienable land had, in fact, already been occupied by whites. Despite this in the early 1850s the Griqua flourished. They took up grain farming, bred horses and merino sheep, and traded with the colony, enjoying a certain degree of protection against the Boers. But disaster struck with the Bloemfontein convention of 1854, which led to the foundation of the OFS and allowed the new Boer republic to administer Griqua lands. The Griqua immediately lost any right to compensation for land taken from them. They could see the writing on the wall and in 1858 decided to sell all their land and move, trekking in a long and difficult migration, losing people and cattle all the way, from Philippolis to Kokstad. Adam Kok III insisted that their settlement there should ban both the alienation of land and the sale of liquor. While this lasted Griqualand East – as the settlement was known – was a success but already the British had announced that they were placing the settlement under their suzerainty. After Kok's death the pressure on land from the whites and immigrants from the Transkei proved too much. In 1878 the Griquas rose in rebellion against British rule but this was easily suppressed.

In 1834 Andries Waterboer, leader of another Griqua group to the north of the Orange, had made an alliance with the Cape Governor, D'Urban, but, predictably, this did not long survive the discovery of diamonds in 1867. This first discovery at Hopetown was followed by a further one in 1869 at Pniel, in the border area with the Orange Free State, followed in 1870 by others at what was to become Kimberley. The Pniel discovery was claimed by the Griqua (now ruled by Andries's son, Nicholas), the Tlhaping, the Transvaal, the OFS and, independently, by the diggers themselves, who attempted to create an independent republic. The Kimberley find was situated on the border between Kok's and Waterboer's Griqua, and was claimed both by the OFS and the Waterboer Griqua. Waterboer's interests were defended by a lawyer who demanded land to the east of the Orange-Vaal confluence as his fee so that even when the Griqua won the case, they still lost land. The boundaries of Waterboer's territory, Griqualand West, were then drawn up, and Waterboer quickly asked for and got a British protectorate, proclaimed in 1873. Even this did not help: the Griqua soon lost their land as it was engulfed in a diamond rush. The Mining Board created in 1874 bitterly opposed any Griqua claims to mining rights and effectively restricted mine ownership to whites. By the end of the 1870s the Griqua were dumped into locations, allegedly in order to protect them from losing more land. The Griqua, now robbed of their land, rose in rebellion in 1878–9 and were easily put down. In 1880 Griqualand West was incorporated into the Cape.

## The Sotho and the Pedi

Moshoeshoe, the Sotho leader, is often and rightly admired for the skill with which he preserved his territory and his nation's independence. At first it looked as if the pattern seen elsewhere would engulf the Sotho too: during the Trek Moshoeshoe gave the Boers transit rights but they began to build permanent buildings. Moshoeshoe took the strategic view that the Boers were the greater threat and so, artfully, got the Cape Governor involved in delimiting Sotho borders and, at his suggestion, set aside a tract of (alienable) land for white settlement between the Orange and the Caledon in 1845 – but did not encourage his people who occupied this territory to move. In 1848 Moshoeshoe supported High Commissioner Harry Smith's annexation of Trans-Orangia in the face of bitter Boer resentment and when, the next year, a new demarcation of borders removed a hundred villages and thousands of his people from Moshoeshoe's jurisdiction, Moshoeshoe swallowed even this bitter pill in order to keep his alliance with the British against the Boers. He could not, however, restrain all his subordinate chiefs and in 1851 and 1852 two British expeditions were organised against them, both of them repulsed by Moshoeshoe's troops. Moshoeshoe then adroitly reconciled with the British just before the British left Trans-Orangia in 1854, leaving the Sotho face to face with the Boers.

In 1858 conflicting land claims in the lower Caledon led to the first attack from the OFS, which was again repulsed by the Sotho. In 1864 the Boers, this time much better prepared, launched a new war of attrition and by April 1866 Moshoeshoe had to sign away two thirds of his arable land and 3,000 cattle. But the alienated land lay empty and the Sotho attempted to reoccupy it. In 1867–8 Boer commandos mounted punitive expeditions into these areas, killing and chasing away the Sotho but at this point Moshoeshoe's long courtship of the British paid dividends for the British now put the Sotho directly under their High Commissioner in the Cape. In 1870 Moshoeshoe died – just as the full rigours of colonial rule were being imposed, including a hut tax and obligatory labour service. Moshoeshoe's son, Letsie, accepted these changes but the chiefs wouldn't: a minor revolt in 1879 was followed by a full-scale rebellion in 1880, the so-called 'gun war', caused by the attempt by the colonial authorities to disarm the Sotho. The Cape government decided to get rid of the troublesome territory and returned it to the British, who made Basutoland the first of their three southern African protectorates, thus preventing any more inroads into Sotho territory by anyone.

The story of the Pedi followed a sadder and more familiar pattern. Before the Trek the main danger to the Pedi were the formidable Ndebele but, to their great relief the latter moved off to get away from the advancing Boers. The Pedi leader, Sekwati, seeing the Boers as allies, signed an agreement with Hendrik Potgieter in 1845, ceding some of his territory to the Boers. The Boers interpreted this as a transfer of freehold – a concept unknown among Africans, the Pedi seeing it as merely a lease. Meanwhile, the Boers at Ohrigstad, regarding the Pedi as tributaries of the Swazi, secured a grant of the Pedi land west of the Steelpoort river from the Swazi king, Mswati.

Inevitably, relations between the Boers and the Pedi deteriorated. In 1852 Boer commandos attacked the Pedi settlement, Phiring, but the Pedi repelled the attack and then withdrew to their mountain stronghold, Thaba Mosega. A treaty of 1857 recognised Pedi independence and defined the boundaries between them and the Boers.

Sekwati died in 1861 and was succeeded by his son, Sekhukhune, though only after seeing off a tough challenge from his brother, Mampuru. Uniquely among Africans of that era, from the late 1840s on – and with strong encouragement from Sekwati and then from Sekhukhune – the Pedi went to work as migrant labourers as far away as Port Elizabeth, and later in the diamond mines, mostly in order to buy firearms. These arms gave the Pedi a real edge over their neighbours and when they clashed with – and roundly defeated – the Swazi in 1869 the Boers began to see them as an uncomfortably powerful presence. Relations between the Pedi and the Boers were also aggravated by Sekhukhune's expulsion of missionaries and their followers in 1864. He had at first tolerated the missionaries but had come to distrust them as the number of their converts grew, particularly among this own family, for he believed they were working for the Transvaal's interests. Worse still, Sekhukhune's treaty with the Transvaal did not define their mutual boundaries and large numbers of white farmers had moved into his territory, claiming it as theirs. This brought up difficult questions not only about land but also about taxation and labour dues, both of which Sekhukhune flatly refused to provide for he did not recognise Transvaal sovereignty over his land.

In May 1876 President Thomas Burgers of the South African Republic declared war on Sekhukhune. The Boers and the Swazis, who supported them against the Pedi, did not manage to defeat the Pedi militarily but did finally starve them into signing a peace treaty in 1877, though whether Sekhukhune understood that he had thereby agreed to recognise the Transvaal's suzerainty is unclear; at any rate he later denied it. A few months later in May 1877 the British annexed the Transvaal and Sekhukhune quickly asked for their protection against the Boers. But 1878 found the British at war with the Pedi, for they feared, probably wrongly, that Sekhukhune was supporting Cetshwayo. The first British attack was repulsed and the next followed only in September 1879, after the end of the Anglo-Zulu war and the capture of Cetshwayo. The British mobilised a force of nearly 14,000 people, the majority of them Swazi and other Transvaal Africans. Even so the Pedi held out until November before Sekhukhune was captured and imprisoned in Pretoria. The war had cost him the lives of three brothers and nine sons. His old rival, Mampuru, was appointed Paramount Chief of the Pedi. In 1881, when the independence of the Transvaal was restored, Sekhukhune was released but in 1882 Mampuru had him killed. The paramount chieftaincy of the Pedi was split, both administratively and politically, and steps taken to ensure that no such dangerous challenger could ever arise again.

## The Swazi and the Venda

The Swazi were the only big and relatively strong African group not to opt for any form of military opposition to the advancing tide of Boer or British power. Their king, Mswati, who took over from Queen Mother Thandile in 1846, played his cards well. The Swazi established good relations with the Ohrigstad-Lydenburg Boers, gave them land between the Olifants and Crocodile rivers, and signed a treaty with them in exchange for cattle and support against the Zulu and the Pedi. Hendrik Potgieter's Boers, who had acquired land from the Pedi, also turned out to be a common opponent for both the Lydenburgers (who were in dispute with him) and Mswati, whose brother, Somcube, nearly toppled Mswati from power, thanks to Potgieter's support. In 1855 Mswati gave away land along the north bank of the Pongola for Boer settlement in order to strengthen his position against the Zulus.

In 1875 a new treaty was signed with the Transvaal according to which the Swazi accepted a semi-dependent status by agreeing to the appointment of a Transvaal official to supervise their external policy (although not to rule them). They also agreed to keep their trade routes open to the Boers and allowed a railway to be built through their territory. In exchange the Swazi received assurances of support against the Pedi and the Zulus. In 1879 they helped the British against Sekhukhune and Cetshwayo. Despite this and despite British backing during the 1880s they lost land to the Boers in the west and to the Portuguese in the east. By the end of the 1880s Swazi authority had been completely undermined by land, mineral, trade and other concessions as settlers, mineral prospectors, traders and others crisscrossed their strategically placed territory.

In 1893 the British government agreed that the Transvaal should administer the whites now resident on Swazi territory. Only at this point did the Swazi refuse to comply – but it was too late. The following year the British government and President Kruger of the South African Republic agreed that the SAR would establish a protectorate over the Swazi – without asking for Swazi consent. However, the collapse of the SAR in the Anglo-Boer War saw the Swazis, now with a much reduced territory, become a separate protectorate under the Crown – a status which prevented further colonial depredations. In that limited sense, at least, the Swazis' steady refusal to take up arms paid off.

The story of the Venda repeats the story of other mountainous chiefdoms in the era of conquest. They felt relatively secure in their Soutpansberg refuge and maintained relations both with the Tsonga in the east and, to the south, with the Boers who had settled at Schoemansdal at the foot of the Soutpansberg. Thanks to their redoubt and the firearms which they bought from both parties, the Venda were able to withstand the growing colonial pressures. In the early 1860s, however, the Boers began to intervene in Venda affairs, backing a rival to the popularly supported Paramount Chief, Machado. Machado responded by sacking Schoemansdal in 1867. The Boers had to flee – but later returned and tried to establish control over Venda territory all the way to the Limpopo. After Machado's death his heir, Mphephu, continued to oppose incorporation into the Transvaal but he was defeated in 1898 and had to flee across the Limpopo. The Venda were the last African chiefdom to be incorporated into white-ruled South Africa. With that white rule became coterminous with the country.

The litany of conquest records a cruel and cynical process. Treaties were ignored, laws changed, agreements made and applied to people who did not understand their contents and land relentlessly appropriated.

But it is difficult to moralise about the process. The conquered societies themselves operated according to similar principles: a drought or cattle disease simply meant you pillaged the cattle of the neighbouring community, leaving them to die of starvation. No white leader killed as many Africans as Shaka did. And some African societies were quite willing to indulge in slave raiding and slave trading: had the practice not been abolished by the British it would undoubtedly have continued. For some of the colonised, moreover, colonialism did bring education and higher life expectancy.

Much the same could have been said of colonial conquest almost anywhere in Africa, but several things made South Africa unique. First, there was no single colonialism but instead competing forms of white rule within the same arena, a competition which ultimately eventuated in a large-scale and bitter war. Second – and this was to create an explosive dynamic lasting another century – the ultimate objective of British colonialism, far more than the conquest of this or that African group, was the conquest and colonisation of the Boers. So great was the drama of this colonisation of one white group by another that for many years this seemed to overshadow the colonisation of the black majority. For even after the Anglo–Boer War was won and lost, an intense struggle between competing sections of white society continued for several more generations – an event unthinkable elsewhere in Africa.

This in turn was possible because South Africa experienced white settlement on a scale not seen anywhere else in Africa, with a correspondingly profound economic impact. The transformation wrought by white rule was so great in South Africa that not only the country but all its people were changed profoundly, making these early struggles seem impossibly distant today. If one compares this with, for example, the not atypical experience of Guinea where Samory Touré fought the French until 1898 and Sekou Touré won independence from them in 1958, one can see how brief and shallow the colonial experience often was. In South Africa white rule began far earlier, lasted far longer and was utterly transformative in its character. While today's African nationalists often call for 'transformation' and use the phrase '*Mayibuye Afrika*' (Come back Africa) these are sad and self-deceiving themes. For in South Africa, more than anywhere else in Africa, transformation took place long ago and there can be no going back.

# VI

## TOWARDS ONE COUNTRY

ⓐ ⓐ ⓐ

The coming of the British changed South Africa utterly: it was now in the mainstream of the world's most powerful imperial state. Even the Cape colony changed in character. The arrival of the British 1820 settlers had brought increased demands for popular participation – and created a press. The first government newspaper – *The Cape Town Gazette and African Advertiser* – appeared in 1800 and the first independent newspaper, *The South African Commercial Advertiser*, in 1827. The first newspaper in Dutch and English, *Die Zuid Afrikaan*, followed in 1830. During the 1840s extensive road construction began and small towns grew up around Dutch Reformed churches. The colony exported wheat, wine and, above all, wool. Wool was produced mostly in the eastern part of the colony and exported from the new harbour at Port Elizabeth. The future University of Cape Town was founded in 1829 as a college and by the 1850s a network of Anglican schools had emerged.

In 1853 a new constitution gave the Cape self-government with a non-racial franchise including a small number of non-whites. Tighter administrative control was established over the provinces and the newly conquered territories and in 1866 the newly acquired Ciskei was given two seats in the Cape parliament, with the Transkei following suit soon after. Although the number of non-white voters was not allowed to expand – indeed, stricter qualifications were later enacted – the granting of the vote, in however limited a fashion, to a conquered population was an unusually liberal measure in an age when segregation and discrimination were the universal norm.

By mid century the big British banks had arrived at the Cape. They were followed there and to Natal by representatives of other major

British companies, while local businesses began to grow in size too. Gradually they spread throughout southern Africa – including the Boer republics – strengthening and uniting the region's economy. Similarly, British culture and the English language were now predominant in the Cape, though in the 1870s an Afrikaner cultural renaissance began.

This was based not on the high Dutch spoken by the small, well-educated elite of white Dutch speakers but on a simplified and Creolised version of Dutch, born in the streets of Cape Town among its multi-ethnic lower classes. Rather as black American slang travelled from the back streets up the social scale in twentieth-century America, so Afrikaans was taken over as the new 'people's language' and nurtured by the new Afrikaner nationalist movement. The first Afrikaans newspaper appeared, *De Afrikaanse Patriot*, as also an Afrikaner school history and several other school textbooks in Afrikaans. The movement began in the Cape but soon spread to the Transvaal and the OFS. In 1880 the Afrikaner Bond was started with the goal of uniting Afrikaner nationalist movements in all the different territories.

Meanwhile more British immigrants came to Natal, some 5,000 arriving between 1849 and 1852. They mostly engaged in maize, wool and stock farming though by the late 1850s the province's potential for large-scale sugar cultivation had become apparent. Regular coastal traffic between the Cape and Natal opened up in the 1840s but the great handicap – not removed till the 1890s – was the sand bar at the entrance to Durban harbour, which made entry difficult for all but shallow-draft vessels. Politically, Natal evolved along the same path as the Cape, securing a governor and executive council in 1856. Theoretically, before 1865 blacks enjoyed the franchise there too, provided they possessed a property worth at least £50 or paid £10 a year in rent – though in 1865 the law was amended to make the extension of the black vote virtually impossible. In 1893 Natal was given responsible government and a parliament.

From 1860 on Natal's Indians began to arrive – mainly from southern India – as cheap indentured labour for the sugar plantations. Their five-year contracts gave them the option to stay for another five years – or go back. They worked under appalling conditions, were treated badly and the majority remained poor. However, from the early 1870s those who had skills were offered land on completion of their contracts and Indian immigration started to grow. Wealthy Indian traders began to come of their own accord – for which reason they were called 'passenger Indians'. They moved beyond Natal's borders into the Transvaal and the Orange Free State, and began to compete with white traders. By

1900 Natal's Indian population numbered about 100,000, far surpassing the whites. One of the new arrivals, a young lawyer, Mohandas Gandhi, spent twenty-one years (1893–1914) in Natal, where he developed his philosophy of non-violent resistance to oppression.

By 2000 there were around a million Indians in South Africa, almost 90 per cent of them in KwaZulu-Natal, the vast majority Hindus but with around 200,000 Moslems. There are another half-million Moslems among the so-called Cape Coloureds but Islam had arrived there quite independently. It had reached Cape Town with the slaves from Indonesia and Malaysia, and had spread fast. Most of the 'passenger Indians' were also Moslems.

The story of nineteenth-century South Africa is one of colonial expansion followed by incorporation. For the British followed in the footsteps of the Boers and made several attempts to unify South Africa into a single country before finally achieving this objective by war. Long before African societies were politically incorporated into the British Empire or the Boer republics, however, their social incorporation had already moved on apace. They were very different societies from what they had been seventy years earlier. The old order was undermined not only by outright conquest and colonisation but also by new social and ideological forces developing within African societies and, indeed, countrywide. By the end of the century a single country with common or at least comparable problems was already visibly rising from the ruins of the pre-colonial era.

Several factors helped pull the country together. The first was that, whatever the differences between Briton and Boer, the new order they installed was equally revolutionary in African terms, being based on written laws, contracts and constitutions. Both sought to regulate by law the lives of their newly acquired subjects, previously constrained only by custom and tradition and, however much they kicked against it, all African societies had to come to terms with this new order, backed up as it was by unarguable military supremacy. True, rural Africans in remote areas might have relatively little contact with this new order at first but when even so mighty a figure as the Zulu king could be felled and exiled by it, there was no question of anyone avoiding submission to it.

Boers and Britons alike brought Christianity with them and it was stunningly successful. It mattered little whether Africans first adopted it as an escape route from war or the unlimited power of tribal rulers, to seek new and more powerful protectors or to gain an education. Similarly, although relations between the different Christian denominations were not always good, and the relations between the missionaries and the colonial or Boer authorities were often frankly bad, the key fact was that Christianity of one variety or another was a ubiquitous presence in the lives of Africans, Boers and Britons alike. The expansion of the Cape was also a religious expansion: in 1785 it had only six parishes but by 1860 it had sixty-four.

The first missionary to arrive in South Africa (in 1728) was Georg Schmidt of the German Moravian Society. The belief spread that all baptised slaves had to be set free, so that the burghers' hostility led to the mission's abandonment in 1744, though the GMS returned to South Africa in 1792. The London Missionary Society began its work in the Cape in 1799 and by 1816 had twenty missionaries in the field. The Church Missionary Society arrived in 1821. From the early nineteenth century on, the missionaries moved into the interior. They preferred to operate through the chiefs but their teaching, their introduction of a new way of life and their independence offered an escape route for dissidents within tribal society and this often led to conflicts.

Although some missionaries quarrelled with colonial officialdom, almost all believed in the superiority of European culture and supported the extension of colonial rule. This did not seem to hinder their growing success among Africans. By the later nineteenth century, black Christians were playing a notable role even in those African states which were still independent. When Moroka II, chief of the still independent Rolong of Thaba 'Nchu, died in 1880, the ensuing succession struggle was fought out between two Christians, one an Anglican, educated in Cape Town and Canterbury, the other a Methodist.

Some Christian converts became famous. Tiyo Soga, a Xhosa converted by Scottish missionaries and educated in Scotland, was ordained in 1856 as the first black South African minister of religion. He became a missionary himself and translated religious literature into Xhosa, but was also known as a writer and composer in his own right. His significance lay in his innovative development of Africanist thought, for he seems to have been the first black African to think and write of Africans as a single community rather than a conglomeration of different tribes. Proud of his roots, he strongly urged his mixed-race children (his wife was a Scot) to choose to be African, not white. Another striking figure was Nehemiah Tile, a Wesleyan who founded the Thembu Church, perhaps the first independent church in South Africa, the precursor of many. In 1881 John Tengo Jabavu, the son of Mfengu Methodists and a prominent African teacher, became the editor of the

Xhosa section of the *Christian Express* published by the Lovedale mission, and in 1884 he founded the first African newspaper, *Imvo Zabantsundu*. In 1876 Elija Makiwane founded the first African organisation, the Native Education Association. All these early black intellectuals were mission products.

Property qualifications kept most Cape Africans off the voters' roll but in 1882 a political party, Imbumba yama Nyama, was founded in deliberate imitation of the Afrikaner Bond and demanded a wider franchise to bring in more blacks. Its spectacular popular success (*Imvo Zabantsundu* was founded to support the party) merely frightened the whites and led to the Registration Act (1887), the Franchise and Ballot Act (1892) and the Glen Grey Act (1894), which raised the qualification bar in order to curb the growth of the black electorate. In 1889–92 a new African organisation, the Native Congress, was created to challenge Jabavu's group. Led by a group of Xhosas headed by Jonathan Tunyiswa, in 1897 the Congress started its own paper, *Izwi Labantu*, thanks in part to a grant from Cecil Rhodes.

Christianity – and the literacy and education it brought – introduced wholly new factors into African society but already the development of a labour market and of labour migrancy was utterly transforming that society. Even before the Trek when communities suffered famine, war or displacement they tended to collapse into offering themselves as labourers in the colony as the price of survival, but during the Trek and the colonial expansion which followed it this practice became far more widespread. More often than not this was the result of the loss of land. Indeed, the whole process of expropriating African land was carried out with the dual aim of acquiring more land for white settlers and forcing blacks to become wage labourers on the new farms. But while wage labour made the labourer dependent on white employers it also subverted all the bonds and hierarchies of African society and the resources it offered an individual could be commuted into anything money could buy. Thus it offered opportunity as well as exploitation – which is why many, like the Pedi, sought it voluntarily.

All these tendencies worked in the same direction, slowly amalgamating a diverse and divided region into a united whole – the slow pace ordained by its simple agrarian economy and a far lesser white population than had swarmed into other parts of the New World. In 1853 a Russian writer and traveller to the Cape, Ivan Goncharov, lamented that 'There is no gold here and the crowds will not rush here as they did to California and Australia'. In fact, the first diamonds were found in 1867 and the diamond rush was on. By 1871 the white population in the Kimberley diamond fields had reached 25,000 and the black population 50,000, numbers which continued to grow. Whites came from around the world but within southern Africa the Pedi, Sotho and Tswana supplied the largest contingents, with Natal and the Cape providing most of the educated black Christians employed as artisans and clerks. Apart from the actual diggings, diamonds also brought large numbers of unskilled jobs in trade, transport, road building and construction. Work on the mines was hard and dangerous but it paid well and, from the beginning, as still today, was accompanied by diamond smuggling.

Diamonds changed South Africa for ever. Foreign and domestic investment poured in on an unprecedented scale, the transport system was sharply upgraded to cope with increased movement of people and goods, while the expanded market for food brought higher prices and profits for farmers. Even traditionally subsistent African farmers were stimulated to grow cash crops but the same dialectic which had seen the drive for a wider African franchise produce the opposite result was to cripple African commercial agriculture. For farming was still by far the biggest sector of the economy and the upward lift it now experienced saw a renewed drive to push Africans off the land and into the white farms and mines. This conflict of interest became a major motive force of South African politics. Gradually those Africans with commercial agricultural skills were forced into sharecropping: Charles van Onselen's memorable biography of one such sharecropper, Kas Maine, shows how skilled some were and what a long (though hopeless) rearguard action they fought.

Many Africans who came to work on the farms and in the mines did not see themselves as permanently quitting one way of life for another. They came in order to work for a season or two to earn money for a particular purpose. Often, they used their wages to buy a rifle and pay *lobola* (the bride price). Having earned enough to do this they would return home, sometimes to communities that had not yet been colonised – in which case they might use their newly acquired weapons precisely to resist such colonisation.

The diamond fields were claimed by several parties, not only by Waterboer's Griqua and the republic of the Orange Free State, but also by the Transvaal, the Tswana and the diggers themselves who proclaimed their own independent republic at Klipdrift. The British entrusted the judgement to a 'neutral' party – the Lieutenant-Governor of Natal, Robert Keate, who awarded most of the diamond fields to the Griqua and kept open the trade routes and roads passing through their territory from the Cape Colony to the north. But the spoils were too rich for this 'Keate award' to last and in 1871 the British annexed the new colony of Griqualand West.

The new colony was racked by tension. The number of claims which could be registered in any name or company was limited and neither competition nor output was regulated. This quickly led to over-production and a calamitous drop in diamond prices. Moreover, in the liberal Cape spirit access to the diamond diggings was, at least in theory, unrestricted by race – though most diggers were white. When, however, some Griquas attempted to register their claims, there was a virtual insurrection by the white diggers. The colour bar was quickly introduced and an unlimited number of claims allowed, thus opening the way for big mining companies.

Cecil John Rhodes, a seventeen-year-old Englishman of modest means, arrived in South Africa in 1870. He was to play a major role in changing the face of diamond digging and of South Africa itself. He started on his brother's farm but was soon drawn to the diamond fields. Seeing the cycle of boom and bust, he realised that the future of the mines lay in amalgamation so as to be able to ride out the downturns and cannily used the busts to buy up numerous claims. Unlike the often feckless miners around him, he did not squander the money he made but used it to buy more and more stakes, and to get a degree from Oxford. Rhodes made a key alliance with Alfred Beit, a diamond dealer and business strategist, and with the financial support of Nathaniel Rothschild, Rhodes's De Beers Consolidated succeeded in buying up and amalgamating the whole diamond area, finally buying out his great rival, Barney Barnato, in 1888.

The De Beers monopoly meant that Rhodes could exercise control over the supply of diamonds to the market – and thus the price – and also control wages which, inevitably, was bad news for labour. In order to prevent desertions and diamond theft, and to establish stricter control over their workers, De Beers began to accommodate them in closed barracks which workers could leave only for work. These barracks – the original hostels which have played such a central and unhappy role in South Africa's history – were no better than prisons: they limited the workers' freedom of movement, were overcrowded and afforded no protection from the heat of summer or the freezing winter. Sanitary conditions within the barracks were extremely poor and no women were allowed to enter, creating ideal conditions for homosexual rape and rule by barrack bullies. Naturally, with the workers now virtual prisoners, management was able to cut their wages. But by this time migrant labour had become a way of life, with rural areas increasingly dependent on the backward flow of migrant wages, so that even these miserable conditions did not diminish the supply of labour.

The changes wrought by the discovery of diamonds were dwarfed, however, by the effects of the discovery of gold in the Transvaal in 1886. For whereas South Africa was to account for around 10 per cent of world diamond production, it was to produce more than twice as much gold as the whole of the rest of the world put together. Gold was thus the decisive factor which turned South Africa into an African country *pas comme les autres*. Gold not only brought a large increase in the white population, changing the racial balance sufficiently to guarantee white dominance for another century, but it turned South Africa into a united industrial state.

Gold was discovered on the northern edge of a range of hills called the Witwatersrand (the Rand, as it came to be known) in 1886. The gold rush which followed not only soon brought some 25,000 African workers to the gold mines but many would-be miners from Europe, despite a high mortality rate in the mines due to accidents and disease. The competition for labour between the gold and diamond mines kept wages up at first but in 1895–6 a rinderpest epidemic killed large numbers of cattle, leading to a famine which drove so many Africans to seek work on the mines that the labour shortage vanished, enabling the mining companies to cut wages.

Soon after the discovery of gold it became clear that although the deposits appeared inexhaustible the concentrations of gold in the rock were generally low. The richest deposits lying close to the surface were found at the site of present-day Johannesburg. But unlike diamonds, gold sold in London at a fixed price. It was only with the discovery in the early 1890s of the possibility of industrial mining of deep-level gold ore that the full value of the Transvaal mines became obvious so that large-scale capital did indeed begin to flow in. Within a few years everything was owned by just eight giant gold-mining companies, one of which was Rhodes's Consolidated Gold Fields.

Deep-level mining, requiring sophisticated and expensive technologies, speeded up the consolidation of capital and the industrialisation of the country, and led to the development of a sophisticated infrastructure of railways, roads, coal mines and electric power. By 1898 the Rand was already producing more than a quarter of the world's gold and Johannesburg was booming. Its society had a rough frontier character: there were a lot of guns, fighting, drinking, drunken brawls and prostitution, unsurprisingly in a population with nearly a hundred men for every woman. This burgeoning population needed not just brothels but houses, food, clothes, health, hygiene and entertainment; needed it right away – and had the money to pay for it. Johannesburg, even today, has never quite lost that mining-town feel, a place of almost professional shallowness, where people come to make money, where they flaunt material wealth with glitz and glamour and judge others very largely on whether they have nice houses or cars, a place bereft of interesting scenery or much high culture so that the only thing in town is to have fun with other people and with money. A hundred years on, prostitution, glitz and guns remain central features.

Jo'burg grew at an enormous pace and many technological novelties, such as street lights, were introduced there earlier than in big European cities. Paul Kruger, elected as the first President of the South African Republic (popularly referred to as the Transvaal) in 1883, invested some of the country's unexpected wealth in recruiting able people to government. One outstanding example was Jan Smuts, a Cambridge law graduate who became the Transvaal's Attorney-General in 1897.

The inflow of capital and the explosive growth of Transvaal's economy resulted in a change in the balance of power of the entire region: henceforth it was the Transvaal and not the Cape that defined the pace and direction. Kruger wanted to use this new power to strengthen the SAR's political independence from Britain – which meant, above all, obtaining rail access to a port which was not under British control. Cecil Rhodes and the British were equally determined to frustrate these plans for it rapidly became clear that a rich, powerful and independent SAR would be able to dominate and even swallow the rest of the region.

Already in 1882 construction of a railway from Jo'burg to Lourenço Marques had begun. Meanwhile the Cape government was building three railways, from Cape Town, Port Elizabeth and East London to the borders of the Orange Free State, and the Natal government was building a railroad from Durban to Charlestown on the Transvaal border. For several years both the SAR and the OFS kept the British railways out of their territories. However, lack of funds slowed down the construction of the Mozambique section of Jo'burg's railway while in 1888 the OFS allowed the Cape to extend its Port Elizabeth–Colesberg line into its territory. Two years later the Dutch company which was building the Transvaal leg of the Lourenço Marques line also ran out of funds and was given a loan by the Cape – of which Cecil Rhodes was by then Prime Minister – on condition that before completing the Mozambican railway it would build another one, the continuation of the Port Elizabeth line from the OFS–SAR border to the Rand. To diminish the impact of this blow and increase his options Kruger decided to allow in the Natal line as well. By the mid 1890s all three lines were finally completed.

It was clear that the economies of all the South African territories were becoming more connected and interdependent. The notion of federating South Africa's white states had occurred to British politicians from the early 1850s on when the Sand River and Bloemfontein Conventions had confirmed the independence of the Boer republics. But such notions took on a far sharper cast with the discovery of diamonds: indeed, the granting of full responsible government to the Cape in 1872 to a large extent stemmed from the vision that the Cape would become a nucleus of a future federation of all the South African states. But not only were the Boer republics opposed; so was the first Cape government. However, the new Tory administration which took power in 1874 was more willing to go ahead with federation: Lord Carnarvon, the new Colonial Secretary, had had experience in federating Canada and he decided upon a huge southern African federation sprawling from the Cape to the Zambezi and Delagoa Bay.

It seemed possible. The Boer republics had begun to feel anxious about a co-ordinated black uprising right across the region – in which case, they realised, they would depend almost entirely on British support. Even the Afrikaner Bond, despite its openly anti-imperial agenda, proclaimed as its goal the creation of a united South Africa, independent of Britain and under its own flag, but with the Royal Navy ready to defend its (white) population. In 1873 when the Hlubi under Langalibalele refused to have their guns registered by the Natal authorities and offered armed resistance, volunteers from all the white-ruled states offered their assistance to Natal.

In 1875 Carnarvon mentioned the desirability of federation in parliament and authorised a meeting of representatives of the white-ruled states in Cape Town to discuss the possibilities of confederation. The Cape government, however, remained unconvinced and ultimately the meeting took place in London a year later, though this was solely preoccupied with the issues of defence and a common 'native policy'. Even before this discussion could begin J. H. Brand, President of the OFS, stated that his country did not recognise the territorial claims of Waterboer's Griqua or the Keate award. He finally accepted a settlement of £90,000 for the diamond fields and a promise of more on condition of allowing a railway to be built from either the Cape or Natal through OFS territory.

Carnarvon was not to be defeated. In September 1876 he decided to annex the SAR as the first move to confederation, and in January 1877 Theophilus Shepstone and a small police force set off from Natal to fulfil this task. This move was cunningly predicated on Transvaal weakness: its commandos had recently been defeated by the Pedi and the Zulu danger seemed imminent. Shepstone's party met little opposition. President Burgers, his position threatened by Kruger, offered little resistance; the Executive Council was divided and the '*uitlanders*', the Transvaal's British population, greeted Shepstone enthusiastically. On 12 April 1877 the Transvaal was proclaimed a British colony and Sir Bartle Frere was invited to the Cape in order to become the first Governor-General of the future federation.

At which point things unravelled. The OFS did not recognise the annexation and refused to discuss any plans for federation until such time as the SAR's Volksraad had accepted it. In the Cape the Afrikanerbond and *Die Patriot* denounced annexation, as did the Cape government under John Molteno. Meanwhile Boer opposition to annexation hardened, especially after the new administration committed the classic mistake of increasing taxation without granting elected representation. Moreover, Frere's desperate attempts to incorporate the surrounding African population resulted in an almost incessant African uprising in various parts of the country in 1878–9, which did not add to his popularity either among his superiors in Britain or among the Boers. The British defeat by the Zulus at Isandlwana in 1879 killed the myth of British invincibility, sealing the fate of federation.

The Transvaal Boers met at mass congresses in January and December 1879 (the first just as British troops moved into Zululand) and decided to reconvene their Volksraad and defend their independence. In the middle of 1879 the Cape parliament defeated a motion calling for confederation after the Transvaal Boer leaders, Paul Kruger and Piet Jacobus Joubert, had met with Cape Boer parliamentarians. Despite these clear warning signs the British government – by then the Liberals under Gladstone – attempted to hold on, but the situation quickly became untenable. The Boer uprising against the British began spontaneously in December 1879 and, despite reinforcements from Natal, British troops were severely beaten in several clashes early in 1880. In December the Boer leaders announced the restoration of Transvaal independence – effectively a declaration of war, the first Anglo-Transvaal war.

In February 1881 a British column heading for the Transvaal was attacked by the Boers led by Piet Joubert on Majuba hill near Charlestown. Ninety-two British troops, including their commander, Major-General Colley, were killed and over a hundred wounded – a humiliating defeat which made it clear that it would take a far stronger force to impose Britain's will on the Boers. London had no appetite for that so an armistice was signed, and in August the Pretoria Convention acknowledged the SAR's independence – though with Britain retaining control of the republic's foreign relations and frontier issues while the British Resident in Pretoria would define policy towards the African population.

The Transvaal signed this treaty with great reluctance, perceiving it as a diplomatic setback. But what the crisis had revealed was that with the exception of Carnarvon there was no general British determination to unify South Africa. The bottom line was that there was certainly no willingness to raise an army sufficient to defeat the Boers. So in 1883 Britain retreated further, signing the London Convention which removed their Resident from Pretoria and limited the Queen's 'suzerainty' over the SAR – in return for the delimitation of the Transvaal's western border.

Yet only sixteen years later, Britain was willing to raise an army of nearly 450,000 in order to defeat the Boer republics and unite South Africa. It is too crude to say that the difference lay simply in the discovery of gold. To move such large historical forces there had to be a unifying vision – and this was provided largely by Cecil Rhodes.

Rhodes joined the Cape parliament in 1880, establishing close links with Afrikaner politicians in the Cape, particularly with Jan Hofmeyr, a leading member of the Afrikaner Bond. Rhodes defended the interests of the (mainly Afrikaner) Cape farmers but he also developed and propagated the idea of a partnership of the two white 'races', the British and the Afrikaner, in fulfilling his dream – which was to establish a chain of British colonies 'from Cape to Cairo'. Rhodes's much vaunted principle of 'equal rights for all civilised men' was driven primarily by this idea of unity between Britons and Afrikaners.

While poor and landless burghers in the Cape tended to support Rhodes because such plans promised new land, the unexpected economic boom of the OFS and the SAR – and the inevitable conflict of interest over labour between the Cape farmers and the mining industrialists in the republics – meant that the broader Cape Afrikaner population responded to Rhodes's call too. In 1890 Rhodes sent a 'pioneer column' across the Limpopo into what is now Zimbabwe and by September the flag of Rhodes's British South Africa Chartered

Company was raised over the fort of Salisbury. The occupation of Rhodesia – as it was called – ensured the support of the Afrikaner Bond, a crucial factor in making Rhodes Prime Minister of the Cape. He further strengthened this support when he introduced the 1892 Ballot Bill and the 1894 Glen Grey Bill, disenfranchising a significant number of black voters and limiting black land ownership. Thus strengthened, Rhodes began to work on plans to end the independence of the Boer republics.

The gold and diamond mines had attracted many foreign fortune hunters – 'uitlanders' as they were called by the Afrikaners – mostly of British origin. The uitlanders were particularly numerous on the Rand where they and their mines together contributed most of the SAR's tax revenue. They naturally resented the fact that they were denied the right of citizenship and thus the franchise – for Kruger had no intention of allowing them political power – and they also disliked the use of Dutch in official life and particularly in education. In 1893 they created the Transvaal National Union to advance their cause, which was also taken up by the Cape and British governments – who nagged without effect. Rhodes was determined to go further and to use uitlander resentments as a springboard to establish direct British control over the Transvaal.

The cards fell into place in 1895 when Salisbury's Conservative government came to power in England with the pro-imperialist Joseph Chamberlain as Colonial Secretary and Rhodes's friend and supporter, Hercules Robinson, as High Commissioner for South Africa. The plan was that uitlander leaders would pen a letter requesting the protection of their women and children, and would then start an armed uprising against the SAR. A police contingent of Rhodes's British South Africa Company would ride to their aid from the British protectorate of Bechuanaland, thus distracting at least part of Kruger's forces and preventing the suppression of the uprising. The moment the rebellion succeeded Robinson would offer his mediation on Britain's behalf and propose the election of a constitutional assembly with uitlanders given the vote. This would then decide on the future of the state, presumably choosing closer association with Britain.

The chosen day was 28 December. Rhodes's force was in position, arms delivered to the uitlanders, their letter written and the London Times squared to publish it at the appropriate moment. But, crucially, the uitlanders got cold feet and decided to postpone the uprising, warning both Rhodes and Leander Jameson, Rhodes's close associate and head of the intervention force, waiting in Bechuanaland. Jameson decided to go ahead on his own, hoping that his move would provoke the *uitlanders* to rise. In a dramatic gesture he cut the telegraph wires connecting him to the Cape, so as not to receive Rhodes's instruction to cancel the intervention. The *uitlanders* were, however, encouraged merely to enter negotiations with Kruger: there was no armed uprising. The SAR's troops thus had their hands free to deal with Jameson's raiders and his force was quickly surrounded and forced to surrender.

Rhodes had to resign and suffered a calamitous loss of Boer support in the Cape, while Robinson had to plead with Kruger to show mercy to Jameson's men and in London Chamberlain too was under threat. But in the end none of the conspirators paid the real price – largely because the Kaiser imprudently sent Kruger a telegram congratulating him on his victory. British opinion, shocked by this open German avowal of interest in the Transvaal's gold, immediately rallied behind the Salisbury government – and Rhodes. In the end even the raiders and the *uitlander* leaders got away with a fright and short sentences – for Kruger was determined at all costs to avoid a quarrel with the British.

The next five years saw ever-increasing British pressure on the SAR both as regards its policy towards the *uitlanders* and its independent status in general. Whatever the British government chose to interpret as a deviation from the London Convention, particularly the SAR's dependent status in foreign policy, ended in a confrontation in which, in every case, Kruger backed down. Over *uitlander* rights Britain got nowhere – for Kruger's government considered this issue as vital to the SAR's survival as an independent state. Kruger also resisted great pressure from the mining magnates who wanted to end the dynamite monopoly held by the SAR government.

The situation worsened when Chamberlain appointed Alfred Milner, an uncompromising proponent of the idea of the superiority of 'British race' and of direct British rule, as High Commissioner for South Africa. Milner consciously and consistently pushed the situation in South Africa towards war, rejecting all Kruger's compromise proposals on franchise reform, and astutely prepared British public opinion in the belief that a war to end the Transvaal 'crisis' was both justified and inevitable. Kruger had no illusions and simply sought to buy time while he prepared for war, buying huge quantities of the latest rifles, machine-guns and other weaponry from Germany. Kruger also sought to win the support of Boers living in the British colonies and to consolidate relations between the SAR and the OFS. In 1897 he and President Martinus Steyn of the OFS renewed a treaty of mutual assistance and an advisory council was established to prepare a federation of the two states.

Kruger's last compromise proposal was to offer the vote to *uitlanders* with five years' residence but he demanded in return that Britain observe the London Convention by ceasing to interfere in the SAR's internal affairs and that it drop the underlying assumption of suzerainty over the Transvaal. This proposal met all Milner's demands, yet the British government merely accepted the offer of franchise. This the Kruger government could not accept. The British began to mass troops on the borders of the Transvaal but Kruger decided to give them no time to prepare for military action and issued an ultimatum. This was duly rejected and war began on 11 October 1899.

This war – alternatively called the Boer War, the Anglo-Boer War and the South African War – was to have a profound effect on the whole southern African region and helped shape the future South African state for generations afterwards. It also had a decisive impact on British foreign and colonial policy, and on the theory and practice of warfare throughout the world. Among the war's innovations were Maxim machine-guns, mobile six-inch guns, barbed wire, finely sighted clip-loading rifles with a long, flat trajectory, field telephones, smokeless Mauser rifles, camouflage khaki uniforms – and concentration camps.

During the war's early stages both sides underestimated the strength and determination of their opponents. The Boers thought the British would stop fighting and negotiate peace after the first significant casualties – and they also overestimated the support they would get from Europe, particularly from Germany and Russia. The British, on the other hand, badly underestimated Boer military prowess, their weapons and their sheer grit. Both sides were to pay dearly for these mistakes.

At the outset the Boer republics had a clear advantage: their forces were at least twice as large as the combined British garrison of 15,000 men. They also had an intimate knowledge of the climate and terrain, were fine horsemen and excellent shots – the young Winston Churchill was astonished to see Boer commandos hitting their targets with rifles while riding full tilt. Thanks to Kruger's foresight they were also often better armed, possessing such marvels of German military technology of the time as the rapid-fire Mauser rifle, smokeless gunpowder and long-range artillery. The result was that during the war's initial stage the Boers won on every front. The SAR and OFS forces moved into Natal as far as Estcourt and laid siege to Ladysmith while OFS commandos moved into the Cape Midlands (where they were soon joined by Cape Afrikaners who had risen to support their cause), Griqualand West and Bechuanaland. British garrisons in Kimberley and Mafikeng were besieged, and in December Boer commandos repelled several British counter-offensives.

However, it soon became obvious that the Boer forces did not have a general plan of action, that they preferred defensive tactics and tended to surrender the initiative. Thus while the Boers inflicted a bloody defeat on the British at Spion Kop on 24 January 1900, killing 300 and wounding 1,500, against their own losses of fifty dead and 120 wounded, they failed to develop this success into an offensive or even an advance.

Strictly speaking the Boers had no regular army, merely non-uniformed volunteer commandos who tended to lack co-ordination and discipline. On occasion they would disobey orders or even desert if they felt they had reason to do so – and particularly in order to protect their own homes and families. Boer commandos generally preferred to stay close to home and when they were close enough to the farm of a particular member he would often return there between battles – to rest or just to see his family. It is hardly surprising that the Boers failed to capitalise on their initial success.

The British gradually accumulated manpower, experience and strength. By March 1900 they had 200,000 troops in South Africa; by the end of the war 450,000. The whole Boer population of the two Boer republics was only 300,000 and even though they sometimes used the very old and the very young, together with a number of foreign volunteers, their forces seldom exceeded 60,000 and were often far smaller. British defeats at the beginning of the war prompted them to replace General Buller as their Commander-in-Chief with General Roberts, with Kitchener appointed as Roberts's second in command. The British offensive under Roberts started from Cape Town with their troops advancing along the railway line with the idea of cutting the OFS line south of Bloemfontein, thus isolating the Boer forces in the south. It worked: by February 1900 the Boer General Pieter Cronje capitulated with 4,000 of his men, and on 13 March Bloemfontein was occupied. Johannesburg was taken on 5 May and Pretoria on 6 June. Kruger left for Europe from Lourenço Marques and the commandos began to leave for home.

But this did not end the war, which continued for another two years with increasing bitterness. This new stage of guerrilla warfare suited the Boer commandos better than regular military action had. Their campaign was now led by President Steyn and several generals – Jan

Smuts, Christiaan de Wet, Koos de la Rey and Louis Botha. They co-ordinated their actions as far as they could and conducted their operations not only in the Transvaal and OFS but also in the Cape, helped by Boer insurgents. Apart from attacking British troops, the commandos concentrated on sabotage, destroying railway lines and disrupting communications – so successfully that the British decided the only way of stopping them lay in scorched-earth tactics. They burnt Boer farms, confiscated their cattle, imprisoned the men and sent women and children to concentration camps, thus attempting to rob the guerrillas of their bases. Wherever a railway line was sabotaged the British retaliated by destroying all the surrounding farms: in all, about 30,000 farms were destroyed. By war's end some 28,000 Boers had died in the camps, of which 22,000 were children under sixteen. These appalling atrocities produced a gale of protest around the world, particularly in England.

All attempts at negotiation failed until the situation of the Boers became utterly unbearable. At question was no longer independence, let alone victory, but merely survival. The Boers had precious little with which to fight: they lacked men, horses, ammunition and supplies. Pro-peace sentiment mounted, particularly among the poorer Boers and some 2,000 of them, mainly *bywoners* (landless tenants), joined up and fought for the British. Most of the Boers who fought on were landed farmers. Finally in April–May 1902 representatives of the two Boer governments met in Klerksdorp and after prolonged discussions accepted the peace terms which ended the war.

The war had been enormously expensive to the British taxpayer and had bankrupted and collapsed the two Boer republics. In addition the British had lost 22,000 imperial troops, the Boers some 7,000 men. Many more died in the prisoner of war camps, scattered from St Helena to Ceylon and Bermuda, while the fate of Boer women and children in the concentration camps left the most lasting stain. Nearly a hundred years later it was not difficult to find Afrikaners who choked with bitterness when recollecting what had happened in the camps. To Europeans the war's brutality seemed far more shocking than that of other colonial wars because it was fought between two white Christian nations. But what had it really been about?

It is clear enough that the major interest at stake was the control of gold and diamonds on which the Boer republics had been wholly dependent and which the British hoped would shore up their empire which, by 1900, had just been overtaken by the growing might of

Germany and the USA. But it was also a clash of civilisations, the British with their belief in the civilising mission of British capitalist colonialism, and the patriarchal settler colonialism of the Boers, rooted in the stark imperative of survival amidst a hostile environment in which the Boers' main advantage lay in what they saw as the intrinsic and insurmountable inequality of the races.

As the war's centenary hove into view the museums and historians who wished to commemorate it received a frosty response from ANC spokesmen, who declared there was nothing to commemorate: the war had simply been a struggle between two white groups as to which of them was to expropriate the profits gained through exploiting the blacks. This attitude changed, however, when it became clear that the celebrations had considerable potential in tourist revenue and, particularly, when ANC ministers belatedly discovered what historians had shown some time before, that large numbers of blacks had been caught up in the war, some as soldiers, others as porters and auxiliaries, and many more as its victims. At this the ANC joined in with gusto and in the ensuing torrent of lamentation over the black victims the war's principal antagonists were either depicted as co-equal oppressors or just forgotten. ANC ministers made ringing speeches to commemorate the black dead, of whose fate they had been blithely ignorant only months before.

This pantomime had its serious points. Undoubtedly one of the war's underlying issues had been a struggle over who was going to control and exploit the local labour supply: the conflicting claims of farmers and the mining industry run like a thread through the last century. To that extent it is correct to see the war as one fought by white predators over black bodies. Yet the Boers also fought for the survival of their state and nationhood, their own civilisation. True, their states were founded on land they had stolen or occupied by force – but then the same was true of all the surrounding African states and nations too, just as the Boer struggle against imperial encroachment was very similar to that of other African peoples.

It is salutary to remember that while apartheid may have sought friends for Afrikaners on the right, the Boers were originally a *cause célèbre* of the left. The Boers' resistance to the British became the world's most popular anti-imperial struggle. Like the Vietnamese in more recent time, they were fighting against the world's most powerful and thus most hated imperial power. Pro-Boer sentiment was as widespread as anti-Vietnam war sentiment in the 1960s and 1970s – and was particularly strong in Ireland, Holland, France, Germany and Russia, all of which saw many volunteers leave to fight for the Boer republics, a response matched only by the International Brigade in which left-wingers around the world enrolled to fight for the Spanish republic.

Both sides in the war had made use of the black majority. Most took the imperial side: the Sotho, Zulu, Xhosa and some Tswana all offered to fight for Britain. They were not allowed to fight as distinct units but the British used them widely as labourers, messengers, guards, scouts, watchmen, and some were allowed to carry arms. Boer commandos also used large numbers of Africans as servants and porters but they did not trust them to carry arms. All told, 100,000 blacks and Coloureds were involved in military action with about 30,000 carrying arms. About 14,000 died, mainly of disease though some were killed in action. Over 100,000 ended up in African concentration camps – separate from the whites and with a much higher death rate. Black communities also used the situation to settle old scores and in some instances spontaneously attacked the Boers, as did the Zulus who launched a successful attack against the Vryheid commando, spearing fifty-six Boers to death. Others, particularly in the Transvaal, reoccupied land that had been expropriated from them by the Boers or occupied Boer farms destroyed or deserted as a result of British action. Others again made a commercial killing out of provisioning the British army.

While the African majority clearly chose the imperialist side – a fact glossed over in the centenary celebrations – others were drawn into the war against their will. But despite the large numbers of blacks involved it was never their war. They did not start it, nor could they end it and irrespective of which side won Africans had no say in defining their own future fate. In this sense it was, indeed, the Anglo-Boer War and theirs alone.

Apart from the gold and diamond rushes, the war was when the rest of the world heard of South Africa for the first time. Several European countries sent military observers to report on this revolutionary war whose many innovations foreshadowed twentieth-century war in general. These observers, together with war correspondents and returning volunteers, wrote endless books and articles about the war and the country where it was fought. For the first time South Africa became a household word – for the war, of course, resulted in the country's lasting unification.

The peace treaty was signed in Vereeniging on 31 May 1902. The Boers had to accept the loss of their republics' independence in exchange for the release of their prisoners of war, permission to use their language in the schools and courts, the honouring of the republics' war debts and Boer property titles, a promise of responsible government at an unspecified future date and postponement of black franchise rights until then. Though less than the Boers might have hoped for, this was still a very generous settlement, with the offer of responsible government particularly attractive. The British made this concession only because they were planning to flood South Africa with sufficient British colonists to outvote the Boers. For Lord Milner, the High Commissioner for the two new colonies (called the Transvaal and Orange River Colonies), was bent on a programme of forced anglicisation and wanted to federate them with the Cape, Natal and Rhodesia into a single anglicised state.

Milner was also determined to revive the economies of the two former Boer states – a precondition, he believed, for the future federation. The Vereeniging treaty had allocated £3 million for distribution to Boers, especially farmers, who had suffered losses in the war – but in fact over £16 million was poured into reviving the farms. The drought of 1903–8 made this an uphill struggle but production recovered steadily. Similarly, strenuous effort saw gold production recover to its pre-war level by 1904 and increase steadily thereafter. But both farms and mines needed plentiful African labour and this rapid recovery quickly created an acute labour shortage.

The shortage occurred not just because so many workers had been lost or dispersed by the war but because the war had produced a boom for African farmers. Both sides had needed provisions and with 450,000 extra troops in South Africa, demand for food soared – at just the time when many Boer farms had been destroyed or were inoperable because bereft of their menfolk. African areas, however, went on producing largely undisturbed. Even before the war white farmers, particularly in the Transvaal and OFS, had often let their land out to African tenants in exchange for a proportion of their crops. Some of these black sharecroppers were successful farmers who ran big enterprises, particularly after the war. In the early years of British rule some black farmers clubbed together to buy land or white farms while African farm production also grew in the Eastern Cape and to a lesser extent in Natal. The prospect of growing a little more food for the market also increased the unwillingness of Africans to leave their communal land. This was quite unacceptable to the British government, which wanted Africans as cheap labour, not as independent agricultural producers.

Two measures were introduced to end the labour shortage, both of them disastrous. In Natal a new poll tax was instituted in 1906 in addition to the hut tax already in existence. The hut tax was collected from heads of homesteads according to the number of huts in the homestead. Since each hut was usually occupied by a wife and her children, more huts generally meant more wives and thus greater wealth so that this was a tax paid by older and wealthier men. The new £1 poll tax was levied on men not paying the hut tax – mostly young unmarried men who in practice had been the ones who were already earning the money to pay their richer relatives' hut tax. The introduction of the new tax resulted in huge social tension in Zululand. Many simply refused to pay and the tax collection campaign led to clashes in which two white policemen were killed. When those responsible were hunted down, two were shot dead and twelve more executed. Thus began the Bambatha rebellion.

Bambatha, a Zulu chief in the Greytown area, refused to make his people pay the tax and fled across the Thukela for safety. With memories of 1879 still fresh there was a panicky white reaction and reinforcements from the Transvaal quickly joined the Natal forces. Bambatha was ambushed and killed together with about 500 of his supporters, and the rebellion squashed with thousands imprisoned and not a few executed. The uprising was blamed on Dinuzulu who was tried, found guilty of harbouring the rebels and sentenced to four years' imprisonment. These and similar draconian measures finally achieved the desired result so that within two years some 80 per cent of adult males in Zululand had turned to migrant labour.

In the Transvaal post-war social tension was exacerbated by the displacement of poor whites, the *bywoners*. Farmers returning from the war often evicted these white tenants, partly because by war's end many had changed sides and became scouts for the British but also because the farmers had discovered that black sharecroppers were much more profitable than white tenants. The displaced *bywoners* flocked to the cities and the mines but attempts to substitute them for unskilled black labour failed miserably. They insisted on higher salaries to enable them to support their families; they expected better food and accommodation than their black colleagues; and they utterly refused the inhuman working conditions inflicted on black workers. Moreover, they all had the vote and thus could not be ignored in the way blacks could. They were simply uneconomical.

This failure left many poverty-stricken whites unemployed at the same time Milner had decided to resolve the labour crisis by importing Chinese workers. About 60,000 Chinese arrived between 1904 and

1907 – by which time African recruitment had begun to grow steadily again. But the widespread white protests against the arrival of the Chinese forced Milner's administration to draw a strict line between qualified and unqualified labour, and to promise that only whites would perform the former, while the blacks and Chinese would perform the latter.

These early industrial disputes along the colour line had an epochal significance. It should be realised that in racial matters South Africa was notably more liberal than the American South all the way through to the end of the nineteenth century. In America, however, the pattern of industrialisation was to weaken the colour bar and gradually see the AFL–CIO become the champion of civil rights for blacks. In South Africa the opposite happened. These early battles in the industrial labour market saw the white working class opt solidly in favour of the colour bar. Once that option had become both clear and unchangeable any white political party had to take it into account.

The anti-Chinese agitation had fatally weakened Milner: the mining magnates may have welcomed Chinese labour but both Afrikaners and English speakers in the Transvaal had drawn together to oppose it, while back in England the move was widely denounced because of the inhuman conditions in which the Chinese worked. Crucially, Milner had also failed to stimulate the hoped-for mass immigration of English speakers, so he sought to anglicise the Boer community by law. His attempt to introduce compulsory English in government schools produced enormous bitterness: the story of the Afrikaans child made to sit in a corner with a dunce's cap for speaking his mother tongue was to ring down the years. The Afrikaner community responded by establishing a parallel, Christian–National system of education whose implicit nationalism undermined Milnerism while English speakers, still resentful over the Chinese issue, failed to give Milner's policy unanimous support – thus sealing the fate of his reforms.

The sheer anglocentric arrogance of Milner's policy was utterly self-defeating. It was itself a major factor behind the revival of Boer nationalism and ultimately helped bring Afrikaner parties to power everywhere save Natal. The danger that this might happen in the two former republics was obvious but Milner was determined to prevent it happening in the Cape. There, however, the war had consolidated the Bond's following so Milner attempted to suspend the constitution in order to prevent this party from coming to power. In this he was supported by the Progressive Party, which had been launched by Rhodes in 1898. Although this move failed, the disenfranchisement of the pro-Boer Cape rebels allowed the Progressives to win the 1904 elections. L. S. Jameson, who became Prime Minister, realised the necessity of reconciling the Afrikaners and thus reduced the disenfranchisement. But attitudes had already hardened and in the next election his party was defeated by the South Africa Party, led by John Merriman, in alliance with the Bond – which thus became part of the new government formed in 1908.

In the Transvaal Boer leaders had met in May 1904 to form a new organisation, Het Volk (the People), under Louis Botha and Jan Smuts, and in the Orange River Colony a similar gathering took place seven months later to form Orangia Unie (United Orangia) under former President Steyn and J. B. M. Hertzog. Both parties expressed their strong opposition to the importation of Chinese labour and declared their resolute defence of Afrikanerdom against Milner's efforts at anglicisation. The language and the church were at the heart of Afrikanerdom's political and cultural revival. The heated debates over which language to choose as a national tongue saw the supporters of Afrikaans win a victory for bilingualism.

All three Afrikaner parties were shrewd enough, however, to see the need for co-operation with the British in order to win power and, in the case of the Transvaal and the ORC, achieve responsible government. Louis Botha and Jan Smuts were the strongest promoters of the conciliatory line but they also realised that while Afrikaners were united not only by language and history but by a common religion, English speakers were not united at all. Thus Het Volk and Orangia Unie attempted with some success to divide the English speakers along class lines and recruit the poorer ones.

Two parties representing English speakers had emerged in the Transvaal in 1904. The larger, the Transvaal Progressive Association, representing diverse *uitlander* interests – including the all-important Chamber of Mines – favoured representative government but wanted to delay responsible government until its control by English speakers was guaranteed. The smaller Transvaal Responsible Government Association was keenly in favour of responsible government right away – which created a basis for co-operation with Het Volk. In the name of this co-operation the Afrikaner party dropped its criticism of the Chinese labour policy (which the 'Responsibles' supported) and they in turn refused to support Milner's anglicisation policy and agreed to the exclusion of all non-whites from the franchise. The various labour groups which had sprung into existence after the war also tended to support Het Volk and the 'Responsibles', rather than the 'Progressives', making this lower-class coalition a significant political force.

Negotiations on responsible government had been dragging on for some time when a new Liberal government came to power in Britain in 1906. It decided to grant responsible government to the Transvaal right away – officially because it was felt that nothing less could unite the war-torn country. In a secret memorandum, however, Winston Churchill, Under-Secretary of State for the Colonies, wrote that the measure was the only way to maintain British influence and that the government was 'absolutely determined to maintain ... a numerical majority of a loyal and English population'. This was to be achieved through a particular system of constituency distribution and provided that English speakers in the Transvaal worked together: it was the besetting fault of all such schemes that they assumed a degree of English-speaking solidarity which never existed. In 1906 responsible government was granted and in 1907 Het Volk romped home in the election with a huge majority, further strengthened by a significant vote for its allies, the 'Responsibles' and Labour. The Transvaal's new constitution, based on a whites-only franchise, had driven a coach and horses through the stipulation of the treaty of Vereeniging linking the enfranchisement of the black population to responsible government. The ORC was granted self-government in 1907 and held its first general election in 1908, Orangia Unie winning a similar absolute majority.

Responsible government in the Transvaal and ORC, both led by Afrikaner governments, and the Afrikaner Bond's victory in the Cape, transformed Boer attitudes towards a South African federation, even one within the British Empire. Paradoxically the economic case for closer union derived not from the compatibility of the interests of the various territories but from the opposite. There were conflicts over customs duties, tariffs, transport costs, the respective costs of farming and mining production and competing demands for labour – but precisely for that reason Milner and his associates, the so-called 'kindergarten', insisted that only closer union could avoid these clashes developing into serious conflicts and they assisted High Commissioner Lord Selborne in drafting a memorandum on this subject.

The memorandum was well received by the Bond in the Cape and Jan Smuts approached the new Premier, Merriman, to negotiate for unification. Smuts had played an important role in achieving responsible government for the Transvaal and the ORC; now he pushed ahead towards unification. Following his suggested procedure, the parliaments of the four territories sent thirty representatives to a National Convention charged with the task of drafting a constitution for the future Union of South Africa. It met in late 1908-9 and worked out what became the South Africa Act of 1909. Now that three of the four South African territories were under the control of Afrikaner parties, Natal alone could not hope for the strongly federal structure it had wanted, particularly given that Smuts and Merriman were determined on a more centralised state.

The Union was to have a bicameral parliament comprising a Senate and a House of Assembly. The franchise for the House of Assembly was a matter of furious debate: neither Natal nor the Transvaal was prepared to have any form of Coloured franchise, while the Cape refused to disenfranchise the Coloureds already on its voters' roll. Only the danger that the Convention might collapse made both sides agree that the status quo in all territories should remain as it was, with the Cape retaining its limited non-white vote. Coloureds could be elected to the Cape Provincial Council but not to the Union parliament. It was decided that the basis for the distribution of seats was the number of the total white male adult population. Finally, the Convention decided that parliament would sit in Cape Town, the executive in Pretoria and the judiciary in Bloemfontein. On 31 May 1910 the Union of South Africa came into being with Louis Botha as its first Prime Minister.

There was no black representation at the Convention and whatever the debates, the actual outcome was much closer to the principle of total exclusion of the black population adhered to in the Transvaal and the OFS (which reverted to its old name) than the slightly more liberal laws of the Cape. Unsurprisingly, politically conscious blacks objected strongly to the nature of the new state. The ORC Native Congress called for a black Convention to discuss the situation. Representatives of black organisations throughout South Africa met in Bloemfontein in March 1909 – while the National Convention was still in session in the same town. The Native Convention passed resolutions rejecting the projected constitution, and criticising the colour bar and the exclusion of blacks. It decided to transform itself into a permanent body and elected Dr Walter Robusana, a Cape representative, minister of religion and Xhosa author, as its Chairman. In 1912 the Native Convention renamed itself the South African Native National Congress, the early form of today's all-powerful ANC.

This was not the only form of protest. The Cape's African newspapers, *Imvo Zabantsundu* and *Izwi Labantu*, criticised the constitution. The African Political Organisation, representing the Cape Coloured population, organised many meetings to press for the extension of the Coloured vote. John Tengo Jabavu, Robusana and Dr Abdullah Abdurahman, leader of the APO, travelled to England, as did a liberal white politician, William Schreiner, in order to advance their objections against the constitution. In London they linked up with the Indian leader Mohandas Gandhi but even their combined opposition failed to make any impression on the British government. The Union, designed by and for the whites only, steamed ahead unabated.

British liberals were well aware that they were abandoning black South Africans to the mercy of the whites and felt guilty about it. They consoled themselves that Britain had retained control over the protectorates of Basutoland, Swaziland and Bechuanaland, and hoped that more liberal impulses would gradually come into play within South Africa itself. As indeed they eventually did – eighty years later. In one sense the creation of the Union was thus a great betrayal. It may be, however, that from a future vantage point this will come to seem less significant than the fact that the century of British rule had transformed South Africa from a polyglot assortment of undeveloped territories into a single modern state with a developing industrial base and infrastructure. Everywhere in Europe as well as Africa, after all, franchise arrangements were to change dramatically in the course of the twentieth century but today, well after universal suffrage has arrived in South Africa, the country still bears the distinctive stamp of that modernity and unity which makes it unique on its continent.

# VII
## A WHITE WORLD WITHOUT END

ම ම ම

The economic thinking behind the creation of the Union proved to be correct: with artificial barriers removed the economy grew fast despite a recession, the First World War and the Depression. The war hit some sections of the population hard but the economy did not, of course, receive any physical damage as it did in Europe, and some sectors benefited from war orders and supplies. The value of gold production grew from about £35 million in 1911 to nearly £99 million in 1939 and in the same period the number of manufacturing industry units more than quadrupled. Agricultural production grew steadily with maize, the staple African diet, rising from 863,000 tons in 1911 to nearly 3 million tons in 1939 – this despite the simultaneous increase in African migrant labour which bled African rural areas of manpower. Wool remained a major export even though its relative worth peaked in the 1870s and was then overshadowed by gold. In the same period the length of South Africa's railway lines increased from 7,500 miles to over 13,000 and the value of exports nearly doubled.

According to the first census taken in 1911 the Union had some 6 million people, of whom over 4 million were Africans, 1,200,000 whites, 526,000 Coloureds and 152,000 Asians, mainly Indians. By 1936 the number of Africans had grown to 6.6 million, whites to 2 million, Coloureds to 770,000 and Asians to 220,000 – a total population of 9.6 million. Significantly, in that year the vast majority of Africans still lived in the rural areas – 2,420,349 in 'Crown Locations' and 2,053,440 on white farms. The number of wholly or partly urbanised Africans – living in the cities and towns, in the mining and other industrial compounds and with construction firms – was just 1,404,343.

Given this large and rapidly increasing African population and the increasing dependence of both agriculture and mining on African labour, one might have expected that 'Native' policy would have been the main issue on the agenda of all political parties. That this was not so – that in fact the political elite remained immersed in disputes which now often seem arcane – was a testament to the feeling of effortless and timeless white superiority which infused all political players. No sooner was Union achieved than South African politicians from Smuts down began demanding the incorporation of the three British protectorates and Rhodesia – Smuts even had in mind a vast federation of white-ruled Africa running as far north as Kenya. The fact that such schemes would have involved adding enormous extra numbers to the African population and virtually no extra whites at all was a matter of complete indifference to Smuts and his successors. After all, was not the rest of Africa governed by European colonial regimes with far smaller numbers of whites? It was simply unthinkable that this white supremacy and white control could ever end. It was not just a fact; it was right, indeed it was deserved and it was the natural order of things. Such was the lasting mood.

The first national government was formed by the South African National Party, which was created by the merger of Het Volk and the National Party of the Transvaal, the Orangia Unie of the OFS and the South Africa Party of the Cape. The party won the first national election in 1910 and its leader, Louis Botha, became the first Prime Minister while his deputy, Jan Smuts, headed the Defence, Mines and Interior Ministries. The government represented a broad span of Afrikaners and English speakers, united only by their acceptance of the idea of Union and of keeping non-whites in their (subordinate) place. The opposition consisted of the Unionist Party, representing urban and industrial English speakers, whose views differed little from those of the ruling party, and a small Labour Party, representing white workers.

The emergence of the South African Party government under Botha and Smuts, who both saw white South Africans as a single united nation and believed South Africa's future lay in a close association with the British Empire, made it seem, for a few brief years, that South Africa had surmounted the divisions of the Anglo-Boer war. But such huge social convulsions are not so easily smoothed over. The OFS leader, Barry Hertzog, a Boer war hero and Minister of Justice in Botha's government, became the spokesman of a resurgent Afrikaner nationalism. He advocated the separate-but-equal development of the two groups of the white population, for without such separation the Afrikaner nation and Afrikaans language would disappear. Hertzog was the first of many to insist that Afrikaner nationalism only fulfilled itself when Afrikaners were in power. He insisted that the Union be governed by 'true Africans', i.e. Afrikaners (though he was prepared to include English speakers who somehow became 'true Africans'), and that the Union should align itself with the British Empire not as a matter of allegiance but only if and when its government saw fit. Botha felt such statements were unacceptable and dropped Hertzog from the government. In 1914 Hertzog formed the National Party which aimed at protecting specifically Afrikaner interests and the ruling party became known simply as the South African Party.

Hertzog's NP was the first Afrikaner nationalist party organised as a nationwide force, appealing not just to Tranvalers or Free Staters but to Afrikaners everywhere, capitalising on the shared memories of suffering at the hands of the British during and after the Anglo–Boer War and a deep indignation that Afrikaners were still the poor relations within the white community.

Relations between the SAP government and the NP opposition soured further during the First World War when the British asked for South Africa's active participation, beginning with the invasion of German South-West Africa. Even some members of Botha's Cabinet opposed the decision to enter the war. Generals Christiaan Beyers, the Commander of the Active Citizen Force, Jacobus ('Koos') de la Rey, a member of the Senate, Solomon ('Manie') Maritz, commander of the forces in Upington which covered the frontier with South-West Africa and Christiaan de Wet, who was by then in the opposition, all opposed South Africa's participation in the war. De la Rey was killed at a road block – the NP never accepting that this was an accident – and the rest went into open rebellion. Maritz and his men even went to fight for the Germans, while other officers gathered their own commandos within South Africa in the hope of restoring the Boer republics. The rebels were easily suppressed and lightly punished, none serving more than two years' imprisonment. One exception, however, was Jopie Fourie. Unlike other rebels in government service, he had not resigned before joining the rebellion and was thus executed for treason. The NP naturally exploited public sympathy for the rebels' sufferings and made large gains in the 1915 election.

Both Botha and Smuts led successful military campaigns in South-West Africa, thus identifying themselves completely with the imperial cause. In 1916 Smuts was appointed commander of the imperial forces fighting in German East-Africa and Botha sent a South African brigade to Europe. The government's pro-British stand was strongly supported by the Unionists and even non-white organisations expressed their support and temporarily withheld criticism of the government. During the war many Africans and Coloureds served in the army as non-combatants both in Africa and Europe.

Although the SAP government was more liberal than its Nationalist successor, the fact is that it enacted three of the cornerstone acts of white supremacy. These were the Native Land Act of 1913, the Native Affairs Act of 1920 and the Native (Urban Areas) Act of 1923.

Of these the Land Act was the most fundamental. Hitherto, although most Africans still held land communally through the chiefs, it had also been possible for them to purchase land privately from white owners or agencies so that, for example, by 1905 Africans owned 230,000 acres in Natal alone. With the advent of industrialisation and intensified farming the whites were no longer prepared to tolerate this situation: they needed African labour for the mines, industries and farms. Accordingly the 1913 Land Act introduced a much stricter racial delimitation of land and put an end to private African land ownership and to sharecropping, offering in exchange merely a slight enlargement of the native reserves. The African franchise in the Cape, which was tied to the land, was left alone for the moment, as were some sharecroppers on white farms in Natal and the Transvaal but Free State farmers signalled what was to come by evicting their squatters en masse.

The Native Affairs Act of 1920 introduced a uniform system of managing the native reserves through a system of district councils. According to the act a Native Conference of African Leaders, appointed by the government, was to meet annually in Pretoria together with the Native Affairs Commission, an all-white body whose task was to report to Parliament on native affairs. This completed the separation of African and European administrative systems from top to bottom. The Natives (Urban Areas) Act of 1923 separated native locations from towns administratively (territorially they had been separated earlier, purportedly on hygienic grounds, for locations were invariably the first places to succumb to epidemics). Other laws passed by the SAP government were aimed against black labour, prohibiting strikes by contract workers, reserving several categories of jobs for whites only and making access to other jobs dependent on qualifications which black youths seldom had.

The government's policy towards Indians was not just discriminatory but left no doubt that Indians were not really wanted in South Africa at all. In Natal (where 90 per cent of Indians lived) they had to pay a special racial tax of £3 a head, their movement between the provinces was restricted, as were their property and occupational rights – and there were anyway restrictions on Indian land ownership per se. An Indian man married to several wives in India could bring only one with him to South Africa and in 1912 further Indian immigration was prohibited altogether. Smuts supported all these measures despite strong opposition from the Indian government. His defence was that rights granted to Indians would have to be granted to Africans as well, which was unthinkable in view of their numerical predominance over the whites. This logic, though a true reflection of the colonial mentality of the time, carefully concealed the fact that whites, particularly those in urban areas, feared economic competition from the Indians – for despite all the restrictions they laboured under the Indian community not only invested massively in education but showed such enterprise that Indian businesses were everywhere growing at an amazing pace. Gandhi, who had by then developed his philosophy of non-violent opposition, organised effective campaigns of civil disobedience – *satyagraha* – against these discriminatory measures and petitioned the Indian government. A compromise was reached in 1914 when the hated Indian tax was lifted and resident Indian husbands were allowed to bring in their wives and children from India. All the other restrictions remained in place, however.

Discriminatory legislation of this kind was most popular among poorer whites who were most exposed to African and Indian competition but even so the white working class had grievances aplenty. In 1913 a strike to demand recognition of the white miners' union soon developed into riots in Johannesburg. With no police force in place the government invited British troops to suppress the uprising. They opened fire but left the city before crushing the uprising, thus allowing the strikers to seize control of the city. Botha and Smuts rushed to Johannesburg, agreed to union recognition and established a committee to investigate the miners' grievances. The miners returned to work but in January 1914 strikes started again in Natal, quickly growing into a national strike. This time the strike was crushed by the government's recently founded defence force. Smuts ignored all legal procedures and deported the strike leaders.

Despite this clear lack of scruple Smuts had gained enormous prestige as a war leader and in 1917 he became a member of the Imperial War Cabinet. His international reputation was such that his pamphlet proposing a league of nations had wide influence and it was Smuts, too, who originated the notion of the League's mandate system, which eventually led to South Africa being given a League mandate to administer ex-German South-West Africa. This was, though, a major disappointment to Smuts who had hoped simply to incorporate this territory into the Greater South Africa he continually dreamed of.

Busy with such grandiose but fruitless schemes, the SAP leadership had paid insufficient attention to the home front and lost the 1920 election to Hertzog's Nationalists, though the SAP hung on to power thanks to a deal with the Unionists and Independents. Botha's death soon after the end of the war had seen Smuts become Prime Minister and he now desperately attempted to reunite the SAP and the National Party. But Hertzog and the Afrikaner nationalists now smelt victory and wanted nothing less than the restoration of two independent Boer republics. This Smuts could not concede: if he stood for anything now it was the British Empire. Instead, he merged the SAP with the Unionists, which completed the party alignment that had been developing since the Anglo-Boer War. The new SAP, which easily won the 1921 election, now clearly represented the interests of big capital and of urban, middle-class English speakers while the NP was the party of rural and poorer Afrikaners.

The post-war economic crisis throughout much of the Western world inevitably affected South Africa too and quickly led to a major political crisis. At the end of 1921 the Chamber of Mines decided to abandon the arrangement which reserved all skilled and semi-skilled jobs for the whites, and unskilled jobs for blacks. Since blacks were paid far less than whites the Chamber decided to make savings employing black workers in place of whites wherever it could, starting in February 1922. There was no greater way to provoke white workers than to suggest that they would be thrown out of work while blacks took their jobs and by January white workers across the Rand went on strike. This turned into a full-scale insurrection – 'the Rand revolt' – with workers' commandos establishing control over the greater part of the Rand by March – under the slogan 'Workers of the World Unite for a White South Africa'. Smuts proclaimed martial law and brought in tanks and artillery; even so it took his troops several days to suppress the uprising. Several workers were killed, many were jailed and four of the strike leaders were executed. Seething with bitterness, the workers had to give in.

Despite the fact that the strikers were fighting for the colour bar they received the wholehearted support of the Labour Party and the Communist Party of South Africa, which had been founded in 1921.

The prevailing view on the left was that the Africans were 'not ready' for class struggle and that the task of challenging the Rand mining barons therefore had to rest with the white working class. Naturally, the strike was not supported by black workers – who had already given every sign of understanding the class struggle, whatever the left might say. The NP had also supported the strike for their social base, which meant they too were an embryonic labour party (they had supported the Russian revolution of 1917). They were instinctively anti-capitalist and anti-imperialist, tending to argue that capitalism and imperialism (and thus Britain) were indivisible, in very much the same way that the ANC were later to argue that apartheid and capitalism were indivisible.

The strike had a huge political impact. The communists belatedly realised the need to work among black workers and prevent the working class being so easily divided on racial lines. The government, the Chamber of Mines and the NP all received a sharp lesson that the maintenance of the colour bar was essential to buying the support of white workers. One outcome of the strike was an electoral pact between the Labour and the Nationalist Parties signed in 1923. This alliance was only natural: the two parties shared a part of their electorate or usefully complemented one another (the rural NP poor and the urban LP poor). This alliance won the 1924 general election, gaining massive white working-class support and also the vote of a part of the Coloured working class which had previously voted for the SAP.

The political fault lines of the Rand revolt and the speed with which it resulted in the NP's electoral victory provided such a powerful object lesson in the way that class and racial politics could be combined to deadly effect that it did much to define the future course of South African history. Although the SAP had been the first to introduce segregationist legislation and to legislate quite nakedly in the interests of one racial group and against others, the NP openly proclaimed this direction as its main goal and took it to new extremes. This was not yet the age of apartheid but from 1922 on segregation, discrimination and *baaskap* (mastery) were official policy. Undoubtedly Smuts would have argued that only by legislating in the interests of the most advanced section of the population could one make the country as a whole advance. Behind such rationales lay extreme racial selfishness and, what was worse, a sort of bullying of the weaker and less educated sections of society.

During its first term the Hertzog government passed several brutally racist laws, justified by heady talk about '*die volk*' rather than by Smuts's high-minded pursuit of abstraction. (Even today South Africans of all races cite Smuts's philosophy of 'holism', which is not, of course, a philosophy at all, merely meaning to take things in the round.) The Mines and Works Amendment Act (1926) prohibited the employment of Africans and Asians in skilled jobs. The Native Administration Act (1927) put all African affairs outside the Cape under the direct jurisdiction of the Governor-General, without the need to refer any matters of native policy to parliament. In the same year the government passed the Immorality Act, making extramarital sexual relations between whites and Africans a crime. In 1926 Hertzog proposed four interconnected bills aimed at tightening the racial distribution of land; at further reducing the already minuscule African representation in parliament (where blacks could, in any case, only elect white representatives); and at removing Coloured voters in the Cape from the common voters' roll. These bills, however, met such stiff opposition from both the Native Conference and the SAP that Hertzog withdrew them for the while.

Hertzog's government also tried to foster industrial development – and white employment. In 1928 it established the Iron and Steel Corporation (ISCOR) and established protective tariffs for a whole range of secondary industries. It also pursued an active 'affirmative action' policy for whites, ousting black workers to make way for whites in state-owned or controlled enterprises and encouraging private busi-nesses to pursue the same policy. 'The native cannot blame us', argued Hertzog, 'if in the first place we try to find work for our own class.' In fact, the post-1994 ANC government was to pay him the highest compliment of all by exactly imitating these policies.

In 1926, Hertzog achieved what he deemed to be another victory. Following his proposals the Imperial Conference in London adopted the so-called Balfour Declaration which proclaimed full equality between Britain and its dominions. Hertzog decided this was a de facto proclamation of South African independence and thus the fulfilment of an old Afrikaner dream. However, this merely convinced many of his supporters that he had sold out to the British Empire like Smuts before him: for them nothing less than an independent republic outside the Empire would do.

For Afrikaner nationalism was still gathering momentum. With the upheavals of the First World War fresh in mind a number of younger, educated Afrikaner professionals, mainly teachers and civil servants, had founded an organisation called Young South Africa to promote the Afrikaner cause, particularly Afrikaans culture and language. The organisation, later renamed the Broederbond (the Brotherhood), became a secret society (clearly in opposition to the strong Masonic lodges then found among English speakers), bent on stretching its links into every sphere of society. The Broederbond established secret cells within important organisations and institutions, and developed a set of secret rituals for the initiated – but at the public level it also waged an energetic campaign to propagate the Afrikaner cultural tradition and historical legacy. This campaign was aimed at developing Afrikaners' self-consciousness: they must see themselves as a distinct and separate group, not only in terms of language, culture and religion but also politically, thus counterpoising them against all other racial groups in the country, including non-Afrikaner whites. By the 1930s the Broederbond had established separate organisations for young Afrikaner boys and students, and gradually it sought to build a 'total society' of cradle-to-grave organisations, rather like European socialist and communist movements, so that members could live every aspect of their lives within the *volk*.

In 1929 the Broederbond established a cultural body, the Federation of Afrikaans Cultural Associations (FAK), which was, in fact, its public façade – even the membership of the executives of the two bodies was the same. The FAK organised cultural festivals, radio programmes and other cultural activities centred on a romanticised version of the history of the *volk*. It also held congresses through which Broederbond ideas and policy were fed into the broader Afrikaner community, for the Broederbond had set itself quite consciously to become the collective brain of Afrikanerdom. By 1939 the FAK had hundreds of affiliated cultural bodies. The Dutch Reformed Church, under Broederbond influence, became a hugely powerful vehicle spreading the notion of a united, disciplined *volk*. Naturally the movement soon honeycombed both the electorate and the leadership of the NP.

The NP won the 1929 election under the banner of '*die swart gevaar*' (the black peril), using Smuts's vision of a 'great African Dominion stretching unbroken throughout Africa' to depict a South Africa drowned in a vast 'black kaffir state'. In fact, the two main parties did not really differ much: both stood for racial segregation in all spheres of life, but the NP made a virtue out of ignoring the interests of the black population completely and outspokenly. With poorer whites only too susceptible to such propaganda, the Labour Party lost ground which it was never to recover.

With this fresh mandate Hertzog's government pushed through more segregationist measures, imposing control over the African influx to urban areas (by the Native Urban Areas Amendment Act, 1930) and strengthening the native authority in the Transkei, which further entrenched the division between two administrative systems. The year 1930 saw the tightening of the Riotous Assemblies Act while the Native Service Contract Act (1932) sought to assist farmers (whose workers were usually the worst paid) by allowing recruitment of farm labour in urban areas and the use of labour provided by farm workers' families, including children. The NP did not touch the qualified franchise for Africans in the Cape – but swamped such voters by removing the property qualifications for white males and enfranchising white women.

However, the Nationalists had come to power just as the Depression began and South Africa was already far too integrated into the world economy to escape its effects. The collapse on Wall Street saw the price of two of South Africa's main exports, diamonds and wool, collapse too. Farmers with export crops were the first to suffer, as foreign demand dropped and cheap imports poured in as other countries dumped their surpluses. There were increasing demands for South Africa to follow other Western nations into protectionism and competitive devaluation, especially after Britain went off the gold standard in 1931. Distress among poor whites was such that the census showed that the number living in rural areas had actually increased – and for a modern industrialising economy re-ruralisation is a trauma, as urban unemployed scramble desperately back on to farms where at least they might hope to eat. But inevitably the whites shifted the burden on to blacks wherever that was possible. In Durban, for example, the huge dry docks were built by white workers using spades: both black workers and tractors were pushed aside to make more jobs for whites.

The government insisted, despite furious opposition, on keeping the gold standard as a matter of principle: it was a matter of pride for the NP not simply to follow Britain's example. If the world's biggest gold producer went off the gold standard what message would that send? But this was mere foolishness given the growing economic distress on every side. The government maintained the gold standard right through 1932 but then defeat in a key by-election showed that the farmers were ready to throw the government out if the gold standard was not abandoned – which it duly was in March 1933. Immediately conditions eased.

Hertzog and Smuts, both facing internal dissension within their own ranks, decided to form a coalition – which easily won the May 1933 election. At the end of 1934 they merged their parties to form the

United South African Nationalist Party, soon known simply as the United Party. This 'fusion' accepted the principle of South Africa's Commonwealth membership – Smuts's inevitable price – which, however, proved unacceptable to the NP hard core, to whom it simply meant partnership with the enemy. In mid 1934 the opponents of fusion, led by D. F. Malan, broke away to form the Purified Nationalist Party, which quickly became known as just the Nationalist Party.

Although fusion received more support among the SAP leadership than among the NP, the new fusion government, in which Hertzog was Prime Minister and Smuts his deputy, was closer to the goals of the old NP than those of the SAP. The fact was that the SAP had been traumatised by the ease with which *die swart gevaar* had swept it from power and realised that but for the economic crisis it might never have shared power again. In practice this meant that whenever the threat of *die swart gevaar* loomed, the SAP – now the UP – tended to back down.

The fusion government's large parliamentary majority enabled Hertzog to push through several segregationist laws that he had dreamt of since the late 1920s. The most important of these was the Native Representation Act (1936) which closed the common roll to Africans in the Cape and introduced communal representation for the entire African population. Cape Coloureds were left only with the right to vote for three white MPs and two members of the Cape Provincial Council. Africans in the country at large were allowed just four white Senators as their representatives. African reaction to this law was one of outrage and despair – for it was now brutally obvious that the government, far from evolving towards more progressive policies, was heading steadily backwards.

A Natives' Representative Council was set up under the Secretary for Native Affairs with an elected majority – though this hardly mattered, for it was purely consultative. The Natives Trust and Land Act (1936) purported to compensate the Africans for the loss of the common roll franchise by slightly increasing the territory of the native reserves. This was wholly insufficient to bring any relief: the reserves had to support ever larger numbers of people. More important, this act finalised the principle of territorial segregation while the Native Laws Amendment Act (1937) introduced influx control into urban areas.

The Depression brought a further twist to the complex dialectic of class and ethnicity. Because Afrikaners were poorer and less educated than English-speaking whites they tended to bear the brunt of hard times, but they were encouraged to see their situation in nationalist rather than class terms. The great issue of the day for nationalist ideologues was 'the poor white problem' and how to prevent this group from being forced down into the (black and Coloured) groups below. In this way the 1930s provided fecund conditions not just for the continuing growth of Afrikaner nationalism but for its refinement into a new Afrikaner ideology which sought to sanctify their suffering at the hands of the British, and to insist on their Calvinist mission and their special destiny in Africa through their covenant with God before the battle of Blood River. Both the Broederbond and the Dutch Reformed Church helped develop and entrench this ideology, which was based on a very selective and distorted reading of history.

The cultural organisations associated with the Broederbond popularised this ideology for mass consumption by staging events glorifying the folk culture of this freshly reimagined group. Most notably, in 1938 a replica of the ox-wagon Trek took place to celebrate the Trek's centenary – again a slightly made-up notion, for the trekkers had left the Cape over a period of years, not all at once in 1838. The participants started in Cape Town and rolled all the way to Pretoria or to the Blood River battleground by multiple routes in order to traverse as many towns on the way as possible. The event was an instant and lasting success though the few English speakers who took the benign propaganda seriously enough to attend the Pretoria finale were shocked to find themselves the target of vocal popular hostility. In the wake of this second Great Trek a new paramilitary organisation, the Ossewabrandwag (Ox Wagon Sentinel) was formed in order to promote Afrikaner unity. It developed an even more extremist mode of nationalism than the Purified Nationalists and was soon competing with them for the heart of Afrikanerdom. (Following Marx's dictum that history ultimately repeats itself as farce, 1988 saw a third Great Trek in which the extremist AWB pushed a strangely tinny ox wagon all the way to Pretoria, amidst popular derision.)

During the 1930s, too, the Broederbond began to work methodically to develop Afrikaner-owned businesses, banks, companies and community self-help societies in order to provide jobs for poor Afrikaners and generate wealth for the Afrikaner middle class, the key being to keep all resources within the community and gradually to undermine what was seen as the economic monopoly of 'the English' – a phrase indifferently used to denote the British or English-speaking South Africans. (Hendrik Verwoerd was once told that in the cricket test match then being played in Durban, the English were batting. 'Our English or their English?' he asked.) The first such community organisation, Santam, grew from the Helpmekaar movement, created to help the families of the victims of the Afrikaner rebellion during the First World War, to become a major insurance company. Other Afrikaner financial institutions, such as the Volkskas Bank and Sanlam, followed thereafter. Strong social pressure – amounting to ostracism in the case of dissidents – was used to ensure that every Afrikaner banked, borrowed or insured himself with the appropriate ethnic institution.

The (Purified) National Party began as a small organisation based mostly in the Cape (where Malan came from) but in the climate of rising nationalism he naturally earned respect for his lonely stand. Malan and other NP leaders joined the Broederbond and mixed freely in the nationalist mainstream. Thus from the first the Afrikaans media divided its sympathies between Hertzog's and Malan's brands of nationalism. Inevitably, as Afrikaner nationalism took its final shape, the movement was influenced by the upsurge of fascism in Europe, whose hostility to British imperialism naturally commended itself to Afrikaner ideologists. Some openly admired Hitler and the Nazis: there was a feeling of closeness between German and Boer-Dutch origins and a natural symmetry between notions of an Aryan super-race and doctrines of white supremacy. Many Afrikaner nationalists disliked the Jews – the cartoons of 'Hoggenheimer' (Oppenheimer) were typical of the attitude to 'Jewish capital' in general. This was less due to systematic anti-semitism than to a belief that Jewish capital was a key component of British imperial capital.

Afrikaner nationalism was later to pay heavily for these apparent connections to Nazism. Its opponents, particularly those in the ANC and the Communist Party, repeatedly insisted that their enemy was Hitlerian and that apartheid was comparable to the Holocaust, a crime against humanity. This made for effective propaganda but it entirely mistook the nature of Afrikaner nationalism. It was not really ever a South African equivalent of the Nazi Party; indeed, it was a lot closer to a European Labour Party in many respects. One has to remember that Indian, Egyptian and other nationalists expressed similarly misguided admiration for Hitler because they too – like Afrikaner nationalists – opposed British imperialism. But Afrikaner nationalism had no equivalent of the SA or the SS, there was no thought of a 'final solution' for anyone and no plan for aggressive war. It was a movement of the poor and not quite so poor, whose main strength lay in the countryside. Its leaders and activists were often country lawyers or small-town preachers and teachers, the epitome of church-going respectability. It saw itself not only as a very moral but a righteous movement. The real comparison is with African nationalism. As the ANC swept to power in

1994 it too was a movement of the poor and not quite so poor disproportionately drawn from the countryside, with small-town preachers, teachers and lawyers prominent within its leadership. It too was immensely self-righteous, repeatedly asserting that it held 'the moral high ground'.

The UP government did not take the NP seriously until the 1938 election when they won no less than twenty-seven seats, considerably assisted by the successful voortrekker celebrations that year. The movement of Afrikaners to the towns was, Malan suggested, the new Great Trek, and their struggle for jobs and against the *swart gevaar* their new battle of Blood River. The NP and the Broederbond attacked Hertzog for his alliances with Labour and the SAP which had, they claimed, diluted the Afrikaner cause and confused poor white Afrikaners. In 1939 the Broederbond convened the People's Economic Congress to discuss the future of the Afrikaner nation. In the wake of the conference several new institutions were formed, all of them promoting the cause of Afrikaner separatism: building Afrikaans business, helping poor white Afrikaners, and pulling workers away from white trade unions they shared with English speakers and enrolling them instead in the OB's Labour Front or the NP's White Workers' Protection League. But while Hertzog's alliance with English-speaking interests made him vulnerable to Malan's onslaught, Malan's party showed little sign of further progress until the situation was again revolutionised by a world war, just as it had been in 1914.

For war again posed the unavoidable issue. Hertzog and his followers stood for South Africa's neutrality; Smuts insisted on support for Britain – but his resolution in parliament was carried only thanks to the support of Labour and the small Dominion Party, the English-speaking diehards who had refused fusion with the Nationalists. Malan, naturally, supported Hertzog. The Cabinet was split but the Governor-General, Patrick Duncan, refused a dissolution. Hertzog had to resign, Smuts returning to the premiership once again.

These dramas were fought out exclusively within the domain of white politics – for the fact was that those African organisations that existed had no real mass following and could mount no serious challenge. Nonetheless these inter-war years were the formative period of African nationalism, when its main features, demands and alliances took shape. Smuts was keenly aware that the coming together of Malan and Hertzog had united Afrikaner nationalism again, but he was much less aware that a new and far larger nationalist movement was struggling to be born.

The most important black organisation, the African National Congress, grew out of the South African Native Convention which had first met in 1909 to protest against the exclusion of African opinion in the formation of the Union. After the Union had been inaugurated the Convention continued to meet, and in 1911 Pixley ka Isaka Seme, a Zulu lawyer with an American and British education, proposed the idea of the Congress to other leaders and notably to the Tswana journalist, author and translator Solomon (Sol) Plaatje. Accordingly the founding conference of the South African Native National Congress met in Bloemfontein on 8-12 January 1912. John Dube, an American-educated teacher, journalist, minister and editor of the first Zulu newspaper, *Ilanga lase Natal*, was elected the first President, with Sol Plaatje as Secretary General and Seme as Treasurer. John Tengo Jabavu, the senior African intellectual and politician, did not join the Congress and attempted to create his own organisation.

The first major challenge came with the tabling of the 1913 Native Land Bill. At that time British liberals believed that territorial segregation, if applied in an honest and just manner, was the best way to protect native interests. This was, after all, why the three protectorates of Swaziland, Basutoland and Bechuanaland had been held back from the Union, to the furious annoyance of Smuts. Some African political leaders shared this view: Jabavu defended it in his newspaper, *Imvo Zabantsundu*, and the SANNC leadership was divided, with Dube supporting segregation in principle and Plaatje rejecting it. The SANNC took Plaatje's part and sent delegations to plead its cause both to Pretoria and London – in vain. During the war the SANNC refrained from protest action but by war's end, with the real implications of segregationist policy now crystal clear, both the SANNC and Jabavu had become completely disillusioned with the notion that segregation had any redeeming features.

In 1919, following the example of Gandhi's passive resistance movement, the SANNC initiated a campaign against the pass laws. It was relatively successful, particularly in the Transvaal, but the government managed to get tribal chiefs to speak against the movement. True, thousands of mine passes were handed in but the SANNC could not match the success of the Indian campaign. The SANNC lacked the external support the Indian movement had enjoyed from the Indian government and the international publicity it had achieved via the Commonwealth. But the SANNC's greatest weakness was simply lack of mass support. Its leaders were law-abiding middle-class men and they lacked experience in rallying African workers – not surprisingly, for the white authorities were progressively taking steps to make strikes by African workers illegal.

The only organisation with a real rapport with African workers was the Industrial and Commercial Workers' union, the ICU, founded in 1919 by Clements Kadalie, an expatriate Malawian cleric and teacher. The ICU's first big action was to organise a black dock workers' strike in Cape Town in December 1919. The next year it grew rapidly into a national organisation, spreading to all the main urban centres but also recruiting many supporters, particularly in Natal and the OFS, among black tenant farmers and labourers who had been evicted or were in danger of eviction from farms. The ICU also took up the protests of black women against the prohibition of brewing and selling of sorghum beer in the towns, an important source of income for them. Collecting paid memberships was always a problem for the ICU but by 1927 it had sold about 100,000 membership cards.

Organisationally, the ICU was always somewhat chaotic with a large and continuous turnover of membership. Kadalie's foreign origins meant he was viewed with suspicion by some and the ICU was also divided between radicals (headed by communists such as James La Guma, the ICU's General Secretary) and moderates such as Kadalie himself. At the end of 1926 Kadalie got rid of the communists by passing a resolution making membership of the Party and the ICU incompatible. Kadalie wanted to move into the world of respectable trade unionism and gain international recognition. This he never achieved for the truth was that the union was a sort of moving shambles, its accounts and records chaotic, and Kadalie was accused of putting funds into his own back pocket. The Natal branch, led by George Champion, was the most active but split away as an independent Natal organisation, ICU yase Natal. In 1929 Kadalie himself left and attempted to form a new organisation, the Independent ICU, but by the early 1930s the organisation was effectively dead. Champion remained a major, though increasingly conservative, figure in Durban for another forty years.

In 1923 the SANNC changed its name to the ANC but it continued to be a legalistic, middle-class organisation, presenting (hopeless) petitions and memoranda. By 1927, however, the communists began to join the ANC, pushing for a more energetic and radical approach. In 1927 the ANC President, James Gumede, visited the Soviet Union and returned full of admiration for the USSR and calling for closer co-operation with the Communist Party (the CPSA). But the ANC's old guard, led by John Dube, did not share Gumede's views and managed to oust him from the presidency in 1930, losing to the anti-communist candidate, Pixley ka Isaka Seme.

However, the increasingly discriminatory nature of government policy, and particularly the tabling of Hertzog's Representation of Natives and Natives' Trust and Land Bills in 1935, required action. African opposition to the bills was unanimous and emphatic. In December 1935 Seme and Davidson Jabavu, John Tengo Jabavu's son who had succeeded him as the leader of the Cape Native Voters' Association, convened an All African Convention. More than 400 delegates attended, representing the ANC, the Cape Native Voters' Association, the remnants of the ICU, the CPSA and various other organisations. The outcome of the Convention was the usual useless petition and a deputation to Hertzog – but black opposition was clearly coming together. Moreover, in 1937, after the bills became law, most of the Convention's leaders won seats on the new segregated bodies. For at this stage there was no thought of boycotting 'illegitimate' institutions. Many prominent ANC members actively campaigned for white candidates standing for election as 'natives' representatives' in parliament – which in practice meant accepting the segregationist principle that the Convention had just rejected.

The late 1930s saw the ANC's partial revival with the election of Reverend James Calata, an energetic Anglican priest, as its President. Under Calata the organisation returned to having regular annual conferences in 1937–9 but it remained small, weak and middle class, like other early nationalist organisations in the rest of Africa at that time. What made the ANC different was its permanent exposure to the continuous interplay of white politics, far more diverse and intense than elsewhere in Africa, its access to relatively good media and perhaps most important, its unique relationship with the CPSA from the late 1930s on.

Just as white parties argued about the particular form which racial domination should take but not about the fact of it, so the black opposition was, inevitably, also organised on racial lines. The State distinguished between three groups of non-whites – 'natives' (Africans), Coloureds and Indians – though in fact each of these groups was also divided ethnically, religiously and culturally.

The African People's Organisation had been formed in 1902 to promote the rights of the Cape Coloured population. Abdullah Abdurahman, its President from 1905 to his death in 1940, turned it into a powerful national organisation though his moderate views and policies were challenged by the younger generation even within his own family.

His daughter (and Cape Town councillor) Zainunissa ('Cissie') Gool was elected President of the National Liberation League, created in 1935, and joined the Non-European United Front under the chairmanship of Yusuf Dadoo in 1938. The Front leapt into action in 1938–9 when the Nationalists first proposed segregating the Coloureds from the whites in all spheres of life – something actually achieved only decades later under apartheid. The demonstration led by Cissie Gool became a riot and the proposed ordinance was withdrawn.

Gandhi, who had introduced passive resistance to South Africa, left for India in 1914. The South African Indian National Congress, which claimed his legacy, was formed in 1923. In 1926 it sent Abdullah Abdurahman to India to present its case to the British and Indian authorities and to the Indian National Congress there. This resulted in a compromise by the Hertzog government who agreed to assist the repatriation of (the very few) South African Indians who wanted to return to India and, more significantly, to confirm the right of wives and children of Indians resident in South Africa to immigrate there, and to accept previously illegal immigrants as residents. New battles came in 1939 with the introduction of the Transvaal Asiatics (Land and Trading) Bill, which further limited Indian trading rights in the province. Yusuf Dadoo, head of the Transvaal Indian Congress, and Cissie Gool led a passive resistance campaign against the Bill, winning a majority of the Indian community to their side.

Although there were several attempts at inter-racial co-operation within the inter-war opposition, only the CPSA united representatives of all the different racial groups in its ranks as a matter of principle. The CPSA had been set up in 1921 and admitted as a member of the Communist International. Initially the party was almost exclusively white, particularly at leadership level, and was mainly devoted to the interests of the white working class, as became obvious during the 1922 Rand revolt which the party wholeheartedly supported despite its clearly expressed anti-black sentiments. The party saw non-whites as victims of colonial oppression who needed assistance and education in Marxist doctrine – but still essentially as the domain of nationalist organisations. By the late 1920s its work among non-whites had produced a trickle of black members but the party still did not see such work as a priority: the target was the mature white working class.

However, in 1927–8 during the visit to Moscow of Jimmy La Guma, one of the first black communists, the Comintern devised the new slogan of an 'independent native republic', a policy made binding on the CPSA – despite the reservations of some of its leaders – by its adoption at the sixth Comintern Congress in 1928. This slogan attracted a new wave of black activists into the party including such key future leaders as John Biver Marks, Edwin Mofutsanyana and Moses Kotane. Although the party was tiny – membership stood at just a few hundred during most of the 1930s – and divided by endless internal struggles, it remained influential, playing a key role first within the ICU and thereafter increasingly within the ANC.

In 1935 the Comintern called on all member parties – including the CPSA – to create popular fronts against fascism and ordered the CPSA to concentrate on trade union and other practical work. Although greatly weakened by factional struggle, the CPSA revitalised its work with the nationalist organisations. It struck up a working relationship with Cissie Gool, recruited Yusuf Dadoo into the party and managed to get representatives on to the governing bodies of both the All-African Convention and the ANC. Despite their expulsion from the ICU, communists continued to work within both white and black trade unions as individuals, sometimes concealing their party membership. The popular front never materialised but by the end of this period communists had greatly increased their influence within both the ANC and the trade unions.

Most blacks were not politically active: coping with everyday life during the Depression was tough enough. It was during the inter-war period when labour migrancy became a dominant factor in African life. In many rural areas at any given time 30–40 per cent of young men were away in the towns, on the farms or in the mines. This meant that the norms which had guided these rural societies before the twentieth century no longer applied and that the structures that were the backbone of these societies began to collapse. Families were now divided almost as a norm; old patterns of polygamy combined with migrancy to produce a situation in which men were seldom socialised to lasting relationships, in which children were reared by their grandmothers as commonly as by their mothers and in which the majority of women who stayed behind in the rural areas brought up their children alone and in poverty. Much of what can be said about the dysfunctional black American family can be said about the black South African family too.

The black men and women drawn to the towns and mines by hopes of a higher income found themselves in precarious situations. The overwhelming majority of the black population in these areas consisted of males who were increasingly beyond the reach of the mores and disciplines of traditional society. Gangs ruled the day, prostitution and crime were rampant, rape common and drunkenness almost a way of life. The psychological pressure of these rapid and drastic changes was enormous and there were few remedies to help cope with it. By far the most common recourse was Christianity, which provided education and some sort of support system, though many Africans found a radical disjuncture between official Christian doctrine and their actual lives.

The answer was obvious: Afro-Christianity, that is to say independent African Churches based on Christian doctrine but creatively interpreting and adjusting that doctrine and practice in line with the requirements of African society in this new stage of development. Their Africanness usually borrowed from African society as a whole, not from one particular ethnic group, and their ritual was closer to African tradition in a broad sense – emphasising singing and dancing, for example. Their leaders were frequently accused of un-Christian polygamy or witchcraft, often with some truth for many were consciously syncretist. They were, after all, not supported by established hierarchies but were operating in a religious free market so they sank or swam depending on whether their particular mix of beliefs and rituals found a congregation or not. The Thembu Church created by Nehemiah Tile in 1884 was probably the first such movement but by 1892 Mangena Mokone's Ethiopian Church had surpassed it, gathering some 10,000 followers in just six years. There were scores of these Churches, the majority remaining small. Several Zionist Churches (a term borrowed from America, having no connection to Judaism or Israel) sprang up, one of them developing into what is today the third-biggest Church in South Africa with millions of followers.

Afro-Christian Churches were mostly apolitical but some, like the Zionists, were quietist and conservative, a means of adaptation to an often unhappy status quo. A few were militant like the Israelite Church founded in 1918 by Enoch Mgijima, who drew his following mostly from among the landless. In 1920 they settled on common land near Queenstown and refused to heed police orders to leave. When, in 1921, the police attempted to move them they attacked the police – who then shot 163 of them dead and wounded 129 more.

South Africa entered the Second World War just as politically divided as it had been during the First War – and the war itself only deepened these divisions. Smuts had now become an iconic figure. His stature was such that Churchill asked him to act as Prime Minister in his place while he was meeting Roosevelt and Stalin in Tehran, and British Tories commonly thought of him as a likely premier if Churchill were killed. Smuts had given himself fully to the role of an imperial statesman and, disdaining local divisions, boldly led the Union to war because in his view its place was with Britain, fighting for the future of humanity. In 1940–1 South African forces (a majority of them Afrikaans-speakers) fought in the campaign against Italy in Ethiopia; in 1942 they ousted the pro-Vichy administration of Madagascar; they fought in the desert war in North Africa and then, as volunteers, in Europe. Many South African pilots joined the RAF and men such as Johnny Johnson and Sailor Malan were among the top fighter aces of the war. Non-white South Africans also participated, though in non-combatant units – not because they weren't willing to fight but because white opinion would have been horrified had they been armed. Some 9,000 South Africans lost their lives in the Allied cause. It was a noble effort and Smuts was a British hero.

Sentiment among militant Afrikaners was different. What they could see, perfectly reasonably, was that the Union's position on the southern tip of Africa meant that it had little reason of its own to fight: if its young men died it was for Britain and its Empire. This was deeply repugnant to both Hertzog and Malan who had little difficulty in burying the hatchet and reuniting the National Party in opposition to the war. But this Reunited Nationalist Party which came together in 1939 did not last. Despite his aversion to war on the side of the British, Hertzog's dream was still the unity and equality of the English speaker and the Afrikaner, while Malan and his party wanted an independent Afrikaner republic. Late in 1940 the new party collapsed and Hertzog left parliament with the remnants of his followers, founding the Afrikaner Party. But such was the fury against the war – and the accumulated momentum of Afrikaner nationalism – that both Malan and Hertzog were far outflanked by several extremist Afrikaner organisations, some of them openly pro-Nazi, particularly during the Axis triumphs in the early stages of the war which strengthened the idea that the Nazi new order might be the future of humanity.

The first openly fascist and anti-semitic organisation, the Greyshirts, founded by Louis Weichardt in 1933, never gained much support. In 1940 Oswald Pirow, a former Defence Minister in the UP government and an open admirer of Hitler, organised the New Order movement within the National Party with the vision of a white racist state based on the Nazi idea of leadership by the will of the Führer rather than on parliamentary principles. There were several other militant and para-military groups but the most popular was the Ossewabrandwag (OB) under the leadership of Johannes Frederik ('Hans') van Rensburg.

The OB still preached Afrikaner cultural values but had come to the conclusion that it was impossible to achieve its goals by constitutional means. Like Pirow's New Order it was also attracted to the Nazi idea of rule by the will of a Führer. But the OB went further, openly seeking an Axis victory by engaging in sabotage and terrorist acts.

The OB presented a serious challenge to Malan's Nationalists. In 1940 Malan managed to achieve an agreement with some OB leaders, requiring them not to act against fraternal Afrikaner political movements – but he found it difficult to make this stick. After all, if the Axis won, the OB would expect to take over South Africa completely – and it thus offered hotheads like the young John Vorster the possibility of a radical short cut to an independent Boer republic. The rivalry came to a head in July 1941 when the OB undertook to distribute 100,000 copies of the draft constitution of a proposed Afrikaner republic, compiled by the Broederbond. This was open sedition in time of war and the draft had quickly to be withdrawn, but in January 1942 OB members were expelled from the NP. Ironically, what saved Malan was that Smuts had chosen the winning side: from 1943 on it became obvious that the OB was leading the Nationalist cause into a dead end.

The UP, in coalition with the Labour Party and the Natal Dominion Party, won an overwhelming majority in the 1943 election but Smuts too easily assumed the home front was secure. For while the NP had won only forty-three seats, most NP seats that were lost had belonged to Malan's intra-party opponents – the Afrikaner Party and Pirow's New Order lost ground. Moreover Malan, who had focused the NP's campaign on domestic racial and labour issues, had made significant gains in the Afrikaner vote at the UP's expense. With Hertzog now gone and Afrikanerdom reuniting round Malan, the NP was clearly going to be a formidable opponent in 1948.

The war had given fresh impetus to the South African economy. Almost every industry benefited from increased wartime demand. Submarine warfare in the Atlantic meant that import substitution of every kind was essential, particularly since Churchill was happy to see British needs supplied by production well beyond the *Luftwaffe's* reach. Old industries expanded, new factories opened and farmers intensified production to cope with the demand: even Cape snoek were exported to wartime Britain though the fish did not suit English tastes. This production boom naturally resulted in an increased demand for labour, causing the Smuts government to be slow to implement Hertzog's segregationist 'native' bills and even create the impression that it might let them lapse. This was certainly what the white liberals who sat as

Native Representatives, such as Margaret Ballinger and John Rheinalt-Jones wanted – and they were unexpectedly effective in parliament. But pressure from the NP – who had begun to play the 'communist danger' card – forced Smuts to back down. The pass regulations were put back on track and steps taken to prevent the growth of African wages. War Measure No. 145 of 1942 outlawed all African strikes and War Measure No. 1425 of 1945 made trade union activity impossible by prohibiting all gatherings of more than twenty people. A discriminatory law (nicknamed the 'Pegging Act') froze all sales of Durban residential properties from white owners to Indians for three years. Many of these wartime discriminatory measures persisted even after the war's end.

The big difference was that black opposition to these sorts of discriminatory measures was far greater during the war than anything seen previously. At the end of 1940 the ANC had elected a new President General, Dr Alfred Bitini Xuma, who began to transform it into a more centralised and active organisation. A million-member campaign, though it failed to achieve its target, did produce a large number of new members. Moreover, the international atmosphere of wartime popular front, of admiration for the Soviet war effort and the fresh beginning of the United Nations gave a following wind to all black organisations. A new Bill of Rights, influenced by the Atlantic Charter and demanding the end of all discrimination against Africans, was adopted by the ANC and presented to the government (which, of course, threw it in the rubbish bin). The ANC also began to participate in the CPSA's mass campaign against the pass laws and Xuma became Chairman of the Anti-Pass Committee. Though the campaign peaked in 1944, when an anti-pass march in Johannesburg attracted about 20,000 people, it continued after the war.

In 1942–3 the ANC Youth League was founded by Anton Lembede as a pressure group for the younger, more militant elements within ANC ranks. Lembede died soon after but the league's other leaders were to become the most significant black figures of their time – Robert Sobukwe, Walter Sisulu and Nelson Mandela among them. Initially the league was exclusively Africanist, rejecting co-operation with other races and warning against the communists on the grounds of their non-African agenda. All this, however, was soon to change.

Coloured politics had also been shaken by the decision of the Smuts government to create a separate section within the Ministry of the Interior to deal with all Coloured affairs. This sounded ominously as if it might be the precursor to a Coloured Affairs Department, parallel

to the Native Affairs Department, which would thus finalise the segregation of the Coloured community. A strong 'Anti-CAD' movement
sprang into existence and, together with the All-African Convention,
held a conference in 1943 to which they invited several other Coloured
and Indian organisations. The conference launched a new organisation,
the Non-European Unity Movement, but it failed to get many important non-white organisations to join. The ANC did not participate and
the Natal Indian Congress (NIC) – by far the largest Indian organisation, for 90 per cent of South Africa's Indians lived in Natal – agreed
to co-operate only on certain issues.

At that time the NIC was fighting against measures for property and
residential segregation in Natal. Pressure from the Indian government
and the threat of turmoil within the Commonwealth led to a compromise being reached in 1944 but this soon broke down as the
government brought in other measures attempting to restrict Indian
property purchases. Unperturbed by the strong reaction from the Indian
community, Smuts introduced the Asiatic Land Tenure and Indian
Representation Bill which restricted the right of Indians to own land
to certain areas of Natal, offering a measure of indirect community
representation as a consolation. When the bill became law in 1946 the
NIC, now under the militant leadership of Dr Gangathura Mohambry
Naicker, termed it the 'Ghetto Act' and launched a passive-resistance
campaign. But, fatefully, by pushing through discriminatory policies
against both Africans and Indians, Smuts had created a united, inter-
racial opposition. In March 1947 Naicker, Dadoo of the Transvaal
Indian Congress and Xuma of the ANC – all three of them medical
doctors – signed a declaration of co-operation, nicknamed the 'Doctors' Pact'.

The CPSA had greatly enhanced its standing during the war. Once
Hitler attacked the Soviet Union in June 1941 the CPSA had at last
found itself in the political mainstream, for its call for unity behind
the anti-fascist cause coincided exactly with the policy of the Smuts
government. The communists took full advantage and even wooed
white anti-fascist opinion via such front organisations as the Friends of
the Spanish Republic, the revitalised Friends of the Soviet Union and
the powerful ex-servicemen's organisation, the Springbok Legion.
More important, however, was the party's continued work with black
organisations. By now CPSA leaders regularly sat on the ANC executive. They also started to work with the Youth League, toning down
its Africanism and introducing its leadership to Marxism. The CPSA
consistently promoted the idea of a united front of organisations of all

the oppressed ethnic groups – while quietly resisting identical calls from the Non-European Unity Movement which was not under Communist influence and which, accordingly, soon developed an angry Trotskyite critique of the party's work.

The trade unions, especially the black trade unions, were, of course, a particular CPSA target. During the war the number of African trade unions grew from twenty to fifty with a total membership of 80,000 – almost four times greater than before the war. Prominent ANC and CPSA members won union leadership positions, for both organisations now saw the unions as their mass power base. Although the unions acquired better organisation and improved bargaining skills from this connection, it hardly made their cause any easier: all attempts during the war by the Council of Non-European Trade Unions to have bargaining rights extended to Africans had come to nothing. The greatest problem, of course, was that there was no shortage of unskilled and semi-skilled labour, so all attempts by African unions to negotiate higher wages for their mainly unskilled and semi-skilled members tended to be undercut. But the movement was gaining momentum and where workers had some skills – for example, the miners – the effect could be dramatic, as the strike of 1946 showed.

The Miners Union, with some 25,000 members, had been trying since 1944 to win union recognition and a wage increase. The employers conceded a small increase for overtime work and also favoured recognition of an African miners' union in principle, but were loath to recognise the MU, which was heavily penetrated by communists. So in August 1946 more than 70,000 mineworkers embarked on a well-organised strike. The Rand gold mines were brought to a halt and the Smuts government reacted ruthlessly, the police forcing the workers back to the mines at gunpoint. Inevitably, this led to clashes in which a number of workers at the Village Deep mine were killed and many more wounded.

Such incidents had littered colonial history. But even moderate black opinion was no longer willing to regard them as normal. The Natives' Representative Council which was sitting during the strike decided, on Xuma's initiative, to adjourn if the government did not abolish the pass laws and did not recognise African trade unions. These demands were ignored so the council unanimously adjourned itself. Negotiations led nowhere, for the government was not prepared to budge, and the NRC moved further and further, demanding direct African representation at all levels.

The Smuts government met the rising tide of protest with straightforward repression partly because of the growing pressure of Malan's NP, always ready to suggest that the government was not firm enough against the *swart gevaar*, but also because it had no other conception of how to behave. Smuts tended to assume that white rule was the permanent and natural order of things. In advocating the incorporation into the Union of all the countries to the north as far as Kenya, he had spoken of how the whole area could be 'made into a great European state or system of states during the next three or four generations', arguing that 'in the long run this subcontinent has only one destiny, and it may be delayed, but it cannot be prevented', that destiny being a larger Union where 'a resolute white policy' would always be pursued. This blind confidence in the permanency of white rule now clearly marks Smuts as a man of a bygone era and it is tempting to see his defeat in the 1948 election as a sort of proof of that. But, of course, Malan was no less a man of a bygone era. In that sense 1948 was to bring no answers, no solutions and was to change nothing.

# VIII
## THE APOGEE OF
## WHITE SUPREMACY
ð ð ð

Few people foresaw the result of the fateful general election of 26 May 1948. Smuts had been vindicated by the Allied victory, the economy was booming and white immigrants were pouring into the country, many of them former British servicemen who had first seen Cape Town or Durban from a troopship. South Africa's international standing was at its height. Not only had it been a founding member of the United Nations but Smuts had even been asked to draft the UN Charter. The royal visit of 1947 had been an acknowledgement of Britain's gratitude and affection. Smuts could not have been riding higher.

But he had, as always, neglected the home front. Farmers were displeased with continuing wartime regulations and with government's failure to provide them with sufficient black labour – for war had speeded up black migration to the cities and mines. White workers were unhappy about the wartime loosening of influx control and felt insecure in the face of the vast resulting inflow of black labour into the towns. Afrikaners were dismayed by Smuts's post-war immigration scheme which had resulted in 60,000 immigrants in 1947–8 alone. They saw this mainly British influx plus the royal visit as a sign that the republic they still longed for was being removed for ever beyond their reach. For them Smuts's role in the UN's creation was just a bad joke. Had not the very Charter that he had helped create been used against South Africa by the Indian government – which had immediately complained that Smuts's discriminatory anti-Indian laws infringed it? Moreover, Smuts's application to incorporate South-West Africa

(Namibia) into the Union had been rejected and South Africa had been asked to transfer this territory to UN Trusteeship (a request Smuts refused). What made this humiliation worse was that the ANC President General, Dr Xuma, had travelled to New York for the General Assembly session and lobbied against incorporation. In effect this had put South Africa's racial policies – not just in South-West Africa but at home – on trial before the world, a trial the country had clearly not won.

Xuma's mission was symbolic of the new assertiveness of black South Africans and it was this, more than anything else, which cost Smuts crucial support. In practice the whole 'native policy' of successive governments had rested on the brutality of the conquest and the lingering sense of fear and deference to white rule it had imposed on Africans. As this eroded and the government came under increasing challenge the UP could not offer a clear-cut native policy – and its opponents did. The NP used the wartime popularity of the CPSA as a bogeyman, and particularly against the UP's liberal wing personified by Jan Hofmeyr, Smuts's deputy and putative successor – by 1948 Smuts was seventy-eight – depicting Hofmeyr as a 'kaffirboetie' – (kaffir-lover). As ever, the UP had no real answer to *swart gevaar* tactics and the NP kept up a ceaseless barrage of racist propaganda. The NP was also better organised: unlike their UP counterparts very few NP activists had volunteered to fight in the war and had thus been able to work away unchallenged at grass roots. Moreover the delimitation commission had just redrawn constituency boundaries in a way that favoured the NP. Malan had also managed to neutralise the Ossewabrandwag and had entered an election pact with the Afrikaner Party, which the over-confident Smuts had rejected. For the UP the disaster was complete. It not only lost power but Hofmeyr unexpectedly died in 1948, followed by Smuts in 1950. It was never to have leaders of their stature again.

The NP – the Nats, as they were always called – had learnt their lesson. There had been many births, rebirths and splits – which had cost them power. They now saw unity as paramount and after the disaster over the gold standard they were willing to stay in the sterling area come what may. They were to hold power for the next forty-six years – under the banner of apartheid, literally 'separateness'.

Apartheid doctrine had originated in discussions within the Broederbond in the 1930s, had been further developed by the South African League of Racial Studies and then by a policy commission the Nats had set up during the war. In theory apartheid meant neither discrimination nor the domination of any particular race; the races would simply follow their separate paths in all spheres of life in accordance with (what the Nats defined as) their own traditions and cultures. The Indians – the only exception – were to be excluded from the new dispensation, for they were considered an alien element, not really belonging in South Africa at all.

The doctrine was refined over time, and successive NP governments implemented it differently but two things always remained unchanged. The first was that the doctrine had grown out of a deep underlying racism and no matter how later theorists tried to purge it of this for presentational reasons, both the doctrine itself and all apartheid laws remained racist and discriminatory. The second was that the Nats never wanted a complete separation of 'races': they needed black and Coloured labour in what they termed the 'white' areas, on the mines and farms and in the cities. Inevitably, however illicit, this meant that a great deal of racial mixing went on right through apartheid. Had apartheid involved simple territorial separation it might conceivably have worked but the decision, from the start, to opt for economic integration remained the policy's Achilles heel.

Since racial classification was to be the cornerstone the NP rushed through the Population Registration Act (1949), registering every citizen under a racial category – a remarkable enterprise in an already Creolised society. At first classification was done on the basis of visual examination alone; later various pseudo-objective criteria were added (measurements of the skull, the degree of curliness of one's hair, etc.). But there was no pretension to scientific rigour: the racial categories were just the groups known by everyday practice – whites, Africans, Indians and Coloureds. The result was that members of the same family were sometimes classified differently and that reclassification became a permanent feature of life. This bizarre and often cruel process had to proceed without researching family trees for many Afrikaners might themselves have fallen foul of such a test. A white thus reclassified as, say, Coloured, would have to move to a Coloured area, use Coloured schools and other services, suffer job discrimination, the loss of the franchise and, often, family break-up. There were many suicides.

Those registered as Africans ('Bantu') had to carry passes at all times. The Abolition of Passes and Consolidation of Documents Act (1952) replaced the multiple passes Africans had previously carried with a single 'reference book', bearing a photograph of the owner, his full record of his employment, tax payments, criminal offences, etc. African women, previously exempt from such a stipulation, now had to carry passes too. This was the key instrument of influx control. All mixing of the races now had to stop: the Prohibition of Mixed Marriages Act (1949) outlawed marriage between the races and in 1950 the Immorality Act was extended to outlaw extramarital sex between whites and Coloureds.

Next came the tightening up of territorial separation. The Native Laws Amendment Act (1952) restricted the rights of Africans to reside in urban areas to those born there; those who had lived or worked there for at least fifteen years; and those who had worked there for the same employer for at least ten years. Rights of residence in a particular town were valid for that town only and were not transferable to any other, thus tying black residents to particular places. The Group Areas Act (1950) gave the authorities the right to resettle or evict Coloureds or Indians who lived in or close to white areas and forcibly resettle them into 'their' group area. This act was used both against individuals and whole communities, causing enormous suffering and bitterness.

The most notorious GAA forced removal was the destruction of District Six, the traditional Coloured suburb in central Cape Town. This large area, the heart of a vigorous subculture and community life, was designated for whites. Not only were Coloureds forcibly evicted but the whole area was razed to the ground, leaving only a few deserted churches in the midst of a wasteland. Coloured leaders passionately implored whites not to settle there, hinting that such a betrayal would not be forgotten, with the result that neither businesses nor private individuals would touch it The area remained a vacant and desolate reminder of apartheid ruthlessness until well after 1994. Such sensitivity was unique. Having arrived less than a century before, Indians had no such long-held traditional area in Durban and white Durbanites had few qualms about taking over Indian property in Riverside or the Berea.

African townships had been uniracial from the time they first emerged. Even so, the NP was determined to consolidate white areas by removing black settlements situated too close to them. The Native Resettlement Act (1956) allowed the authorities to withdraw existing property rights and remove their owners. Several African townships in Johannesburg were removed in this way, most notably Sophiatown, in north-west Johannesburg, razed to the ground as 'slum clearance'. Sophiatown was home to Johannesburg's longest-established black residents and, as the centre of black township culture and politics, was a tempting target. The government changed the name of the area to Triomf (Triumph) and settled it with whites. The former residents were moved to a new township called South-West Townships (Soweto).

A similarly bitter battle was fought to raze Cato Manor in Durban with the residents forcibly relocated to Kwa Mashu Township. More than a generation later Kwa Mashu remained Durban's most militant township, for the scar of forced removal never really healed.

Segregation in urban areas was completed by the Reservation of Separate Amenities Act (1953) requiring any place used by different races to be equipped with separate 'amenities', including separate toilets, entrances, counters etc. The law specifically stipulated that such amenities did not need to be equal. In 1957 similar requirements were extended to cultural facilities, parks etc. These two laws resulted in the 'whites only' and 'non-whites' signs which adorned virtually every nook and cranny of every town. Such signs were not only insulting and overtly racist but the segregation in sports and culture closed off two routes to success taken by many blacks even in pre-Civil Rights America.

The most destructive Act of all, which still hangs like a lead weight on the country's future, was the Bantu Education Act (1953) which barred Africans from acquiring skills or knowledge that could not be used in the native reserves or in the service of the whites in white areas. Notoriously, Hendrik Verwoerd boasted that there was no point, for example, in Africans doing maths or acquiring other such skills which could only result in inflated expectations and frustration. Moreover, the Act placed African education under the Department of Native Affairs, not the Department of Education. All black schools, including missionary schools, were allowed to teach only the government-approved syllabus, which leaned heavily on menial skills and Afrikaans. Much of the teaching was done in local languages, thus barring students from English – the country's only international language. This also meant that virtually all (the often excellent) mission schools closed, an unparalleled act of educational vandalism. This was, in effect, an attempt to set the cultural clock back to the immediate post-conquest period.

In 1959, despite bitter resistance from the English-language universities, the Extension of University Education Act was passed, segregating higher education. It introduced tertiary institutions for each racial group, including a raft of 'tribal colleges' in the black 'homeland' areas, pathetic mockeries of universities, usually staffed by third-rate Broederbonders. Moreover, the previous trickle of black and brown students into the country's English-language universities now stopped, the sole exception being the all-black medical school of Natal University – which thus became by far the country's most important black educational institution.

The Prevention of Illegal Squatting Act (1951), aimed against Africans still living on farm, mission or church land in rural areas designated as white, extended segregation to the rural areas. Under it the Minister of Native Affairs was entitled to remove Africans from any land in designated white areas, with resettlement camps to be created for those thus removed who had nowhere to go.

Inevitably, these measures were greeted by a storm of protest by black nationalists, liberals and the left so the government simultaneously took steps to suppress such voices. The Suppression of Communism Act (1950) outlawed the CPSA and allowed for communists to be deprived of their civil liberties by banning orders. Communism, however, was defined so vaguely that the Act could be – and was – applied to anybody who made a political nuisance of themselves. The Native Labour (Settlement of Disputes) Act (1953) made any strike by Africans illegal while the Industrial Conciliation Act (1956) excluded Africans from the definition of 'employees' completely, thus making conciliation and arbitration unavailable for them. The racially mixed trade unions that existed were forced to form separate branches for white and non-white members and the executive committees of such unions had to be exclusively white. Under the Act the Industrial Tribunal could examine any industry or job and proclaim them exclusively reserved for whites.

Finally, once territorial segregation had been enforced and the Natives' Representative Council abolished, the native reserves had to be governed in line with 'tradition' so the Bantu Authorities Act (1953) established an administration in the reserves dominated by chiefs with expanded powers. But the chiefs were still appointed by the government, which defined their duties and jurisdiction. This, of course, bore no relationship to any 'tradition' at all.

A major obstacle to complete separation of the races, however, was the fact that, entrenched by the constitution, Coloureds were still on the common voters' roll and had direct representation on the Cape Provincial Council. And changing the constitution would require a two-thirds majority of both houses of parliament – which the Nats did not have. The government decided to ignore this requirement on the grounds that South Africa was a sovereign state and its parliament a sovereign body. So in March 1951 the Separate Representation of Voters Bill was passed by both houses, removing the Coloureds from the common roll and introducing indirect representation for them instead. However, the houses sat separately, not together, as the constitution required, and in both cases the bill passed by simple majorities.

A group of Coloured voters challenged the resolution in court and won. The government then decided to force through the High Court of Parliament Act, proclaiming parliament itself a high court – with the ability to override inconvenient lesser courts. However, the High Court of Parliament Act was itself pronounced invalid by the appeal court. The government had to back down. Even its own supporters were now divided, and foreign investors had been panicked by this cavalier attitude to the constitution and what it might mean for property rights.

Malan finally decided that instead of attempting to change the rules it would be easier to change parliament. So he enlarged both houses of parliament and the appeal court, packing them with NP supporters. With a two-thirds majority thus ensured, the bill was finally passed in 1956, and the appeal court dutifully threw out an appeal. A separate Coloured Affairs Department and Council on Coloured Affairs were created soon after.

Malan retired in 1954, aged eighty and, fearing the harder-line Transvaal Nats, tried hard to secure the election of Eben Dönges, his successor as Cape NP leader. But the Transvaal Nats, resentful that he had always maintained a Cape majority within the Cabinet, were simply stronger and their leader, Johannes Strijdom, became Prime Minister.

Strijdom's closest associate was Dr Hendrik Verwoerd who, as Minister of Native Affairs from 1950 on, had been the key architect of the apartheid legislation above. Verwoerd remained in the same ministry under Strijdom, himself becoming the NP's Transvaal leader, and on Strijdom's death in 1958 he became Prime Minister. Formerly a professor of psychology and newspaper editor, Verwoerd devoted his entire career to the elaboration, defence and implementation of apartheid. A ponderous, boring speaker, he was at the same time a man of intellect, energy and passion. He became the most dominant figure in Afrikanerdom after Paul Kruger. When he came to power in 1958 political change in Africa was gaining pace, with Ghanaian independence in 1957 clearly inaugurating the era of decolonisation. Verwoerd responded to this challenge by introducing the idea of self-government for the African reserves and by proclaiming South Africa a republic.

In 1956 the Tomlinson Commission had reported exhaustively – and not very favourably – on the case for separate African 'homelands', the last form of direct African representation having disappeared with the abolition of the Native Representative Council in 1951. Verwoerd simply brushed aside Tomlinson's warnings as to the homelands' lack of feasibility. In 1959 the government passed the Promotion of Bantu

Self-Government Act which ended indirect African representation in the Union parliament and stipulated the development of 'Territorial Authorities' in eight self-governing Bantu homelands (the word 'Bantu' was substituted for 'native' in all official parlance) which, it was now decided, would eventually become fully independent states. This was Verwoerd's reply to Harold Macmillan, the British Prime Minister, who had spoken of the 'wind of change' in Africa during his visit to South Africa in 1960 and had warned that Britain could not support apartheid. Verwoerd averred that the homelands policy was designed exactly in the spirit of the changes on the continent, not in contradiction to them.

It had not required Britain's change of policy in Africa to convince Verwoerd that South Africa must achieve its own 'independence' as a republic, whatever the consequences that might bring for its Commonwealth membership – for the hard core Transvaal Nats had never lessened their commitment to a republic, despite Malan's attempts to get them to play the issue down. The new republican constitution stipulated the equality of English and Afrikaans speakers, leaving all power exclusively in white hands. Only whites were allowed to vote in the referendum on the issue of the republic in October 1960 – a bold gamble by Verwoerd, for the NP at that stage still owed power to the electoral weighting of rural constituencies and had never achieved a majority of the popular vote. Even the fact that South-West Africa's whites were allowed to vote in the referendum too still saw the 'Yes' vote win by only 52 per cent. Verwoerd then applied for South Africa to remain in the Commonwealth as a republic. Ironically, Nkrumah's Ghana was accommodating but Nigeria threatened to walk out if South Africa was allowed to remain a member. Verwoerd quickly withdrew his application. On 31 May 1961 the country was proclaimed the Republic of South Africa – outside the Commonwealth.

By 1963 the Transkei – the first of the homelands – was proclaimed a 'self-governing territory within the Republic of South Africa'. The government of this 'self-governing territory' was elected by its Legislative Assembly, in which chiefs had a built-in majority – thus allowing Pretoria to push in its presidential candidate, Kaiser Matanzima, despite the fact that a majority of the elected deputies supported his opponents. The whole homeland structure was completely artificial, depending entirely on the back-up and subsidies of the South African state – but it incorporated a tiny elite of homeland leaders and their cronies, and gave them an interest in maintaining the homeland myth.

To a large extent the dream of apartheid was a Transvaal dream.

There were very few Coloureds or Indians in the Transvaal: NP leaders there were used to a stark and simple confrontation of black and white. Here the logic of separation seemed straightforward and it was no accident that no less than six of the ultimately ten homelands were within the Transvaal's borders. In effect this simple black-white division was then imposed on the Cape, where the fact that a majority of the population was Coloured meant the doctrine hardly fitted at all, and on to Natal where the presence of 900,000 Indians also greatly complicated matters. But power, wealth and half the country's white population lay within the Transvaal. It was the Prussia of the new South Africa and Verwoerd was its Bismarck.

Amazingly, for a time it seemed that apartheid might work. The majority of white voters either bought into Verwoerd's experiment or, at least, were content that white supremacy was being so firmly defended: every successive general election returned the NP to power with an increased vote. The UP dwindled partly because it was terrified of the efficacy of *swart gevaar* tactics and offered little serious alternative. Even when it did fight hard – to save the Coloured vote – this nearly split the party for the fact was that liberal instincts among whites were rare. Thus the white opposition group, the war veterans' Torch Commando, carried out loud protest campaigns and night torch demonstrations against the removal of the Coloured vote – but ended in farce when the organisation could not agree on admitting Coloured ex-servicemen into its own ranks. Coloureds deserted it and its numbers collapsed.

The Coloured vote issue and the government's attempts to change the constitution by illegal means brought another white liberal organisation into existence in 1955 – the Black Sash. Women, drawn mostly from the English-speaking upper class and wearing black sashes, began to stage silent protest demonstrations on public occasions. There were also other signs of stronger opposition. The Liberal Party was formed in 1953 with a programme of a non-racial qualified franchise, soon changed to a programme simply calling for universal suffrage. Containing many of the country's leading intellectuals of all races, the party gained respect among blacks and Indians but was viewed by most whites as a sell-out.

The UP, desperate to find a way to oppose Verwoerd's policy without exposing itself to *swart gevaar* tactics, found it in his plans to add more land to the native reserves before granting them self-government. The Tomlinson Report had argued that even in 1951 the reserves could support only 51 per cent of their population. Even with additions to the reserves still pending from the 1936 Land Act there would still be an excess of at least 200,000 families there, so Verwoerd had to offer some minimal gesture towards making the reserves sustainable – though in fact it was soon obvious that Tomlinson had grossly underestimated population growth in the reserves and that any attempt at self-sufficiency was bound to produce starvation. Even so, the UP objected to additional land being granted to the reserves if plans for their independence were to go ahead and South Africa was thus to be 'partitioned'.

Divisions over this issue caused the UP to split in 1959 with a liberal minority of MPs leaving to form the Progressive Party. The PP called for a united state with a non-racial qualified franchise and constitutional protection of minorities. The Progs (as they were called) managed to re-elect only one of their original MPs in the 1961 election, Helen Suzman, who remained the sole root-and-branch opponent of apartheid in parliament for the next thirteen years. But the Progs were important. For the first time a truly liberal perspective had gained an electoral base and attracted supporters among white professionals and the younger intelligentsia. Slowly its ideas began to make progress within the white mainstream.

Meanwhile the NP victory of 1948 had strengthened the hand of the ANC Youth League, enabling it to take over the ANC leadership at its annual conference in 1949 – which adopted the Youth League's Programme of Action, proclaiming the right of Africans to 'self-determination'. With Youth League support, James Moroka was elected as the ANC President General while Walter Sisulu became the ANC's Secretary General. Several other Youth League members were elected to the national executive.

Even before the Suppression of Communism Act was passed, on 20 June 1950, the CPSA dissolved itself in an attempt to protect its members and assets. This did not help, for the government quickly made the Act retrospective and extended the definition of a 'communist' to include anybody who had ever belonged to the party. Two communist MPs, Sam Kahn and Fred Carneson, lost their seats, and Brian Bunting and Ray Simons, who had been elected to replace them, were prevented from entering parliament. Individual party members continued their work within the trade unions and the ANC, gradually converting several prominent ANC leaders to their cause – including Walter Sisulu. Party publications were banned, resurfaced in a new guise and were banned again. In 1953 the party was secretly resurrected as an underground organisation, now called the South African Communist Party (SACP). From then on all its most important work was done through and in the name of the ANC and the trade unions, in which it played the role of ideological leader and strategist.

Using the Suppression of Communism Act, the government began to step up pressure on the trade unions. Despite tough resistance – dozens of trade union leaders were banned – by 1957 all trade unions had been forced to segregate their membership. The strikes of the early 1950s were mostly political: the successful boycott of municipal buses in Johannesburg, for example – a protest against rising transport costs – was organised by communist-led trade unions. For months people walked long distances from townships to work and back, often walking two hours each way, and finally won. On 1 May 1950 a strike was organised by communists within the ANC and the Transvaal Indian Congress in support of three of their comrades on whom restriction orders had been served. Clashes with the police left eighteen strikers dead, and on 26 June another strike, to mourn them, was called, this time by the ANC. A further strike to protest against the removal of Coloured voters from the common roll was held on 7 May 1951 and another protest campaign was organised on 6 April 1952 – the anniversary of Van Riebeeck's landing.

The success of these protest actions led the leaders of the ANC and the South African Indian Congress to launch the Defiance Campaign on 26 June 1952. The idea of the campaign was to break apartheid laws and regulations, publicly but peacefully, and be prepared to go to jail for this in the spirit of Gandhi's *satyagraha*. It was hoped that with sufficient mass support the whole apartheid structure would collapse under the pressure. The campaign was an enormous success. Starting from Port Elizabeth and East London it spread throughout urban South Africa, steadily gaining momentum. Non-whites publicly burnt their passes, occupied 'whites only' seats in buses, parks and other public places, and used other 'whites only' facilities, while Indians and whites entered black locations without permits. More than 8,000 people, including the campaign's leaders, were arrested, charged and imprisoned. The ANC's membership at the height of the campaign reached 100,000 for the first time.

But in October violence broke out in Port Elizabeth, when township crowds attacked the police and government buildings. Similar incidents took place in Kimberley, East London and Johannesburg in November. In East London a white nun was killed and the police responded with gunfire, killing about thirty people. Although the riots had not been instigated by the campaign organisers they showed the limits of such tactics in a black culture where violence was never far from the surface, facing a police force only too willing to use force. By year's end the campaign had run out of steam and ANC support dwindled. Dr Moroka, compromised by his own unwillingness to risk going to jail, lost the ANC presidency to Chief Albert Luthuli. White voters reacted with increased support for the Nats in the 1953 election, which in turn enabled them to proclaim a state of emergency and to impose heavy sentences for incitement or breaches of the peace.

The ANC was at a crossroads. At its Cape conference Professor Z. K. Matthews of Fort Hare University, who had been one of the authors of the Bill of Rights adopted by the ANC in 1942, suggested that the ANC convene a national conference and adopt a charter – a declaration of rights for the South African nation irrespective of race. The idea was taken up by the ANC, the SAIC, the South African Coloured People's Organisation and the Congress of Democrats, a radical white front organisation created in 1953 consisting mainly of the SACP plus fellow travellers. After several preliminary meetings the Congress of the People – about 3,000 representatives of different organisations of all races – met at Kliptown in June 1955. The Liberal Party was invited only at the last moment and did not participate as an organisation, although some members did attend: the party saw its late invitation and much else about the congress's organisation as proof that the SACP was in control of the event. The congress discussed and adopted the Freedom Charter – which was indeed drafted by white communists, though the pretence had to be gone through that it was based on black suggestions. The charter became one of the major documents in South African history, accepted as part of their own programme for decades ahead by all the participating organisations, collectively known as the Congress Alliance.

The Freedom Charter began: 'We, the people of South Africa, declare for all our country and the world to know: – That South Africa belongs to all who live in it, black and white, and that no government can justly claim authority unless it is based on the will of the people …' It further stipulated the main principles: 'The People Shall Govern'; 'All National Groups Shall Have Equal Rights'; 'The People Shall Share the Country's Wealth'; 'The Land Shall Be Shared Among Those Who Work it'; 'All Shall Be Equal Before the Law'; 'All Shall Enjoy Equal Human Rights'; 'There Shall Be Work and Security'; 'The Doors of Learning and Culture Shall Be Opened'; 'There Shall Be Houses, Security and Comfort'; 'There Shall Be Peace and Friendship'. The charter ended with the declaration: 'These freedoms we shall fight for, side by side, throughout our lives, until we have won our liberty'. The charter's communist authorship was seldom visible except in the demand for nationalisation ('transfer to the people') of all the country's mineral wealth, banks and 'monopoly industry'.

The government's response was predictable. The police raided the homes and offices of Kliptown participants, arrested 156 prominent members of the Alliance and charged them with high treason. This was the longest political trial in history, lasting until 29 November 1961. Gradually the number of the accused was reduced and finally all were acquitted of the original charges. But the trial had drawn world publicity and became part of the legend of the unfolding struggle.

Not everybody in the ANC was happy about its co-operation with other anti-apartheid organisations, for the influential role of white communists had been noticed not just by liberals but by Africanists. For them Marxism was an alien, European ideology and the communists were there only to use Africans for their own purposes. This group within the ANC leadership – mostly within the Youth League – was not prepared to accept the thesis that 'South Africa belongs to all who live in it'; they held that Africa was for the Africans – the only truly indigenous people. The debate about the charter within the ANC was so intense that its 1955 national conference could not reach a decision and the charter was only endorsed in 1956. However, the disagreement simmered and finally came to the surface in November 1958 when Robert Sobukwe, Potlako Leballo and other Africanists were driven from the hall where the ANC's Transvaal provincial congress was meeting. In April 1959 they formed the Pan-Africanist Congress with Sobukwe at its head and the Africanist values of the pre-1949 ANC Youth League as its programme.

At the end of 1959 the ANC decided to stage a national protest campaign against the pass laws and for an increased minimum wage. The campaign was to start on 31 March 1960. The PAC, however, intercepted the initiative and announced its own anti-pass campaign – to start ten days earlier, on 21 March. On that day the PAC leaders and their following throughout the country defied the pass laws and many were arrested. The campaign was peaceful, however, and people dispersed when threatened by the police. But at the Transvaal township of Sharpeville the police opened fire at a crowd of demonstrators gathered outside the police station who, according to the police, were threatening to pull down the fence. Sixty-nine people were killed and 180 wounded, shot mostly in the back – a clear indication that the crowd was actually fleeing when most of the shooting occurred. Later the same day shooting occurred in Langa, a Cape Town township. There a crowd of several thousand people had, at the urgings of a PAC activist, Philip Kgosana, agreed to disperse – but when they heard the news of the massacre at Sharpeville their mood changed to one of anger. The police opened fire, killing three people and injuring forty-seven. The crowd went on the rampage, burning municipal buildings and attacking the police.

In this situation the ANC leaders could not but join the campaign. On 27 March Luthuli publicly burnt his pass book. He also proclaimed the next day a day of mourning and called on people to stay at home. Many responded, including some whites. But the same day saw the government introduce legislation to ban both the PAC and the ANC. However, without waiting, the police detained over 18,000 people on 30 March. The same day a PAC-led march to Durban city centre was fired on by white army reservists, while in Cape Town 30,000 township dwellers marched to parliament to protest at the arrest of their leaders. Kgosana joined the march and after negotiation with police Brigadier I. P. S. Terblanche was able to persuade people to disperse peacefully in exchange for a promise of a meeting with the Minister of Justice. He returned later in the day for the promised meeting, only to be arrested. The government meanwhile ordered army reservists to cordon off the Cape Town townships of Langa and Nyanga, and proclaimed a state of emergency in almost half of South Africa's magisterial districts. The last incident in the unfolding crisis was an attempt on Verwoerd's life on 9 April. Badly wounded, Verwoerd survived and the culprit, a white farmer, was declared insane.

Sharpeville and its aftermath had an enormous effect on South Africa, both domestically and internationally. The crisis received huge international publicity, exposing the nature of the regime and tainting its apartheid policy beyond repair. Moreover, whereas foreign investors had previously taken the view that apartheid seemed to be compatible with both stability and rapid economic growth, this now seemed in doubt and capital flowed out. For similar reasons Sharpeville also produced a real crisis of confidence among whites and emigration soared. Black nationalists, on the other hand, received what they took as final proof that the government had left no legal channel for the peaceful expression of black political feelings. The government itself was determined to learn nothing but even it could now understand that apartheid had caused enormous frustration and anger within the black population and that this was potentially a powerful weapon for any political force able to use it.

Before Sharpeville there had been occasional explosions of African violence in various parts of the country but these had normally been spontaneous, uncoordinated and often not clearly political. Thus in January 1949 in Durban anti-Indian rioting by Africans cost the lives of 142 people with more than a thousand injured, a pogrom sparked off by a trivial incident between an Indian shop owner and an African youth. The riots had clearly derived from the enormous social tensions in both communities, and particularly from African anger at the way Indians had risen through their midst and were rapidly becoming economically dominant. African and Indian political leaders came together quickly to stop the bloodshed and devised the convenient myth that whites had somehow manipulated Africans into rioting. This myth, though still repeated today by politicians, has never really been believed by any community in Durban itself. In 1959 a police raid on a shebeen in Cato Manor, Durban, also triggered off a spontaneous riot which left nine policemen dead.

Opposition to the 1951 Bantu Authorities Act often took the shape of a struggle for or against particular leaders and this too could easily erupt into violence. In July 1957 the government appointed Moroamoche Sekhukhune as head of the new tribal authority of Sekhukhuneland, but suspended him in November. He appealed and won, but instead of being reinstated was deported. A retired policeman was appointed in his place but the Pedi refused to recognise his authority. In May 1958 riots followed, and several people were killed. Similarly, when the controversial chief Botha Sigcau was appointed to head the new administration in Pondoland in 1957 he too was not recognised by the local population and riots followed. The anti-Sigcau opposition then moved to the hills and formed a 'mountain committee' which claimed to be the legitimate administration. It attempted to establish its authority by burning its opponents' huts and conducting its own courts to intimidate those who obeyed the government. The stand-off continued until June 1960 when the government destroyed the rebels' stronghold in the hills, using aircraft and armoured vehicles. In Thembuland opposition to the new legislation was led by Paramount Chief Sabata Dalindyebo. In 1962 his supporters, influenced by PAC militants, were caught by the police as they gathered at the homestead of Dalindyebo's main rival, the government-backed Chief Kaiser Matanzima, in order to kill him.

Violence also occurred when women were first compelled (in 1956) to carry passes or 'reference books'. A peaceful protest march of 20,000 women to the Union Buildings (the seat of government in Pretoria) was organised on 9 August. As the campaign spread, however, it became more violent as women burnt their passes and in some instances stoned government officials. In particular Hurutshe Reserve, in the Western Transvaal, became the centre of violent opposition. A pass-burning campaign ended in 1958 with the police sealing off a particularly defiant location. Many inhabitants fled to Bechuanaland.

Sharpeville, however, had been no local incident but a national confrontation over a key national policy and its effects were quite different. The shootings, their own banning, and the rivalry between the two organisations led both the ANC and PAC to conclude that violence was now the only way; indeed, that revolution was at hand. In March 1961 the ANC convened a conference of some 145 black organisations with a few whites and Indians also present. Nelson Mandela, one of the founder members of the ANC Youth League and a former head of the ANC's Transvaal branch, was elected Secretary of a new National Action Council (the names of other members of the council were kept secret). The conference demanded that a new all-race national convention be convened, and threatened the government with demonstrations and a general strike on Republic Day, 31 May 1961. The government rejected the demand and the strike went ahead, though with limited success. Mandela went underground to prepare for a guerrilla war.

The idea of the ANC going underground is associated with the 'M-Plan', adopted by the ANC's national executive as early as 1953 and named after Mandela, its author. In fact, the plan was mostly about strengthening the party organisation by basing it on a cell structure at grass roots. Although it was envisaged that the ANC might one day have to go underground, just as the SACP had, and that the cell structure might help it to operate in such a situation, the plan was no secret – it had been discussed quite openly as a way of boosting the party at grass roots. Nor did this structure suddenly spring into action after Sharpeville, when the ANC and the PAC were banned. Indeed, the state of emergency caught both organisations on the hop. Some ANC and PAC leaders – most notably Oliver Tambo, the ANC Deputy President – went into exile to represent their organisations abroad and also as a form of insurance in case the internal leaders were all imprisoned. This trickle of political émigrés gradually became a flood, many of them leaving the country illegally. After the government lifted the state of emergency on the eve of Republic Day, several (illegal) meetings were organised but protests then petered out. For secretly a group within the ANC was preparing to launch a small illegal organisation to start the armed struggle. In South African conditions – with the enormous superiority of the army and police – this could only mean a sabotage campaign.

This organisation, *Umkonto we Sizwe* (The Spear of the Nation), or MK, was formed in November 1961, the same month when the Treason Trial ended in a flop. MK was formed as the military wing of the ANC but the national executive, according to Mandela, did not readily embrace the initiative, deciding only not to discipline those who opted for violence. The first bombs exploded on 16 December 1961, just as Albert Luthuli, the ANC's President, returned home from his trip to Oslo to receive the Nobel Peace Prize, awarded to him for fighting against racial discrimination by non-violent methods. The liberal tradition within the black community was still alive and after the banning of the ANC and PAC there was a flood of black members into the Liberal Party. The open recognition of the association between the ANC and MK came only in 1963, at the ANC's first post-Sharpeville conference held in Bechuanaland. Unlike the ANC, MK was open to all races. The PAC formed its own military wing, *Poqo* (We Go it Alone). Some Liberal Party members, not to be left out, founded the African Resistance Movement, a mainly white organisation also dedicated to sabotage.

The approach of MK and Poqo to sabotage was different. Poqo did not have a proper underground structure or even a plan and most of its top leadership was in prison or in exile. It was guided mostly by spontaneous anger against the regime and against whites generally. Poqo murdered pro-government chiefs and killed or intimidated collaborators. Twice it made attempts on Kaiser Matanzima's life. Poqo was also prepared to kill whites indiscriminately. Two attacks particularly excited white fears: the murder of two whites and an assault on three more in Paarl, and the brutal murder of five whites camping in the Transkei, including a woman and two young girls. Potlako Leballo, who attempted to lead the PAC and Poqo from Basutoland, merely hastened the movement's demise by boasting publicly about the 'launch' of Poqo in South Africa and calling for vengeance against whites in general, including women and children. In April 1963 Leballo's office in Maseru was raided, and arms, leaflets, membership lists and other documents seized. Mass arrests followed and the organisation was completely smashed.

MK, on the other hand, launched its campaign by exploding home-made bombs directed at targets of only symbolic significance. The idea was that sabotage was to be aimed against installations, not people, so that this national-liberation revolution would be bloodless, sufficient merely to make whites see the need for change. In all the MK carried out some seventy acts of sabotage before its leaders were arrested, with the ARM responsible for a further number. However, the ANC had a longer perspective in mind. Early in 1962 Mandela illegally escaped abroad to speak at a conference of African liberation movements in Addis Ababa, where he spoke of the ANC's intention of returning to mass action campaigns when the opportunity arose – but at the same time he met the leaders of African independent states to discuss the possibilities of training MK cadres and raising funds to buy arms for guerrilla warfare. Mandela also travelled to London to meet British Opposition leaders. Soon after his return six months later he was arrested and charged (amazingly) with inciting workers to stay away from work and with illegally leaving the country. He was sentenced to five years' imprisonment.

The government reacted toughly, passing the Sabotage Act (1962) aimed against 'agitators' who, the government believed, were mostly white. Protest against the bill was widespread but, with the ANC and PAC banned, mainly white. Even the UP opposed the bill in parliament and liberals of every stripe staged protest marches. The new law prohibited the reproduction of any statement made by any banned person and banned persons were forbidden to communicate with one another or to participate in any meeting of three or more people. In 1962–3, 152 people of all races were listed as banned persons and many were placed under house arrest. The Liberal Party, the Congress of Democrats (COD), trade unions, and the Indian and Coloured Congresses were endlessly harassed, and COD was finally banned. By June 1963 over 600 people had been convicted or were awaiting trial under the Act. In May 1963 there followed the General Law Amendment Act or 'Ninety-Day Act' which allowed repeated ninety-day periods of detention without trial or charge and interrogation of detained persons without lawyers present. Only Helen Suzman voted against this bill – which effectively gave the police plenary powers and made it easy for them to torture detainees.

On 11 July 1963 the police raided a farm belonging to the SACP in the Johannesburg suburb of Rivonia. They arrested six members of MK – including Walter Sisulu, Govan Mbeki, Raymond Mhlaba, Ahmad Kathrada and Lionel Bernstein – all of whom had met to discuss 'Operation Mayibuye', a plan for revolution. The whole MK archive of hundreds of documents was captured. Mandela was revealed to be the head of MK, as was the fact that many members of MK's

National High Command, including Sisulu and Mbeki, were communists. Now charged with high treason, they could all be hanged. The prosecution attempted to draw Luthuli into the trial but failed. The trial drew wide international attention culminating in a UN Security Council resolution denouncing South African political trials in general and, with four abstentions, calling on Pretoria to grant amnesty to the defendants. Mandela's five-hour speech, defending the position of MK and the ANC, became the focal point of the trial. Mandela had been important before but he emerged from the trial as the ANC's dominant figure and the major leader of the struggle. The judge decided, however, not to turn the accused into martyrs and sentenced them to life imprisonment rather than to death. Four of the accused managed to escape from prison. The rest, including Mandela and Sisulu, were sent to the Robben Island prison.

A unique case among the 1964 accused was that of Bram Fischer, a successful advocate, who was left to lead the SACP after Rivonia – a trial in which he had acted as advocate for the accused. He himself was subsequently charged with membership of the illegal party – but allowed to travel to London on business, having given his word that he would return – and return he did. He then went into hiding, was rearrested, tried and sentenced to life imprisonment. He remained a shining example of Afrikaner integrity in the cause of black liberation.

In July 1964 came a fateful moment when a bomb exploded at Johannesburg railway station. The bomb had been placed by John Harris, a former Liberal Party and ARM activist. Harris had acted alone – the ARM had already been crushed. But the police rage at this atrocity – and the fact that innocent civilians had been killed and maimed – led to a worsening of repression and the routine use of torture even against white detainees. Harris himself appeared in court with several broken limbs. He was hanged.

The Rivonia trial was the high point of the 1960s struggle but it also exposed the bitter truth: the opposition was slipshod, amateur and ineffectual, and the government was winning. The quiet of the graveyard – and a degree of stabilisation – followed. Faced with the post-Sharpeville challenge, Verwoerd had turned to John Vorster and given him carte blanche as Minister of Justice to crush the revolutionary challenge. Vorster, himself an old OB wartime detainee, worked in tandem with his fellow ex-OB detainee, Hendrik van den Bergh, the head of the security police, and together they made an object lesson of the fact that the ANC and SACP had been foolish enough to challenge them. MK never developed into an effective organisation and the costs of repression were high. The turn towards violence had been a wrong turn: the ANC and trade unions could have achieved far more had they refused that choice. As it was, more than a quarter-century of repression followed, the bleakest period in the whole of South Africa's history.

Vorster and Van den Bergh built up a huge security apparat. Security laws were progressively tightened: in 1965 came 180-day detention without trial and from 1966 on, if authorised by a judge, the period could be unlimited. From 1976 not even judicial authorisation was required. In effect, the police could now do whatever they liked and the number of cases of suspicious deaths of prisoners in police custody began to rise steadily. In 1968 a new intelligence agency was set up, the Bureau of State Security (BOSS), with even broader powers. It spied more and more widely. From then on all political organisations in and out of the country, as well as NGOs and student milieux were heavily infiltrated. In 1963 a censorship body, the Publications Control Board, was established and the press decided to censure itself through the Press Board of Reference. Not only had black opposition disappeared but blacks were fearful, intimidated and silent while the security apparat tore through the remnants of the white left. When that was done BOSS sat atop the pile, growled and showed its teeth, a fearful beast no one could challenge.

In such circumstances the idea of the Bantustans – the separate black homelands – started to win black support as the only avenue left open and a new black elite began to emerge there. The government placed into position its dependent and thus loyal black supporters in the Bantustans: whatever black opposition might emerge, it would have to start by confronting them. Serious white opposition consisted merely of Helen Suzman in parliament, a few scattered liberals and a claque of white communists in exile. Stabilisation was good for business, which boomed. The flight of capital was reversed and by the mid 1960s foreign investment came flowing back in. Verwoerd was thus at the peak of success when he was assassinated in September 1966. As before, the assassin was declared insane. It was almost a formality for the traumatised Nats to turn to another strong leader from the Transvaal, John Vorster.

Vorster now pushed the homelands policy through to its logical end. Neither he nor P. W. Botha were intellectually original men but the last clear orders the apartheid bureaucracy had had were from Verwoerd, which settled that. With the ANC and PAC out of the equation, all that now stood in the way of making the homelands a reality was the cost of making them viable – and demography. The Vorster government had to deal with both.

The Bantustans were supposed to be the national homelands of the main African population groups of South Africa: the Zulu, Xhosa, Swazi, Tsonga, Ndebele, Venda, northern Sotho, southern Sotho and Tswana. The Xhosa were to have two homelands, the Transkei and the Ciskei; the others one each. The Indians, with the option of returning to India, had no need of a homeland in South Africa. The Coloureds, as always, were a problem: they would have to be accommodated within 'white' South Africa – already the Western Cape was turned into a 'Coloured preference area', which meant keeping would-be black migrants out of the Cape. With the exception of the Transkei, Ciskei, Venda and KwaNdebele – all more or less compact territories – the homelands consisted of patchwork quilts of land divided by European farmland: KwaZulu, for example, consisted of eleven separate patches. Nonetheless, the Bantustans were supposed to become economically self-sufficient and independent units. Once this was achieved, Africans would then become citizens of these states and thus foreigners when working in white South Africa where, by definition, they would have no vote or other citizen rights. Ideally, all blacks would live in the Bantustans, keep their families there and come to work in white areas merely as temporary labourers.

The Tomlinson Report had recommended that the government spend £104 million (some R200 million) on the reserves in the first ten years in order to engage the population in commercial agriculture and in 'border industries' to be sited in white areas adjacent to the reserves. But Tomlinson's demographic guesses had been inadequate: by 1970 South Africa was supposed to have 10 to 13 million blacks, while the real figure turned out to exceed 15 million. Worse still, between 1956 and 1961 the government had spent only £7.9 million of the scheduled £104 million. Despite the passage of the Bantu Investment Corporation Act (1959) and the Bantu Homelands Development Corporation Act (1965) by the end of 1966 only 45,000 jobs had been created in the reserves and adjacent areas – less than Tomlinson had envisaged for just one year. No wonder, then, that despite all the government's efforts the African population outside the Bantustans did not diminish.

The Vorster government pressed on with this fantastical experiment. Incentives were now offered to white entrepreneurs to develop businesses inside the Bantustans and simultaneously new restrictions were imposed on the African population in white rural and urban areas. It was made extremely difficult for skilled Africans to work in towns and more and more categories of job in those areas were listed as those for which the employment of Africans was banned. Some of these restrictions began to be a burden even to the whites. In 1970, for example, the employment of Africans as clerks, shop assistants and receptionists was to be banned. This law was adjusted and amended months later because of the objections of white employers: even so it never became operational. Yet any African who did not have a job at any given moment – including, for example, widows, the aged and the unfit – was to be removed to one of the Bantustans. Even where such people had previously had the right to live in a town they now lost it. In rural areas African peasants working the land independently, as well as farm workers and their families whose service was not immediately required, were also removed. This process – 'black spot removal' – was ethnic cleansing, pure and simple. There was not enough agricultural land in the Bantustans for all these people and they had to sell whatever cattle, sheep and goats they had.

The government realised that the patchwork-quilt nature of the Bantustans robbed them of credibility: even so sympathetic an outsider as Margaret Thatcher, staring at a map of Bophuthatswana, would later say, 'Can't you get all those bits joined up?' But attempts to consolidate the territory of the Bantustans were never more than partially successful because of opposition from white farmers and because economically South Africa was already a scrambled egg which could not be unscrambled. The only sort of tidying up which could be done was 'black spot removal'. Already by the late 1960s about half a million people had been moved to the Bantustans and in the next decade, according to the Surplus Peoples Project, a further 3 million were moved.

This was social engineering on a grand scale and it was grotesque. Africans thus moved were put into resettlement villages or camps usually situated in remote and unpromising areas that others in the Bantustan did not want. Such people had lost their familiar surrounding, their friends and whatever social function they had had in their previous environment. The government did not provide them with proper housing, although it was now spending more money to accommodate them. They could not become farmers because there was not enough agricultural land even for those already in the Bantustan. They had no jobs and little prospect of getting any. Even with the increased funding of the border industries, only about 8,000 jobs a year were provided for Bantustan residents between 1960 and 1972, while even Tomlinson (with its lower population estimates) had posited the need for 50,000 jobs a year. The only areas where border industrialisation worked at all was where Bantustans were situated close to existing industrial centres.

The political progress of the Bantustans was also much slower than one might have envisaged, given the importance attached to it by the government. Transkei was the only territory with a Legislative Assembly until 1971 and also the first homeland to gain full independence in 1976. By 1984 four Bantustans – Transkei, Ciskei, Bophuthatswana and Venda – were independent. The other six – KwaZulu, Kwa-Ndebele, Lebowa, Gazankulu, KaNgwane and Qwaqwa – remained self-governing territories. Naturally, with a degree of power and patronage on offer, internal Bantustan politics began to emerge, both around the competition for internal control and around the question of relations with Pretoria. There could be no real opposition to apartheid policy at the level of homeland leadership but each of the leaders played his own political game within that limit.

Kaiser Matanzima supported the homelands policy wholeheartedly. Despite the fact that Transkei was completely dependent on Pretoria, Matanzima took various symbolic steps to demonstrate his independence. He insisted on liquidating 'white spots' within the Transkei; demanded the incorporation of further parts of South African territory into his homeland; and introduced English instead of Xhosa as the medium of instruction in Transkei schools. In many cases his example was followed by other homeland leaders but Matanzima got so carried away by his independence that he even broke off diplomatic relations with South Africa for a while. The fact that there was no 'petty apartheid' in the homelands saw Matanzima and several other homeland leaders make deals with the hotel magnate, Sol Kerzner, to open casinos (which were illegal in South Africa) to entice whites from Durban or Johannesburg to come and gamble. Typically, interracial sex tourism was part of the lure for many.

On the other hand, Mangosuthu Buthelezi, Chief Minister of KwaZulu – the man who wielded the real power behind the Zulu King Zwelithini Goodwill Bhekuzulu – played a more sophisticated and complicated game by attempting to use the Bantustan system to serve his own ends and those of the wider black cause. Buthelezi, himself an ANC member, had sought Oliver Tambo's advice before taking the opportunity to become KwaZulu's Chief Minister. Tambo was keen that he do so, for it was obvious both to the ANC and the government that the entire apartheid policy rested on what the Zulus –

the biggest of South Africa's black nations – would do. If the two biggest groups, the Xhosa and Zulu, both accepted independence, apartheid might work. If the Zulus, of all people, enjoying a reputation as a proud warrior race, refused independence, it was difficult to see how it could ever work. KwaZulu had become a self-governing territory in 1972 but Buthelezi resolutely opposed 'full' independence and made sure that the KwaZulu Legislative Assembly prevented King Zwelithini from accepting the honour. Buthelezi, moreover, openly challenged the whole system by proposing the idea of a federation of homelands to his counterparts in other Bantustans. When, in 1976, Vorster rejected the idea, Buthelezi suggested instead a political alliance, the Black Unity Front. At the same time he repeatedly used the forum which KwaZulu provided to make public demands for Mandela's release, the unbanning of the ANC and to broadcast his rejection of apartheid in general. This created an extremely difficult situation for Vorster. On the one hand this show of public defiance gave Buthelezi nation-wide publicity and support as the leading anti-apartheid spokesman of the black cause – a hardly tolerable situation. On the other hand, Vorster knew he had to resist the temptation to arrest Buthelezi for that would both make him a martyr and undermine the homelands policy.

Buthelezi's relations with the ANC were complicated, however. In 1975 he obtained the blessing of the ANC's exile leadership to re-establish Inkatha, a dormant Zulu cultural movement, with the notion that this would grow into a sort of legal internal wing of the ANC. Inkatha immediately adopted the ANC's colours, flag and anthem, and old ANC stalwarts flocked to join it. But Buthelezi was playing a difficult game, not only because he continually risked Pretoria's wrath but because the exiled ANC came increasingly to suspect that he was building his own power rather than theirs, a suspicion not lessened by the fact that many of the ANC leaders in exile were Xhosas.

Despite its extension of the 'grand apartheid' of independent home-lands, the Vorster era was also when 'petty apartheid' began to fray. In many public places the infamous 'whites only' signs were removed – they had become internationally embarrassing – and segregation no longer observed. In some cases the regulations were dropped, often they were simply ignored. Even where high-profile visibility made retreat embar-rassing – as in international sport – pressure from the international sporting boycott mounted by anti-apartheid forces abroad meant that desegregation, gradually and unevenly, began. Simultaneously Vorster tried to break out of South Africa's isolation in Africa, meeting with the heads of state of Lesotho, Botswana and Swaziland, maintaining relations with Malawi and, surreptitiously, with Côte d'Ivoire. Such diplomacy meant the desegregation of some of South Africa's top hotels, either by proclaiming the hotels to be 'international hotels' or designating distinguished black guests as 'honorary whites'.

This development met resistance from right-wing Nats. In 1969 Albert Hertzog, leader of the right wing and son of Barry Hertzog, quit the NP to found the Restored National Party (Herstigte Nasionale Party or HNP) to fight for a return to strict Verwoerdian apartheid. The new party failed to win a single seat in the 1970 election but its birth signalled the fact that the monolithic unity of Afrikanerdom was beginning to give way to a more pluralist reality. Already, even in the 1960s a new generation of Afrikaner intellectuals – the so-called 'Sestigers' – had emerged, often willing to argue for individualist and non-conformist positions. Although their criticisms were tepid their influence on Afrikaner culture and society was considerable. Gradually, the notion of open discussion and dissent within Afrikanerdom was re-established. By the 1970s there was openly acknowledged division between pro-reform *verligtes* (enlightened) and *verkramptes* (hardliners). In the 1974 election the Progressives suddenly leapt from one seat to seven, one of the new MPs being Dr Frederick van Zyl Slabbert, an emblematic figure of the new and more liberal generation of Afrikaners.

Anti-apartheid dissent was endemic on the non-Afrikaans university campuses. After the Rivonia trial the National Union of South African Students (NUSAS) was the most radical voice left in society, provoking Vorster to launch an investigation into its activities in 1972. But even NUSAS was not radical enough for black students. In 1968 Steve Biko, a medical student from Natal University's Non-European Medical School, founded the all-black South African Students' Organisation (SASO). Though influenced by the American Black Power movement, Biko and his followers developed a peculiarly South African form of Black Consciousness, embracing African, Indian and Coloured students not only into one organisation but also into one self-definition, that they were all black. The ideology of Black Consciousness (BC, as it was known) was projected as the ideology of all non-white South Africans and consisted in asserting black values, black pride and a black challenge not only to the white apartheid state but also to the liberal views of many white sympathisers. BC purported to be non-racial but its appeal to a younger generation was often that it legitimated their rejection of all things white and insisted that they would determine their own destiny.

With the lack of any other credible political leadership and the younger generation burning with anger, BC spread like wildfire on the tribal college campuses, the black universities located mainly in the homelands, and from there it quickly reached the townships and the schools. Ironically, at first the government did not mind: convinced that its troubles came mainly from white communists, it saw BC as a welcome counterweight – and even a partial affirmation of the need for separate black homelands. Moreover, the BC movement did not try to mount an organisational challenge: there were no mass demonstrations or protests and it did not even have a political programme. Its method lay simply in 'conscientising' its following through a network of classes throughout the country.

By 1972 SASO was at the height of its influence and power. The BC mentality, language and behaviour became an important factor in South Africa's cultural life and began to influence the media. Black music, black dance and black dress had become fashionable among the younger generation of urban blacks. The government quietly dropped the old 'non-white' and substituted 'black' in its own language, matching what had already happened in the media. Meanwhile, black journalists had become crucial allies in spreading the BC message and the Union of Black Journalists, created at that time, became a powerful pressure group in the media. In mid 1972 SASO launched the Black People's Convention and attempted to get other black organisations to affiliate with it. The Natal Indian Congress, which had revived after a period of inaction, was invited to join but its leadership remained faithful to the Congress tradition of non-racialism. Even so, many of its younger members left to join SASO or the Convention. By mid 1973 a network of regional youth organisations was formed and an umbrella body, the National Youth Organisation, was created. From mid 1974 the South African Students' Movement (SASM) began functioning among schoolchildren.

It was a heady brew. 'Conscientisation' in combination with the growing anger and frustration of the new generation of urban blacks was bound to spill over into violence at some point, but the BC movement was, naively, unprepared for such a development apart from vague notions that the revolution would arrive at an appropriate moment. Trouble began at the University of the North at Turfloop. Following the expulsion of a student for a defiant speech at a graduation ceremony in May 1972, students boycotted lectures and the university had to be closed. When students were readmitted in June – by which time all black campuses were ready for solidarity action – they learnt that twenty-two student activists, together with the original 'culprit', had not been readmitted. More than 500 students then left the university. About a hundred Fort Hare students and thirty Zululand University students followed their example. Although SASO had not initiated the incident, it negotiated on the students' behalf and thus revealed its leadership role. So in March 1973 Biko and several other BC leaders were banned. During 1973 more clashes between students and university authorities occurred elsewhere, and several hundred more students abandoned their education. Some of the drop-outs, particularly from Turfloop, found teaching jobs in the Soweto schools. For that generation of school-goers – who were only a few years younger – they were heroes and role models. Then came the dramatic news of the Portuguese revolution and the victory of the guerrilla movements in Angola and Mozambique. The effect on black South Africa was electric: suddenly it was clear that white power could be overthrown, that revolution was not a dream but a credible possibility.

In May 1976 SASM held a conference at which the government's enforcement of instruction in Afrikaans was denounced. The law that half of the subjects in school had to be taught in Afrikaans had existed for decades but had not been observed – until then. Not only were there not enough teachers with the requisite Afrikaans but the language itself was now hated as a symbol of oppression. On 13 June a SASO branch at a Soweto school decided to demonstrate against Afrikaans on 16 June. An Action Committee was formed under a final-year student, Tsietsi Mashinini, and on the morning of the sixteenth thousands of Soweto schoolchildren converged to march towards Orlando stadium. Police attempted to disperse them, failed and started shooting into the crowd. A twelve-year-old schoolboy, Hector Petersen, was killed. The picture of two other youths carrying his dead body was shown by the media worldwide and remains to this day the symbol of the Soweto uprising. The uprising spread to about a hundred urban areas and continued for almost a year. By late February 1977 more than 600 people were dead even by the official count, the vast majority being schoolchildren. The uprising was surprisingly well co-ordinated despite its spontaneous character and the fact that it was driven by young people without much experience of political organisation. In early August the Action Committee was renamed the Soweto Students' Representative Council and it was this organisation that for almost a year functioned as a real power in townships. The Black Parents

Association offered logistical support and acted as a welfare organisation – but it did not give the students any advice; on the contrary it looked up to them for directives. For the remarkable result of the uprising was that the young were now seen – against all the traditional norms of African society – as playing the leadership role.

The students moved through a whole range of forms of protest. Administrative buildings were burnt, collaborators with the regime were targeted, some of their houses torched, and councillors made to resign. Funerals of victims were turned into protest demonstrations. Police brutality prompted more displays of student militancy. Students demonstrated their power over the townships by boycotts and stay-aways. Municipal beer halls were told to close and the majority did: those that didn't suffered bomb blasts. Township shebeens – illegal drinking establishments – did not co-operate and many were smashed. In some cases the success of the stay-aways was helped by intimidation. On one occasion Zulu migrant workers from one of the hostels clashed with the students and the local residents who supported them but after this students took great care to earn the support of hostel dwellers though, oddly, they made no attempt to work with the trade unions or ordinary workers. But inevitably the movement began to burn itself out from weariness and repression. When the SSRC called for a boycott of the November 1976 exams the response was ragged and poor.

One after another, BC leaders were arrested or killed or had to flee. Biko was arrested on 18 August 1977 and died on 11 September in Pretoria Central Prison after being savagely beaten and then driven naked on the floor of a police car from Port Elizabeth to Pretoria. Biko's death in police custody was predictable – but by then he had become an internationally known figure and the news of his death was met with worldwide indignation and protest. In October 1977 nearly all BC organisations were banned – but the damage was done.

During the uprising the students had not sought direction from the exiled ANC or PAC. But both organisations enjoyed an almost mythical prestige and although BC was wary of communist influence within the ANC some of its leaders had made contact with the ANC abroad before the uprising. Despite his reservations, Biko himself had begun to try to establish contact with ANC and PAC underground structures from 1975 on, without much success. However, during and after the uprising several thousand young men and women fled abroad, many of them straight into the arms of the ANC: whatever their preference might have been, the PAC structures in exile were much weaker than the ANC's and BC had no exile structures of its own. And, of course, the ANC's Marxism-Leninism, its range of contacts with the European labour movement, with the Soviet bloc and around the Third World gave the movement an unparallelled range and sophistication. True, the ANC had atrophied in exile, was riven with informers and factional politicking – and its own guerrilla efforts were largely ineffectual. But it was established and occupied the ground. The ANC had watched the Soweto events with alarm, seeing BC as a major rival and a sign of how badly it had lost contact with grass roots South Africa. Now, suddenly, it found itself recruiting another large army of youngsters, eager for battle. History had, by accident, given it yet another chance.

# IX

# ECLIPSE AND VICTORY

ⓐ ⓐ ⓐ

At the time of the Soweto uprising ANC structures inside South Africa barely existed. Any former ANC member – often hot off Robben Island – who tried to revive ANC activities was rapidly caught (usually they were followed from prison), tortured if necessary and quickly broken. This caused dismay among the organisers of the burgeoning black trade union movement which had sprung into existence after a wave of strikes in Durban in 1973. Inevitably, the ANC and MK would attempt to recruit among the more promising shop stewards of the labour movement which would immediately mean that they too were detained and tortured. The exiled ANC, meanwhile, kept its head in the sand and insisted that the only real trade union movement was the South African Congress of Trade Unions (SACTU) – actually a mere empty shell of a few communist unionists in exile. Accordingly, the unions organised in the Federation of South African Trade Unions (FOSATU) were denounced by the ANC and SACP as employers' stooges and even the SACP member, Ben Turok, was actually expelled from the party for making a donation to union funds. This was an indication of how badly fossilised in a Stalinist mode the exiled ANC and SACP had become. Typically, both movements supported the Soviet invasion of Hungary in 1956 and Czechoslovakia in 1968.

The problem was that the ANC and SACP leaders who were not on Robben Island were in exile: there was no middle ground. Exile was not a well-planned retreat: people used any available means to escape and then found themselves scattered between London, Lusaka, Dar-es-Salaam and Moscow. The organisation's revival in exile had taken much time and effort and owed much to Oliver Tambo, Mandela's law colleague and friend. The first meeting of the ANC in exile was convened in October 1962, in Lobatse, Bechuanaland. About fifty leading ANC figures were present – many of them communists – some soon to be tried and sentenced to life imprisonment. Many more went into exile after the Rivonia trial. The first ANC headquarters in exile was in Tanzania, first in Dar-es-Salaam, then at Morogoro where the enlarged ANC National Executive met in 1965 and 1966, together with representatives of MK, the SACP, the Indian and Coloured Congresses and SACTU. It was agreed that these organisations would not create their own centres in exile but simply use the ANC's. In practice this strengthened the SACP's grip over the whole Congress alliance: the party was well represented on the ANC executive, had complete control of MK and SACTU and a large influence within both the other two Congress organisations. In addition, of course, the SACP had privileged access to Soviet bloc aid and its cadres were also better connected to the European left.

The PAC established its own organisation abroad. Attempts to create a united front of ANC and PAC failed completely. The PAC leadership itself was divided and its different factions frequently fought one another. In 1967 the PAC held a conference in Moshi, Tanzania, at which Potlako Leballo defeated his rivals to become the new PAC leader but his pronouncements about killing white women and children caused further divisions and made the Zambian government so nervous about possible retaliatory action by Pretoria that in 1968 it banned the PAC, arresting the organisation's entire male membership and evicting it to Tanzania. The Organisation of African Unity, which had hitherto supported both the ANC and PAC, now ceased its support for the PAC. The PAC made several attempts to infiltrate guerrillas into South Africa but without success. It remained financially and organisationally weak and staggered from one leadership crisis to the next. Its shambolic state reflected the extreme fissiparousness of black elite politics, which lacked the unifying strand either of a charismatic leader or the interlinking SACP network – and its organisational discipline – which was the secret of the ANC's unity.

Well before Rivonia, the ANC had established relations with the Soviet bloc – both in consultation with the SACP and as a separate organisation. Both parties received Soviet financial assistance, logistical support and military training – support which was crucial to the very survival of the ANC in exile. From 1963 on – when Soviet aid began – it received $300,000 on top of the $56,000 allocated that year to the SACP (which had begun to get funding earlier). In 1965–6 the ANC received $560,000 and the SACP $112,000, and after this both the

SACP and ANC continued to receive regular financial infusions from the Soviet Union until the early 1990s, as well as supplies of arms and military equipment. The military training of ANC and SACP cadres in the Soviet Union began in the 1960s and continued into the 1990s, with 95 per cent of all ANC members in exile thus trained. Soviet operational assistance was diverse and multiple. In 1969, when the Tanzanian government began to object to the ANC's growing military presence in the country, the ANC's entire military wing was evacuated from Tanzania to the USSR and supported there for several years. Soviet military specialists assisted in planning and carrying out multiple attempts by MK to infiltrate guerrillas into South Africa. The Soviet government and Soviet agencies also provided facilities for numerous internal and international meetings which the ANC held or in which it participated. Again in 1984, when Pretoria signed the Nkomati peace accord with Mozambique, outlawing the presence of MK in that country, Soviet aeroplanes relocated the entire ANC leadership and MK camps from that country to Angola, and provided military supplies and training there. This support was particularly vital during the 1960s and 1970s when South Africa's future was still far from clear, and when no other states or parties offered similar assistance.

The ANC's decision to launch MK had been taken in shock and anger in the wake of Sharpeville, partly out of concern that the PAC might outflank the ANC – as it had in the pass-burning campaign – and partly on the analogy of the Algerian FLN which had won independence in 1962 by means of armed struggle. These were not very sound reasons for adopting similar methods in a country whose terrain offered little help for guerrillas and with no neighbouring states able or willing to act as guerrilla sanctuaries in the way Egypt had for the FLN. However, with the ANC inside South Africa smashed or in jail, the exiled ANC had only the guerrilla struggle left as a weapon.

By 1967 the first echelon of MK fighters had finished their military training and were sitting around in Tanzania doing nothing. Morale and discipline were deteriorating and there was increasing restlessness over alleged corruption within the ANC leadership. So in 1967 it was decided to incorporate one MK detachment into a unit of the Zimbabwe African People's Union (one of the two liberation movements in Zimbabwe) guerrilla forces which was to move from Zambia into what was then Rhodesia. Having crossed the Zambezi river, this detachment was to split. One group of about thirty men was to reach Wankie game reserve in order to establish a permanent guerrilla base there. A larger group of about fifty under the command of Chris Hani was to penetrate South Africa in order to form MK units there. This meant the guerrillas would have to battle the Rhodesian forces before even getting to South Africa – and the guerrillas would then have to sustain themselves there while recruiting and training others. Such a plan could only have been born out of revolutionary enthusiasm, inexperience and naive incompetence. Some of the guerrillas were killed, some were captured and spent the next thirteen years in Rhodesian prisons, and only a few managed to get to South Africa where, of course, they were all caught. A lucky few, including the later MK and SACP leader, Chris Hani, escaped to Botswana where they were imprisoned for eighteen months.

When Hani finally returned to Lusaka, he wrote a memorandum criticising the ANC leadership, the situation in the camps and the planning of the Wankie operation. In response Tambo convened a consultative conference of the whole ANC – not just its NEC – in Morogoro in April 1969. This – the first full ANC conference to meet since 1959 – had to deal with serious internal problems and a worsening international situation for just before the conference fourteen heads of African states had signed a manifesto calling on the South African liberation movements to find non-military solutions to their problems and, with certain provisos, to open a dialogue with the Pretoria government. That Vorster's detente policy had already managed to get fourteen states willing to take such a line was deeply threatening to ANC militants and particularly the SACP – for whom there would be no place in any compromise.

The Morogoro conference discussed and passed a programme document, 'Strategy and Tactics' drafted by Joe Slovo, the SACP leader who was also one of MK's leaders. Naturally, there was no place in it for any notion of compromise with Pretoria. The document stressed the importance of political leadership in the struggle and defined the aim of the struggle as 'the national liberation of African people'. It artfully conflated race and class by calling the 'African people' 'a dispossessed and racially oppressed nation'. It was also resolved, after a long and difficult debate, that the ANC would open its membership to Congress alliance members in exile, that is to say, to Coloureds, Indians and whites. Clearly this would see more SACP members move powerfully into the ANC and probably dominate it. Africanists within the ANC opposed the resolution – but so did some communists who felt that the ANC should preserve its identity as a specifically African nationalist movement, independent and separate from the SACP. Others openly insisted that the SACP must play a 'vanguard' role within the ANC – and the SACP was already strong enough within the ANC to win this battle. One concession was made: only Africans could be elected to the NEC, a rule which remained unchanged until 1985. This was, though, largely cosmetic: when the new and smaller NEC was elected, communists constituted a significant part of its membership and it now had to share power with a new body, the Revolutionary Council which, though headed by Tambo (re-elected as ANC Acting President in Mandela's absence), consisted of representatives of the three other Congress Alliance organisations, every single one of whom was a communist.

Communist dominance within the ANC always had its opponents. In 1975 eight members of the ANC leadership – some of them communists – were expelled for challenging the Morogoro line and denouncing the decision to open membership to non-Africans and particularly to white communists. The eight expelled Africanists tried to form a separate organisation, just as the PAC had in 1959, but with no success. They disappeared into the political wilderness and the role of the SACP and the nature of the alliance forged at the Morogoro conference were reaffirmed. Not only was SACP membership – the sign of the true militant – the fast track to revolutionary promotion within the movement but those who challenged the party's position got nowhere.

Although MK continued to try to penetrate South Africa in order to establish a base inside the country all such attempts were unsuccessful. Shortly after Morogoro a party of MK guerillas infiltrated South Africa but the whole group disappeared. Another attempt, 'Operation J', was initiated by Joe Slovo and planned for more than a year. The idea was to transport several dozen MK guerrillas to South Africa by sea. The SACP bought a yacht, manned it with a crew of Greek communists and sent it off from friendly Somalia – but the yacht's engines failed and the plan had to be abandoned. In 1975 the Afrikaner poet, Breyten Breytenbach, attempted to show that non-communists were willing to engage in guerrilla tactics too. Tambo gave the go-ahead to his group, 'Okhela', but it was quickly sabotaged by the SACP who were utterly unwilling to see non-communist whites gain influence within the ANC. The security police were tipped off and as soon as Breytenbach entered South Africa he was put under surveillance and his whole network rolled up. Several MK operatives who attempted to enter South Africa on an individual basis were captured and either killed or sentenced to long jail terms. Smaller operations were more successful: ANC and SACP publications, pamphlets and leaflets were smuggled into South Africa and distributed there.

When the thousands of Soweto refugees began to emerge from South Africa, it was only the ANC that had the structures, the international support system and the theoretical foundation for a guerrilla struggle all ready and laid out. Of course, its facilities were inadequate – until 1976 the ANC leadership was dealing with only a few hundred fighters – but other organisations had nothing at all to offer to the new generation. So, despite the fact that most had been BC followers till then, this new generation had little option but to join the ANC. The result was that from the late 1970s on the ANC effort in building up its organisation was rewarded with success. In 1977 the ANC opened a school at Morogoro for this younger exile generation, the Solomon Mahlangu Freedom College, named after a young MK operative who had been caught and executed that year. The same year saw military camps opened in Mozambique, bringing the war closer to the South African border. The ANC's prestige increased, thanks largely to the Soweto rising, and Oliver Tambo was invited to address the United Nations in 1977, a year which also saw a new wave of MK bomb blasts, several guerrilla clashes with the police and more terrorism trials.

The ANC also made renewed efforts to create political structures within the country. From 1978 Mac Maharaj, having served his term on Robben Island, began working on this aspect of ANC activities under the Revolutionary Council. By 1983 a new Politico-Military Strategy Commission was created to work with legal and semi-legal organisations within the country, particularly the trade unions, and to intensify ANC propaganda. The Commission was headed by Tambo and consisted of Joe Slovo, Joe Modise and Thabo Mbeki. By then communication had been established with the ANC leaders on Robben Island and opinions exchanged. Meanwhile, conditions for the Robben Island prisoners had been considerably improved as Pretoria responded to world pressure. The prisoners could now communicate freely with one another and the older generation's ideology, knowledge and political experience was passed on to younger newcomers.

However, the era ushered in by the Soweto rising also brought fresh problems for the ANC. The new exile generation was far less educated and politically sophisticated than the old one. Discipline in the MK camps – always a difficult issue – became a critical problem, with major mutinies put down with terrifying ruthlessness. One Angolan camp, the notorious Quatro, was set up as a punishment camp and appalling tortures and human rights abuses were the order of the day: to the inmates' horror no one paid the slightest attention to the provisions of the Freedom Charter. Virtually the whole of the ANC exile leadership were guilty of connivance with these abuses, to a greater or lesser degree. Conditions in the MK camps were tough. Some of the new recruits had come to the movement through criminal gangs and brought their habits with them. Harsh conditions, the loss of familiar surroundings and friends, the lack of privacy and the hardships of military training often had dire effects on personal relationships. Moreover, there was a clear pattern of preference for Xhosa recruits and a feeling among Zulus, in particular, that they were being discriminated against.

There was, too, an ever-present paranoia. The ANC leadership spied on the recruits, fearful that they might include spies or mutineers, while cadres were racked by uncertainty about the future and fear of what might happen if they fell into the hands of the regime. It was known that BOSS had penetrated the movement from top to bottom and that many MK infiltrators were rounded up by the police the minute they stepped across the border, clear evidence of betrayal. The result was a permanent and intense climate of suspicion. Accusations of treachery and spying were common, and in some cases justified. The ANC would try such cases with courts which bore all the worst features of revolutionary justice, with the punishment often death. The isolation of cadres, the strict hierarchy of the ANC's structures which practised democratic centralism on the Soviet model, and the fact that ANC congresses or elections for the NEC very seldom took place, all gave the leadership inordinate power. This in turn meant that even ordinary exiles, let alone MK members, were subject to draconian restrictions – they had, for example, to get leadership permission before they could marry or divorce, apply to do a degree or take almost any step in their personal life. The fact that the leadership was the only source of power responsible for every aspect of life naturally led to the development of paternalism and favouritism. Within the leadership personal and factional struggles were ruthless.

Thus the ANC over decades of exile became a movement which preached democracy but was authoritarian, claimed to stand for human rights but abused them, and which espoused non-racialism but was racked by tribalism and referred to its enemy in straightforwardly ethnic terms as '*die Boere*'. Moreover it began to take on many features of the hated Afrikaner nationalists: there was the same paranoia, the same inferiority complex, the same reliance on a secret inner core (the SACP instead of the Broederbond) and the same laager mentality.

These problems were not visible from inside the country where the ANC's popularity grew from year to year. Peace never returned to the townships after Soweto. A new political movement, the Azanian

People's Organisation (AZAPO) was founded in 1978 in the spirit of Black Consciousness but without its success. Even though AZAPO was a strictly Africanist organisation, it declared that it would not participate in any national convention or any form of dialogue unless the ANC was present; an index of how far the ANC had come in the popular imagination. It was now the struggle's talisman, the one organisation which could not be left out. Even when unsuccessful MK infiltration took place and its operatives were caught or killed before they could fulfil their tasks, the simple news that they were in the country, defying the apartheid regime, made them heroes for many blacks.

In the early 1980s several more successful and high-profile operations brought fresh converts to the ANC. The most dramatic were the bombing of two oil-from-coal factories, at Sasolburg and Secunda in 1980, and of the Koeberg nuclear plant in 1982. By this time the government had taken to suppressing news of such sabotage but these acts could not be hidden. In 1980 a group of MK fighters attacked the Silverton branch of the Volkskas Bank, took hostages and demanded the release of their leaders. In 1983 a bomb exploded in a street in Pretoria, killing nineteen people and injuring 200, and in 1984 another bomb targeting civilians exploded in Durban. Such bombings were, in any ordinary sense, atrocities in which innocent civilians were maimed or killed but there was no doubt that they served a political point. In every supermarket or other public place ever-present security guards now frisked every shopper or visitor and the police mounted special exhibits on every wall of what the guerrilla weapons looked like. This all contributed to a general climate of tension and insecurity of which even the most apolitical had to be aware. Each escalation of tension sent more whites fleeing abroad, robbing the regime of their manpower, their capital and their sons as army recruits. And there was no doubt that the simple message of all-out defiance which guerrilla actions sent helped consolidate the ANC's popularity in every township. At funerals for victims of police raids or clashes with the police ANC flags often covered the coffins, the ANC salute was openly given and ANC songs sung. Often, blacks just wore yellow and green clothes so that, set against their black skin, they displayed the black, yellow and green of the ANC flag.

Within the country the only really authentic African voice was that of the trade unions. At first there was a vacuum where trade unions might have been but then came the spontaneous Durban strikes of 1973, involving 146 plants and over 60,000 workers. It was quite obvious that the strikes had not been politically instigated (though Buthelezi supported the strikers) so police reaction was mild, the press and white public opinion were sympathetic to the strikers and in many cases they won pay rises. With the spread of the strike movement to other areas, however, the government started to see it as a more general black challenge. The police began to interfere in labour disputes, strike leaders were arrested and sometimes tortured, and in one case eleven miners were shot dead.

In the late 1970s the government appointed two commissions, one led by P. J. Riekert, another by N. E. Wiehahn, to look into the situation of African labour in general and particularly the issue of collective bargaining. Riekert recommended that urbanised workers be allowed to stay in the towns permanently, together with their families, but that the 'un-urbanised' should continue to be removed. The townships themselves were to be recognised as a permanent element of the urban landscape and should have an administration which collected rents and local taxes. This drove a coach and horses through apartheid: urban workers were no longer to be regarded as migrants but as a stable group living in white South Africa – and clearly a privileged group in that respect. Two years later Wiehahn recommended that African workers be allowed to join or form trade unions. There was simply no other way: employers already had to negotiate wages with African unions, even though they were unregistered and unrecognised.

In 1981 the Labour Relations Amendment Act was passed allowing racially mixed unions. Thereafter black union membership progressed by leaps and bounds and many new unions emerged, some grouped within the (BC) Council of Unions of South Africa (CUSA), others within the more radical FOSATU, which in many cases had unions run by committed young white radicals. The 1980s saw a great upsurge of union and strike activity, with the unions ever more clearly acting as the voice of the unenfranchised black majority. The Riekert and Wiehahn reports were, in fact, a death blow to apartheid. Once urban blacks were accepted as a permanent necessity in white areas and were given the right to permanent residence and to collective bargaining, it was difficult to see how they would not use this leverage to acquire full citizenship. It is still difficult to imagine how the government could concede these reforms without realising that they were bound to be fatal to the system they still hoped to retain.

★

But the government still felt confident of its supremacy. It had no alternative to the plan bequeathed by Verwoerd and so it tended to make piecemeal reforms as they seemed either economically necessary or required to allay ever-growing international pressure: at the least the government wanted to have a presentable case to argue in international forums. Beneath that, in Vorster's case, lay the conviction that the homelands provided one with almost unlimited bargaining opportunities where, as in the nineteenth-century Boer republics, bits of land could be traded and boundaries adjusted almost ad infinitum. But the Soweto rising clearly showed that something else was needed so in 1977 Vorster returned to the recommendations of a commission set up in 1973 to investigate the possibility of Coloured representation at national level, since they did not have a 'homeland' of their own. Vorster gave the job to the Cape NP leader, Pieter (P. W.) Botha. Botha's committee proposed the setting up of three parliaments, one for whites, one for Coloureds and one for Indians. Legislation of common interest to all three chambers was to be presented for consideration to a 'Council of Cabinets' with the State President at its head. The President himself would be elected by representatives of all three parliaments, though with whites having over half the votes in the electoral college. Africans, of course, with their own independent homelands, would have no voice in South African affairs.

This plan was presented to the electorate during the 1977 general election – fought by Vorster on a bitter tide of anti-Americanism in protest at President Jimmy Carter's strong line against apartheid. The NP was returned with a record majority but Vorster did nothing: reform was endlessly postponed for fear of opposition from NP hardliners. In fact, his majority was safe but Vorster, having suffered badly for his OB past, never wished to have the accusation of dividing Afrikanerdom levelled at him again. This was the way it was in those years: everything had to be set by the clock of what was convenient within Afrikanerdom as if South Africa was inhabited by no one else.

Vorster's term of office came to a summary end in September 1978 and he resigned, purportedly on the grounds of ill health. He had, naturally, prepared the succession so that he would be succeeded by the Transvaal NP leader, Connie Mulder, for since Strijdom's victory the NP leadership had effectively been the preserve of its Transvaal branch, a fact greatly resented by the Cape Nats. Mulder, a right winger – a Transvaal leader had to be – had built his Information Department into a fiefdom of extraordinary proportions on the grounds that a better international image was vital to the country's survival.

Not only did it consume large amounts of money but Mulder had information officers in every embassy abroad, effectively giving him his own diplomatic service. Mulder's finger was in every pie. But P. W. Botha, the Cape Nat leader, had built his own Department of Defence into an even more powerful fiefdom and Military Intelligence, which had long been jealous of the rise of BOSS under Vorster, gave him his own intelligence network – which spied on Mulder. In 1977 the trap was sprung: the Auditor-General discovered substantial irregularities in the finances of the Ministry of Information.

This, was the start of the Information Scandal or Muldergate, as it was known. Mulder had, it emerged, spent large sums to buy favourable coverage for South Africa in the Western media, to launch an English-speaking Nat paper in South Africa, *The Citizen*, and to bribe British politicians. On top of this, exchange control regulations had been broken and, inevitably, substantial sums of public money had ended up in private pockets. All this and more was leaked to the press – already furious to find that the state had been illicitly financing their competition – even before a proper investigation began. In effect the leaks were used to force Vorster to step down and Mulder's reputation was also fatally damaged. As a result in the subsequent leadership election Mulder was beaten by P. W. Botha. The whole operation had been a sort of disguised coup, leaving Botha's military establishment in control. The investigation into the scandal which Botha then launched exonerated Vorster but not Mulder, who ultimately quit the NP.

Botha, though no liberal, was forced along the road of reform both by the deteriorating international situation, with boycotts and sanctions an ever-growing reality, and also by the military and technocrats that he brought into the National Security Council which he set up. Faced with a steady border war in Namibia and endless civil disorder in the townships after Soweto, South Africa had become an increasingly militarised society. In the Botha years one saw military uniforms on every street and on every bus. Botha appointed to his own old job of Minister of Defence Magnus Malan, the former Commander-in-Chief of the army and the proponent of a 'total strategy' against liberation movements. The result was a 'national security state', with the sharp downgrading of the NP parliamentary caucus and the Cabinet. The dominance of the NSC reflected Botha's belief that South Africa now faced a state of acute and permanent crisis as a result of the 'total onslaught' against it mounted by communist and radical forces. However, the military securocrats had all read the classic texts about the necessity of winning hearts and minds, and exercised steady pressure for reform, insisting that security could not be achieved unless the country reached a socially defensible situation in which the various interests all had a stake.

This did not constitute an alternative theory to apartheid, so the Verwoerdian vision remained intact – but was increasingly amended. About this Botha was pragmatic – he had no qualms about reaching out to English speakers and the business community, and was far less bothered than Vorster about what the NP right might think. The result was that as 'petty apartheid' was progressively eroded and in many cases scrapped there was a major right-wing reaction. Previously, neither Hertzog's HNP, created in 1969, nor the Afrikaner Weer-standsbeweging (AWB) formed in 1973 by Eugene Terreblanche, had developed a following sufficient to make it to parliament, but the early 1980s saw several new organisations emerge, all determined to defend Verwoerdian orthodoxy. By far the most serious challenge came from Andries Treurnicht, the new Transvaal NP leader, who attempted to use his power in the NP caucus and parliament to block reform.

Botha, however, had the majority of the party behind him and moved ahead. As a first move towards the implementation of the recommendations of his own constitutional committee, Botha abol-ished the Senate, replacing it with the President's Council, an appointed advisory body of white, Indian and Coloured representatives. The 1981 general election saw Botha confirm his mandate for reform, though the Progressives – now the PFP – continued to expand, gradually becoming the official opposition. Botha now moved ahead with the scheme for a new tricameral constitution and executive presidency. In effect this meant attempting to bring in Coloureds and Indians as junior partners in the white-ruled state, an acknowledgement of the need for at least partial power-sharing. Treurnicht, appalled at this departure from Verwoerdian orthodoxy, moved a vote of no confidence in Botha and lost. He then quit the NP to found the Conservative Party, which rapidly captured over a third of the Afrikaner vote. Mulder soon joined the CP.

A whites only referendum on the new constitution followed in 1983. In general the English-speaking business community backed the plan but Afrikanerdom was now deeply divided for the first time since the war. The PFP, now led by van Zyl Slabbert, opposed the new constitution, as did Buthelezi, both arguing that it was absurd and unconscionable to exclude Africans entirely from the new dispensation. But significant elements within the Indian and Coloured communities were keen to be incorporated, although a new mass organisation, the

United Democratic Front, was launched in all-out opposition to the new tricameral system. The ANC from exile denounced the entire reform and vowed vengeance against those Coloured and Indian politicians who participated in the system. (Ironically, within a decade it had made alliances with exactly these elements while bitterly opposing Buthelezi and the liberals who had taken a principled position against the plan.)

In the campaign against the new tricameral plan – the white House of Assembly now being flanked by the Indian House of Delegates (which, under the leadership of Amichand Rajbansi, became such a byword for corruption that it was popularly known as the House of Dogs), and the Coloured House of Representatives – the ANC and UDF called for an election boycott. Botha, trying to win favour with these communities, further relaxed a number of petty apartheid regulations but, crucially, the Group Areas Act remained, as did such symbolically powerful segregation as that of the beaches. Against this the new constitution made both Indians and Coloureds theoretically eligible for conscription.

The ANC's call for a boycott showed how far it had come. Originally the movement had been in favour of maximum participation in every forum possible, trying to use whatever means were at hand. The politics of boycott belonged more with the Non-European Unity Movement in the Cape whose key clientele had been Coloured schoolteachers, the country's first non-white intelligentsia. Coloured history had naturally left this intelligentsia with a strong sense of resentment and, finding itself in a situation where it was small and powerless vis-à-vis white authority, it found that the one way it had of expressing grievance was simply the withdrawal of goodwill and co-operation. The boycott weapon became a virtual epidemic among this group and was later supplemented by the Gandhian tradition of passive resistance. This had not been the ANC's way: hence, for example, Tambo's encouragement for Buthelezi to participate in the KwaZulu homeland. But gradually the use of the weapon had spread and the ANC in exile had called for cultural, sporting and other boycotts of apartheid until the tactic came to seem emblematic of the anti-apartheid struggle. Now, when it called for an election boycott of the tricameral assemblies it was on strong ground, given the history of boycott in both the Coloured and Indian communities, backed up by a strong sense that the government had hardly done enough to win their support – and some trepidation that those who broke the boycott might expose themselves to reprisals. Inevitably, electoral turnout was negligible.

★

The fact that the tricameral plan had had no place in it for the African majority meant that Botha was now condemned to press ahead with the homelands policy. This could only be understood as a concession to the internal politics of Afrikanerdom for it was already obvious that the Bantustan experiment had failed and that with every passing year the increase in population of the homelands made them less and less viable. Nonetheless Botha showed muscular vigour in consolidating the territory of the homelands, adding a farm here, another patch of land there, in evicting hapless African rural dwellers from 'black spots', and in deporting 'undesirable' Africans from townships and squatter camps.

The scale of these removals – and one is measuring human misery – was staggering. Over half a million pass offences a year were punished as Africans increasingly ignored the law keeping them out of white cities. Those caught were then kicked out of the towns. According to official statistics, by 1984 another 2 million people had been forcibly removed – though according to the Surplus Peoples' Project between 1960 and 1982 actually some 3.5 million were removed and another 2 million threatened with removal. The removals continued right through the Botha era and were often carried out with great ruthlessness, as in the case of the repeated bulldozing of squatter settlements in Cape Town. Sometimes people were evicted without any thought as to where they could go. Thus, for example, the Coloured descendants of the 1829 Kat River settlement were evicted from their farms in 1988, when their area was included into the territory of the Ciskei, without any alternative offered to them. In some cases people were moved to empty land with poor soil which, impossibly, they were expected to farm; in other cases they might be moved to well-populated agricultural areas where overpopulation had already resulted in soil erosion. Inevitably, all such cases were disastrous for the homelands, for the people concerned and even for those who had previously eked out a living there. To press on for years with such policies was simply callous.

The Botha government also threw a great deal of good money after bad. Even on the very eve of change, in 1988–9, long after it had become obvious that the homelands were doomed, the government spent R5.5 billion on them, most of it going to those which had accepted independence. There was virtually nothing to show for this money. The population of the homelands had grown so fast (almost doubling in Ciskei in the 1970s, for example) as natural increase was added to the increase due to having 'surplus people' from black spot removals dumped on them. Even if the homelands had been growing fast economically they would have struggled to absorb such numbers but in fact they were not developing at all. Pretoria's money was spent on salaries and other administrative costs, and in many cases was simply stolen. Meanwhile a vast human tide flowed continuously out of the homelands towards the cities, hoping always for jobs, but often having to settle for begging, crime, pilferage and prostitution. Influx control could simply not contain this desperate human tide. Thus, despite forced removals and influx control the population of Crossroads – to take the case of just one Cape Town settlement – multiplied eightfold in the ten years from 1975 to 1985. Naturally, when influx control was finally abandoned in 1986 the flood became a torrent.

The political development of the four independent homelands was equally disastrous. All were ruled through systems of patronage, bribery and a brutal police force. None was a democracy in anything but name.

Ciskei (independent in 1981) was ruled by its Life President, Chief Lennox Sebe. It had an industrial development area and a new capital, Bisho, which enjoyed Sebe's attention and investment but never amounted to more than a small town with government buildings and the regulation Holiday Inn and a casino. Nothing was done to develop the rural areas and the burden of the resettled population made the small territory unsustainable. Opposition was bribed or silenced. However, conflict developed within the Sebe family itself and relations with Transkei deteriorated drastically in the face of Transkeian pressure to unite the two Xhosa homelands. In 1990 Sebe was overthrown in a military coup.

The Transkei President, Kaiser Matanzima, never escaped the shadow of the popular paramount chief, Sabata Dalindyebo, who had failed to win the presidency only due to Pretoria's manipulation. In 1979 Dalindyebo became the leader of the opposition Democratic Party, only to have the majority of its members detained or banned a year later. He fled to Zambia (where he joined up with the ANC) but the DP's popularity made Matanzima's position intolerable. In 1986 Matanzima resigned, producing infighting among his successors. In 1988 General Bantu Holomisa led a successful military coup against Matanzima's latest successor, Stella Sigcau. Dalindyebo had also died in 1986, Matanzima denying him a proper funeral and preventing his son from inheriting the paramount chieftaincy. Once in power, Holomisa invited back Dalindyebo's son, and Dalindyebo was reburied with appropriate honours.

Bophuthatswana received its independence in 1977. It had a democratic constitution and there were many liberal aspects to life in this most prosperous of all the Bantustans – thanks to the fact that it had the world's biggest platinum mines on its territory. Its university, for example, became a refuge for anti-apartheid radicals from South Africa. But Mangope, faced with insistent UDF and ANC pressure, resorted to extra-constitutional means to keep the opposition under control. In 1988 he, like Sebe, was overthrown in a military coup but he appealed to Pretoria for help. The coup was suppressed and Mangope restored to power, though with his 'independent' credentials fatally damaged.

Venda was, finally, that familiar African sight, an authoritarian one-party state, led by Patrick Mphephu until his death in 1988.

In many ways, however, the key homeland remained KwaZulu, which had persistently rejected independence. Buthelezi's hopes of becoming the centre around which black politics would consolidate at a national level had seemed entirely realistic in the mid 1970s. The exiled ANC, always wary lest Mandela cut a deal with Pretoria from his prison cell, had taken a decision not to personalise their cause, which meant that Mandela's name was seldom heard. Thus when the Arnold Bergstrasser Institute carried out a landmark survey of black opinion in 1977 it had to ask how people felt about 'ANC leaders' as a collective group and Buthelezi emerged as the most popular champion of black rights in the country. By 1981, however, similar polls showed that although Buthelezi remained overwhelmingly popular in Natal, on the Reef he trailed 'ANC leaders' by 17 per cent to 42 per cent. He was never to close that gap again. One reason was the impact of Black Consciousness and the Soweto uprising. Buthelezi's refusal to accept independence cut little ice with young BC followers, who gave him a bitterly hostile reception when he attended Robert Sobukwe's funeral in March 1978. But ironically Steve Biko's death in detention in 1977 had done Buthelezi even greater harm. The exiled ANC had been thoroughly rattled by Biko's meteoric rise and by the way the BC current had triggered the Soweto uprising. Once again it feared being overtaken on its left, as had almost happened with the PAC in 1960. In that situation it clung hard to its alliance with Buthelezi. With Biko dead, however, there was no longer a third force to worry about and the ANC exiles became increasingly hostile towards Buthelezi whom they saw as a political competitor. By 1980 the ANC put Buthelezi to the test by demanding he give open support to MK – which, of course, he could not, not only because of his own non-violent philosophy but because Pretoria would hardly tolerate such open support for guerrilla warfare from a homeland leader. With that, the ANC broke with Buthelezi and launched an all-out attack on his support base.

However, in order to secure his base in KwaZulu Buthelezi now strengthened Inkatha by developing the Inkatha Youth Brigade into a quasi-military wing of the movement. The Brigade became the main tool for suppressing the wave of post-Soweto school boycotts. Inkatha membership was enforced first on teachers and then on anybody holding or applying for a job within Buthelezi's homeland administration. Buthelezi also pressed ahead in his quest for a non-violent compromise solution at least where he had control. Since he had steadily advocated the reincorporation of the homelands back into South Africa, in 1980 he initiated the Buthelezi Commission to study the possible merger of KwaZulu and Natal. When the government refused co-operation Buthelezi relaunched this initiative in 1986 in the shape of the Indaba, a major constitutional conference aimed at power-sharing in a combined KwaZulu-Natal which, Buthelezi hoped, would be a model for the country as a whole. The government again refused to participate. After 1994 many whites wondered whether there had been any alternative to the complete defeat which both the NP and the white community had suffered. Looking back it was obvious, viewed from that perspective, that after 1978 the government should have moved vigorously ahead with privatisation, federalism and genuine power-sharing. This was the only alternative future on offer. That alternative was left to die by the scornful rejection of Buthelezi's initiatives.

By the end of the 1980s the situation in the homelands could not have been more different from what the government had intended. Politically and administratively they were a mess and economically they were becoming more, not less, dependent on Pretoria. Some were already seeking reincorporation into South Africa or envisaging such reincorporation in future. Only three homeland leaders had a sufficiently popular base to survive a free election: Buthelezi, who was defying the government; Enos Mabuza, the premier of the tiny Swazi homeland, KaNgwane, who had developed an amicable relationship with the ANC; and Holomisa in the Transkei, which was rapidly becoming the first real internal base for the ANC and PAC. The leaders of the other homelands almost invariably faced opposition movements which were now in communication with the ANC. Ultimately, the ANC was to help set afoot the Congress of Traditional Leaders of South Africa (Contralesa), uniting a large number of homeland chiefs against apartheid. In terms of the original Verwoerdian vision this was nothing less than nightmarish.

But the fundamental crisis of the 1980s lay not just in the homelands but with the regime itself and with South Africa's economy. Throughout the 1970s international pressure had built against Pretoria – Biko's death in 1977 had seen even the French join the UN arms embargo against South Africa – and it was obvious that the situation would only get worse. But, thanks largely to the freeing of the gold price in 1970, the economy was in good fettle at the time of Botha's accession. Thereafter the gold price took off, peaking at $830 an ounce on 31 December 1980. At this stage the government had completely recaptured the initiative. The Soweto rising had been put down. MK's guerrilla efforts were as puny as ever and the ANC had just split its united front with Buthelezi. The economy was growing at 8 per cent a year and the government, like the country, was awash with cash. Ironically, it was the great gold and oil price boom which prolonged the natural life of the Soviet Union, whose economy and society had clearly reached the point of stagnation in the mid 1970s, and the same boom kept apartheid afloat too. Had the Botha regime decided to strike a power-sharing compromise with the black majority it could have done so then from a position of strength – but of course regimes in a strong position seldom see the need for compromise.

By the mid 1980s the bonanza was over. The price of gold fell steadily and the growth rate with it. The extra money was largely squandered on weapons, the war in Namibia/Angola, other military and security operations, corruption and resettlement. In 1982–4 the country was hit by drought. The homelands were particularly vulnerable because the soil had been ruined by erosion, overgrazing and overpopulation. Nineteen districts were declared disaster areas and famine relief programmes were organised. In white farming areas crops failed and the government had to buy maize abroad. White farmers were plunged into debt and although the government increased the controlled maize price, their losses were huge.

Unlike the period after Sharpeville, there was never really a lull in grass roots opposition after Soweto. Despite such key government concessions as the right to choose one of the two official languages, English or Afrikaans, as a medium of instruction, and a substantial expansion of the school system, boycotts, protests and disturbances in education flared up in 1980 and never really went away again. The demands and issues behind this turmoil differed from time to time and place to place but – urged on by the notorious ANC slogan of 'liberation now, education later' – black students and many of their teachers felt that education within the existing system, however reformed, was unacceptable in itself. Often school buildings were damaged or burnt as a vague protest against 'the system' and intimidation to enforce compliance with boycotts or protests became routine. The police and army were used to disperse the students and found themselves more and more on 'township duty'.

In the early 1980s several crises converged. The disturbances in schools, universities and technikons, an upsurge of labour unrest and Indian and Coloured protests against the new tricameral constitution connected with rent and rates boycotts aimed at the new township administrations, general township unrest and the hardship caused by drought and higher food prices. The United Democratic Front grew out of this explosive mix.

The UDF was essentially an umbrella national front inspired by the leadership of the exiled ANC which was by this stage regularly working with different organisations within the country. Already in 1981 a group of ANC supporters in Soweto had organised a campaign against the celebration of the twentieth anniversary of the republic. The activists of this campaign called themselves 'Charterists' – followers of the principles of the Freedom Charter – which was in effect a euphemism for the banned ANC. In the same year the young Indian activists, Valli Moosa and Ismail Momoniat, organised a Charterist conference in Durban, attended by both Indians and Africans. The government, sensing the danger, arrested the organisers throughout the country.

The UDF was launched at a mass meeting in Cape Town, on 20 August 1983. It accepted the Freedom Charter's guiding principles and rejected apartheid and all institutions associated with it. The launch was carefully prepared by a planning committee consisting of Zac Yacoob, Popo Molefe, Valli Moosa, 'Terror' Lekota, Archie Gumede, Trevor Manuel and other activists, mostly young but some older, with Robben Island experience. The organisation, based on federal principles, had branches in every province. It elected three presidents, Archie Gumede, Oscar Mpetha and Albertina Sisulu, and a number of 'patrons', many of them old Charterists, some still in prison. The composition of the UDF leadership clearly reflected the organisers' conscious effort to acknowledge 'the primacy of African leadership' but at the same time, its allegiance to non-racialism. The main speech was delivered by one of the patrons, Allan Boesak, a young Cape

Town cleric. Mandela sent a message of greeting from jail to the new organisation.

The formation of the UDF met with enormous enthusiasm. It was by far the biggest mass movement South Africa had ever seen: at its peak it claimed 2 million members via its (extremely various) 400-odd affiliated organisations. Among these were religious and civic organisations, action groups, youth groups, educational groups, sports clubs, some political groups such as the 'Release Mandela Campaign' – people of all races and all classes, from the townships, suburbs and homelands. Its youthful energy and frequent displays of defiance; its non-racialism combined with a strong sensitivity towards the feelings of the African majority; its all-inclusiveness; its ability to excite mass audiences and to organise campaigns under the single banner of anti-apartheid and its connection with the Congress tradition (particularly the ANC) – all gave the movement a genuine popular élan. Indeed, the UDF – because of its non-racial appeal and its mass nature – achieved nothing less than the creation of a common sense of South African nationhood. Neither before nor since has any movement achieved such a thing, a fact which does much to explain the elation of this emotional moment in South Africa's history. Moreover, while a pervasive sense of danger had been part of the excitement of Congress politics for a generation, what was new about the UDF was that there was now also a sense, for the first time, that the day of the majority's ultimate triumph could not be far away. It was heady stuff.

For while the UDF was not a substitute for the ANC it saw itself as holding the fort for the ANC while it was still banned and its leadership was still in jail or exile. It was with bitter irony that one watched UDF activists denounce any suggestion that the UDF was a surrogate ANC and then, the minute the ANC was unbanned, the same people announce that the UDF had indeed stood for the ANC and that consequently the UDF must now be wound up. For the many liberals who joined the UDF it provided the exhilaration of at last being involved on the same side as the black masses. This created an enormous sense of righteousness, of being on the right side of history. Sadly, it also provided, above all, an education in taking the party line. Many such people learnt to justify violence when it was used by the righteous, that is to say their own, side; to refuse to condemn intimidation or the suppression of free speech if it was deployed against those labelled the unrighteous by the UDF; and generally to slide away from defending the liberal values and human rights they had always stood for.

Immediately after its launch the UDF organised a mass campaign against the tricameral constitution, followed by bitter township battles around a wide variety of local issues, usually starting with a populist refusal to pay rents, rates and taxes to an 'illegitimate' regime. On 21 March 1984, twenty-five years after the Sharpeville massacre, events repeated themselves when police in Uitenhage shot into a peaceful crowd on its way to a commemoration meeting: nineteen were killed and many wounded. The townships exploded in revolt: for now the ANC, through the UDF, had a nationwide network and thus the capacity to orchestrate concerted action in a situation which was only too ripe for it. A wave of mass demonstrations and riots rolled through the townships and the country. ANC banners – and sometimes more daringly still, SACP banners – were displayed in open defiance, people sang ANC songs, gave mass black power salutes and danced the militant toyi-toyi dance. More people were shot and killed during the riots, and every funeral turned into another mass demonstration – sometimes leading to yet more victims being killed. The anger in the townships boiled over. Militant 'comrades' began to kill black policemen, township councillors, suspected traitors and anyone thought to be a 'collaborator'. In 1985 the government proclaimed a state of emergency (which was to last until 1990) and mass arrests and detentions followed. This did little to calm the situation but it did partially suppress it. It remained obvious that the government was barely containing a huge groundswell of popular feeling, one which continued spasmodically to erupt. The police and army were deployed permanently on a crisis footing and deaths in 'township troubles' continued to be common. Many township administrations collapsed and some townships recognised the authority of civic bodies affiliated to the UDF. In the Eastern Cape alone twenty-seven townships passed under the control of 'civics'.

In June 1985 the ANC convened a conference in Kabwe, Zambia, to discuss the situation created by the new mass movement and the first attempt by the government to investigate the possibility of negotiations. The conference decided that negotiations were out of the question until apartheid was scrapped or until it was clear that it would be. Instead, it resolved to intensify the armed struggle with the decision that, for the first time, 'soft targets' could be attacked. This was not meant to imply indiscriminate atrocities against civilians although this was sometimes exactly what occurred. The ANC called on the people 'to make the country ungovernable'. In one sense ungovernability already existed but the fact that the ANC had now publicly put its authority behind this message had a great – and often very destructive –

effect, especially after it was conveyed to ANC followers inside the country by Tambo on the ANC's Freedom Radio. For the first time the conference decided to open the ANC national executive committee to all races, a decision reflected in the NEC then elected.

Neither the UDF structures nor the ANC had complete control over what was happening on the ground: they simply lacked the capacity for that. At the same time the UDF's claim that its campaigns were spontaneous and that the ANC had nothing to do with them was, of course, untrue. Anyone working on a South African English-speaking university campus in the 1980s, for example, became familiar with declarations of boycotts and other forms of protest, typically in the form of an announcement that 'there has been a call for a stay-away'. A vote would seldom be allowed and if one queried who exactly had made the call and in the name of what organisation, one would be met with a stony stare. The reality was a hidden chain of command: somebody phoning from callboxes in Jo'burg, word passed to ideological zealots and an organisation which, though it endlessly stressed the need for 'consultation with the community', was certainly not willing to have its instructions voted down.

The situation in the townships was anarchic and less manipulable. This led the ANC and UDF to deny responsibility for some of the actions taken by various local groups in their name, such as the practice of 'necklacing' those accused of 'collaboration' or being *impimpis* (informers) – that is, burning them to death by putting petrol-filled tyres round their necks and igniting them. The unruly younger generation of township youth who performed such barbaric deeds were, indeed, often beyond anyone's control. Both the ANC and UDF leadership denounced the practice but half excused it by explaining that it stemmed from the people's righteous and uncontainable anger. These dreadful acts were often ordained by 'people's courts', terrifying kangaroo courts with no proper procedure. Inevitably, many local scores were settled this way. Apartheid townships were often ugly, cruel and desperate places in which horrifying levels of interpersonal violence were quite routine and it was no surprise when, whipped to political frenzy, they displayed mass behaviour which was also ugly, cruel and desperate.

The UDF, while initially scrupulously democratic in its non-racialism and about procedural issues, the need to represent different racial groups and the careful phrasing of its resolutions, was highly intolerant of dissident or alien ideas or even the use of terminology other than its own. In practice it turned a blind eye to racism against whites – happily joining in chants led by leaders such as Peter Mokaba of 'kill the farmer, kill the Boer', even though this was originally a PAC slogan and though it was an open secret that Mokaba had been a spy for the apartheid security police. Yet other UDF slogans would be diverse, some even preaching national unity. Theoretically it was in favour of debate and consultation yet this was stillborn by its inability to listen to any arguments from an outsider, let alone an opponent.

A classic case was that of the writer, Conor Cruise O'Brien, who had had the temerity to criticise the academic boycott prior to his visit to the University of Cape Town in 1986. He was publicly attacked, physically manhandled and prevented from speaking by UDF students who later admitted to having received instructions to this effect from the UDF hierarchy. Yet O'Brien had for decades been a strong supporter of the anti-apartheid cause; his good faith was beyond question. In a fashion which was cowardly but all too typical of university admin-istrations of the period, UCT set up a commission of enquiry under two pro-ANC lawyers, Ismael Mohamed and Arthur Chaskalson, who duly refused to defend O'Brien's freedom of speech and, indeed, concluded that the disturbances had effectively been O'Brien's fault. Mohamed was later made Chief Justice and Chaskalson head of the Constitutional Court by the ANC government – truly Orwellian appointments. At Wits University UDF students showed similar sect-arian zeal by preventing the anti-apartheid veteran, Helen Suzman, from speaking.

Such incidents were not unusual. Visiting Natal University at that time the author was quizzed by UDF students as to his attitude to freedom of speech. I was in favour of it. This turned out to be the wrong answer, for freedom of speech would have meant that Buthelezi, among others, would have had the right to address students and this would be intolerable. There must, I was told, only be freedom for those who had hitherto been denied freedom of speech. In fact, the UDF students made sure that only UDF speakers were allowed on campus and even the Democratic Party (the former Progressives) had its meet-ings broken up. The UDF is fondly remembered as a democratic movement by some and it is true that UDF leaders had to consult widely and to be keenly sensitive to popular feeling if their initiatives were to succeed. In this they were far in advance of the exiled ANC, which had no need to consult, no masses to respond to and was naturally commandist in the classic tradition of Leninist democratic centralism. In that respect the nostalgia for the UDF is understandable; yet it was a very limited democracy.

The ANC was able to use the UDF to extend its networks and

influence into every corner of the country – a push which quickly brought it into bitter conflict with Inkatha, which clearly risked losing control of townships and rural areas where it had previously been in undisputed command. Conflict was fierce on the Reef, where Buthelezi had enjoyed substantial support, and often pitted Zulu hostel dwellers against other local residents, but the struggle for KwaZulu-Natal, Buthelezi's power base, amounted to a low-intensity civil war. Inkatha's command had seldom been democratic, resting squarely on the power of the Zulu chieftaincy, and elections to the KwaZulu legislature had usually been uncontested. Now, however, the UDF challenged Buthelezi as he had never been challenged before, beginning with the bussing in of radical youth from Soweto who helped politicise and organise the local youth, calling for the school boycotts which Buthelezi had never allowed in KwaZulu. From there the movement rapidly fanned out to gain the support of many of the Zulu youth restive under the weight of chiefly authority – for in many areas the movement took the character of an anti-chief rebellion. Inevitably, neither Buthelezi nor the Zulu chiefs were willing to see their power undermined on their own turf without a fight.

Despite its former distaste for Buthelezi the government far preferred Inkatha to the UDF and allowed it to bring its 'impis' – a euphemism for the Inkatha Youth Brigade – into some of the disputed townships. Moreover, both in their official and private capacities many policemen gave Inkatha a helping hand, a fact which convinced the UDF (which needed no convincing) that Buthelezi was merely an apartheid creation, a puppet who would disappear once apartheid did. This not only denied credit to Buthelezi for his crucial opposition to homeland independence and his repeated demands for Mandela's release but it deliberately misunderstood the fact that Inkatha's power was rooted in the fabric of Zulu society and that this would easily survive apartheid. However, once the bitter battle at grass roots was joined – a battle in which some 15,000 were to die – it was next to impossible for leaders on either side to stop it.

The UDF was incomparably stronger than any previous movement. The extraordinary range of organisations behind it meant that, for the first time, not only the townships but many rural areas were politicised. Moreover, international anti-apartheid opinion was not only far stronger than before but was willing to fund the UDF or initiatives it supported. A great deal of money began to flow into South Africa from such well-wishers, often via back-channel routes. The UDF was also able to capture and control English-speaking university campuses in a way the ANC had never remotely managed. Perhaps most important of all, it had the backing of the new trade union federation, the Congress of South African Trade Unions (COSATU), launched in December 1985 with 450,000 members, a number which grew steadily to 2 million.

COSATU's existence was itself a triumph for the ANC for it meant that FOSATU, previously the biggest federation, had been forced to abandon its 'workerist' position of promoting workers' interests while refusing politicisation. But it also wanted unity and the formation of COSATU, which placed itself in the Congress tradition, was the price of acquiring the affiliation of the powerful General Workers' Union and, above all, the country's biggest union, the National Union of Mineworkers. COSATU was from the start led by prominent political activists, such as its first two General Secretaries, Elijah Barayi and Jay Naidoo, and Cyril Ramaphosa, the communist NUM leader. Indeed, many of the key COSATU leaders were communists and it quickly adopted a socialist platform. Many of the old FOSATU workerists were startled when Barayi and a few other key leaders flew up to meet the ANC leadership in Lusaka and, on their return and without discussion within COSATU, launched an all-out attack on Buthelezi and Inkatha. This was viewed as a disaster by many union leaders for not only did Inkatha immediately set afoot its own trade union federation, the United Workers' Union (UWUSA) but the battle between Inkatha and UDF was now translated into bitter conflict at worker level, something which union leaders had hitherto striven at all costs to avoid.

The Botha government saw the UDF as part of the 'total onslaught' and reacted with ferocity. By 1987 the whole UDF leadership, some 8,000 people, were banned, imprisoned or otherwise restricted while several other UDF leaders were murdered by police hit squads. From February 1988 all UDF activities were restricted and the organisation was practically banned.

By this time, however, the UDF's own weaknesses had become apparent. Its leadership was in a permanent state of consultation with the exiled ANC and also with Mandela, first on Robben Island, and then, under increasingly liberal conditions, at Victor Verster and Pollsmoor prisons. This added to its authority but also to its authoritarianism. More and more it had become a vehicle through which the ANC conveyed its ideas to the masses without requiring or getting much real feedback. Government repression made the leadership hide its activities at national level, and its communication with the regions consisted mainly of issuing instructions to affiliates without being accountable to them. A lot of money was floating around but the affiliates saw little funding of their activities. Instead, the centre employed more and more 'organisers'. In the late 1980s dissidents within the organisation accused the leadership of being a self-interested 'cabal' and called for a broader front to be formed.

Two UDF leaders who could not easily be banned were Archbishop Desmond Tutu and the Reverend Allan Boesak, who both leant heavily on their clerical celebrity status. As other leaders were eclipsed, they became almost synonymous with the UDF, touring the world demanding sanctions and peddling a mix of politics and religion which occasionally irritated the exiled ANC into pointing out that the two men had 'no mandate'. It was a strange pairing. Both men were past masters at self-promotion and although they maintained a degree of public unity, they greatly disliked one another. Tutu was wont to attend demonstrations and meetings wearing his episcopal crimson, much to Boesak's chagrin for his Coloured branch of the Dutch Reformed Church admitted only of dark suits. In the end Boesak decided to stretch matters by having a suit made of shiny light-grey material – a silver suit, in fact – but events overtook him before he ever got to wear it. He was dogged by sexual and marital scandals and, it emerged, he was also stealing money from foreign donors. Nonetheless, both Boesak and Tutu were crowd pleasers and were often able to assemble vast audiences even after the UDF was wilting under state repression. In effect, they took the UDF through to the new era after 2 February 1990 when the ANC was unbanned. As soon as the ANC developed its presence on the ground it became clear that the UDF's days were over. It was finally dissolved in 1991, Tutu wisely announcing his retreat from the political arena. Boesak, with only a small, obscure church to return to, decided to press on with a political career. But now the rules had all changed and, like that other political star of the 1980s, Winnie Mandela, Boesak met with nothing but discredit and disaster.

Apart from a growing sea of troubles at home the Botha government had also put much effort into its 'total strategy' abroad. This strategy comprised three elements: a general diplomatic effort to convince the Western world that meaningful reform was taking place – which had, even in Vorster's time, led to an acceptance that South Africa would have to move away from apartheid and became simply a plea for more time to achieve reform; targeted strikes against ANC, SACP and MK targets beyond South Africa's borders; and an attempt to maintain a political status quo in southern Africa which would not be supportive of their enemies.

The targeted strikes were the easiest to accomplish: land and air raids hit ANC camps in Botswana and Zambia, and SWAPO camps in Angola. The countries hosting the ANC could do nothing to protect them and knew that they themselves were utterly vulnerable in the face of Pretoria's military machine. This was supplemented by attacks on individual members of the ANC abroad, perhaps the most notorious case being the killing in Mozambique in 1982 of Ruth First, a prominent SACP and ANC member, and wife of the SACP leader, Joe Slovo. However, while such strikes could be made with relative impunity in southern Africa, murders in Western Europe – though they did occur – were more problematic and would lead to grave complications with countries Pretoria was desperate to keep onside.

The great strategic drama lay in Pretoria's long rearguard action in its own region. Once Angola and Mozambique became independent under radical regimes in 1974, Pretoria sought to undermine both governments by stoking internal conflicts. In Mozambique, South Africa supplied the RENAMO guerrilla groups fighting against the FRELIMO government with arms and other materiel while in Angola South Africa's support for UNITA against the MPLA government involved a full-scale invasion of Angola in 1975 and continuing support for UNITA after Pretoria was forced to withdraw from central Angola. Even so, South African troops remained inside southern Angola in order to prosecute the war against SWAPO.

For throughout the 1980s the Namibian border remained a constant drain on the country's human, financial and psychological resources. Pretoria's determination to hold fast in Namibia looks absurd in retrospect. The costs were outrageously high and yet an independent Namibia – with its tiny population and vulnerable economy – could do South Africa little harm. Far more serious had been the 'loss' of Rhodesia, a serious white power to Pretoria's north, a regime with its own formidable army and air force. Both Vorster and Botha had pushed the Rhodesian leader, Ian Smith, towards conceding majority rule, though on the assumption that it could be arranged for either Bishop Abel Muzorewa or Joshua Nkomo to win the elections and keep Robert Mugabe out. When, in the event, Mugabe swept to power, Pretoria had lost control of its whole northern tier.

Nothing as important as that was at stake in Namibia. The problem, to put it baldly, was that P. W. Botha, a former NP organiser, was a man of very limited perspectives and horizons. He stuck to his guns because he lacked the imagination or nerve to do anything else. Nat MPs, though they could see the country burning and the alarming international situation, showed similar parochialism and timidity. They longed to see the back of the bullying P. W. but were frightened of him and, for all their rhetorical nationalism, never dared to put their country first.

Botha's total strategy had been based on the notion that by depicting the ANC – not unrealistically – as being driven by the SACP, he could not only convince his own electorate of his case but Reagan, Thatcher and the West: thus the Cold War was his final safeguard. But Gorbachev's accession to power in the USSR changed everything. Gorbachev wanted to end the Cold War and was willing to co-operate with the West in solving common problems. This was first illustrated in the case of Namibia and Angola where the USSR happily worked with the Western powers to reach a solution. The Cubans and South Africans must both leave Angola and there must be an end to South African prevarication over Namibia. It was immediately clear that the game was up: Pretoria could not resist a coalition of all the great powers. Preparations for elections and Namibian independence were quickly under way.

In South Africa the combination of international and domestic pressure fed press leaks that Botha would make his 'Rubicon' speech in Durban on 15 August 1985, announcing a major departure from apartheid and a major new reform initiative. However, in the run-up to the speech Botha was subjected to strong conservative lobbying from within the NP and was also greatly irritated by leaks to the media of what his speech was to contain. The result was that, in typical style, he lost his temper, tore up his speech and instead came up with little more than spitting defiance. The effect, taken together with the virtually simultaneous decision by Chase Manhattan to call in a loan to South Africa, was catastrophic.

Ironically, the ANC and anti-apartheid movement abroad, which had long campaigned for trade sanctions and disinvestment from South Africa, had failed to grasp the crucial nature of credit: the Chase Manhattan decision was not taken as a result of their lobbying but as a market judgement that the Botha government was heading into a brick wall. Other banks naturally followed suit, while many corporations disinvested too. The result was a collapse in the value of the Rand – from being worth $1.36 in 1981 by 1989, you needed R2.44 to buy $1. This in turn had the effect of multiplying South Africa's foreign debt more than threefold. As capital fled the country so the economic growth rate sagged further – having averaged 5.8 per cent per annum in the 1960s and 3.3 per cent in the 1970s, growth in the 1980s averaged under 2 per cent. Moreover, this sagging growth rate had to support ever higher expenditure on defence – over R9 billion in 1989 alone. The government was on the ropes and, faced with every other sort of challenge, took the easy way out over inflation, which stayed permanently in double figures.

The crisis of 1985 illustrated what had become an iron law of South African political economy, the need for foreign capital. Ever since the discovery of diamonds in 1867, and particularly since the discovery of gold and the need for large capital infusions to finance deep-level mining, the South African economy had lived off a steady inflow of foreign investment. This was a structural necessity, for only a minority of whites and Indians had enough disposable income to save anything. Thus there was never any prospect of South Africa having the high savings ratio which later typified successful developing countries in Asia; which in turn meant that the investment necessary to keep the economy turning could not all be domestically derived. So even the most nationalistic politicians quickly learnt the imperative of attracting foreign capital.

There have, however, been several occasions when the capital inflow has ceased. This occurred at the end of World War I when post-war recession in the rest of the world and a fall in the gold price made more than half the country's gold mines unprofitable. Investment naturally dried up, producing savage wage cuts and, ultimately, the Rand revolt of 1922 and Smuts's eviction from power in 1924. It occurred again during the Depression of the 1930s when the economic crisis brought low the Hertzog government and forced the creation of the fusion government. But the long-lasting crisis of the 1930s also greatly worsened and ultimately politicised the poor white problem, which eventually propelled the NP to power in 1948. Thus a key lesson of South African history is that the country cannot long withstand a cessation of foreign investment without creating a major political reaction and usually the collapse of a sitting government.

Hence the significance of 1985. With the collapse of the currency and of foreign capital inflows, and with no way out of its political crisis, the Botha government had run out of options. The political price for this was to be paid first by a surge in the far-right Conservative Party vote, so that in the 1989 election the NP fell under 50 per cent for the first time in decades – and ultimately by the regime change of 1994. After 1985 it was a matter of the cash register ringing up a transaction which had already long occurred. But Botha was too stubborn to accept the logic of the situation. True, he began to make the first approaches to Mandela and attempts at negotiation with the ANC but he continued to insist on preconditions which rendered such talks stillborn.

The result was a period of surrealism fully worthy of Gabriel García Márquez. On the one hand the government couldn't go forward but it also couldn't go back. A dull repressive gloom hung over the country and its stagnant economy. Botha himself was increasingly ill-tempered. There were endless displays of finger-wagging ego, of self-righteous tirades, of brutal intervention in news broadcasts despite the fact that the electronic media fawned as never before. It was the autumn of the patriarch. But three things were happening.

First, the establishment had understood perfectly well that the political rationale for the Rubicon speech had been that foreign pressure was now overwhelming and that things had to change: this was the era of endless missions to Dakar and Lusaka to meet the ANC by business groups, intellectuals and others, all anxious to declare their good faith to the country's presumed future rulers and to secure their own situation in that future. The ANC, though still caught up in the unyielding and self-righteous postures of the past – nothing less than 'the seizure of state power' would do – began to glimpse a victory it had all but given up hope of.

Second, the establishment of the apartheid state, realising that its days were numbered, began to steal everything that wasn't nailed down and quite a bit even of what was. Corruption became endemic. Capital flowed abroad into secret accounts, many of those involved also making arrangements to emigrate to where their money now was. It was nothing less than the looting of a sinking ship.

In effect, Botha was re-enacting the role of Kruger. Like him, a crude and poorly educated man, Botha found himself under pressure from international forces which focused on the fact that the majority of the republic's citizens were denied the vote. His response was the same as Kruger's: these were not really citizens, these were *uitlanders*, they didn't really belong there. Kruger struggled against his isolation by having bogus little republics set up in order to try to let the Transvaal develop a corridor to the sea, but the British wouldn't let him get away with that. Botha too set up bogus little republics – the Bantustans – and these too didn't pass muster. Kruger desperately tried to develop diplomatic links with Germany, Russia, anyone who might help; Botha placed similarly extravagant hopes that somehow his alliances with

Paraguay, Taiwan or even China would enable him to balance off the mounting international pressures on him. For Kruger it all ended with his exile to Europe. At least Botha ended up in retirement in Wilderness in the Cape.

For not only had the advent of Gorbachev undermined Botha's ability to play the anti-communist card with the West but by 1989 the Berlin Wall was coming down and communism itself was clearly in a state of terminal collapse. In this new environment the remaining constraints on firm Western action to end apartheid all fell away.

In January 1989 Botha had a stroke and resigned the NP leadership. However, he failed to get his candidate, Barend Du Plessis, elected in his place: instead the Transvaal leader, F. W. de Klerk narrowly won. Piqued, Botha then decided, absurdly, to stay on as President. De Klerk was fully equal to the situation and by August had forced Botha's resignation. He then led the NP through a tough election, losing seats to both right and left, with vague promises of a five-year plan to solve all the country's problems.

In fact, de Klerk had accepted defeat gracefully and, having cleared his speech with the Western powers, rose to speak at parliament's opening on 2 February 1990 and, with great calm and panache, announced the end of apartheid, the unbanning of all proscribed organisations, the release of Mandela and the remaining ANC prisoners, a welcome back home of all exiles and the invitation to the ANC and all other parties to talks on a new democratic constitution. By the time de Klerk had finished speaking South Africa had changed completely and for ever.

# X
## THE LIMITS TO LIBERATION
@ @ @

In July 1989, just a month before F. W. de Klerk finally forced Botha from office, the SACP assembled in Havana, Cuba for its seventh congress. Chaired by Thabo Mbeki, the Congress adopted a programme, 'The Path to Power', which again stressed the party's intention to continue the armed struggle until victory and advance to socialism thereafter. Many SACP and ANC activists were stuck in a Stalinist mindset and nourished a particular admiration for Cuba and East Germany – the SACP talked of wanting to 'build East Germany in Africa'; this shortly before the Berlin Wall fell. This was also true of some of the leadership – but not all. The party had struggled to cope with the ideological consequences of Gorbachev's perestroika. Joe Slovo's pamphlet, *Has Socialism Failed?*, published in late 1989, was symptomatic of the party's dilemma. Partly it was meant to explain the new situation to Slovo's disconcerted comrades – but it was also an attempt to reassure those with whom Slovo hoped soon to be in negotiation, by signalling a new flexibility in the party's attitude.

On his way to Havana Mbeki had stopped off in Bermuda to hold discussions with senior Nat and Broederbond figures. How many of his comrades at the SACP congress were privy to these negotiations is an interesting question. Had they all known, some would doubtless have accused Mbeki of being an apartheid agent and spy. But the negotiations – each step of them – were a collective decision of the top leadership, of which the rank and file received mere hints.

Unofficial talks between various intermediaries and proxies of the NP and ANC had been going on since 1984. Mandela, with the ANC's consent, had been involved in unofficial secret talks for three years while still in jail. Both sides hoped that negotiations would weaken and divide their opponents but the ANC were almost pathologically unwilling to believe what de Klerk said. Even on the very eve of de Klerk's speech the ANC leadership did not believe that he would unban the SACP as well as the ANC, and release all political prisoners.

On 11 February 1990 Nelson Mandela walked free after twenty-seven years in jail, amidst a tidal wave of euphoria – and the exiles began to return home. Ironically, the next few years were the most difficult time in the history of South Africa's liberation movement. The apartheid state, its security forces and the Bantustans were all still in place – though fully aware that their days were numbered. The Tripartite Alliance of the ANC, SACP and COSATU were aware that they were the government in waiting, but had none of the institutions, structures or habits of mind necessary to govern. The country was in a situation of dual power and of frantic struggle for advantage between different groups, interests and personalities.

The ANC had to establish control over the UDF, accommodate its MK and other cadres returning from exile, demonstrate its power to the government, and simultaneously show it was ready for negotiation and reassure its activists that it wasn't selling out. Mass campaigns, boycotts and marches in support of the ANC rocked the country, public services were disrupted, universities were permanently in turmoil, strikes shook one branch of industry after another. With everything up for grabs, militant activism, craven opportunism and personal rivalries were everywhere. The ANC had suspended but not terminated the armed struggle and its push for power in areas where it had previously had little support often led to open and bitter conflicts. On the other hand, ANC cadres were also constantly under threat from Bantustan opponents, Inkatha militants, right-wing activists and from the security forces who felt confused and provoked. The country had become truly ungovernable and almost anything could happen: civil war, a right-wing or military coup, a left-wing rebellion, the secession of provinces or just a collapse into chaos.

The question was whether the ANC leadership was really prepared to talk. Nothing could disguise the fact that right up to the early 1990s the ANC had been training its cadres for a military seizure of power in a revolution that would bring in a largely communist government. Soon after his release Mandela announced that nationalisation of the mines, banks and other major industries remained ANC policy but it was soon clear that such aims, along with a great deal else, would have to be jettisoned if all hope of domestic compromise or international support were not to be abandoned. Both the ANC and SACP had remained ideological dinosaurs and now, in their moment of triumph, would have to modernise and moderate their policies quite abruptly, somehow find a way of selling such changes to their followers and simultaneously maintain and extend their control of their new mass party. It was an extremely tall order. To achieve this the ANC would have to lean heavily both on Mandela's unchallengeable appeal and on the iron party discipline which it had always exercised. Luckily, Mandela himself was always obedient to such discipline. This, fundamentally, was why it took the ANC almost two years before it was ready to sit down for talks on a new constitution and even longer to work out what it wanted to do with state power when it got it.

But the Nats were under pressure too. De Klerk had promised a new deal within five years and he couldn't afford another whites-only election. In order to reassure the white, Indian and Coloured minorities, de Klerk promised that he would ensure that the new democratic constitution, now to be negotiated, would include provision for a strong element of federalism, an entrenched bill of rights, blocking mechanisms of various kinds and provision for permanent power-sharing. But de Klerk, having unleashed a tidal wave of change, had almost immediately lost control of events. He was in the position of a man who has shot the rapids in a canoe and who, whatever his previous plans, very quickly finds himself amidst boiling white waters, navigating frantically to avoid whirlpools and rocks just to stay afloat.

The atmosphere of *fin de règne* fired up power struggles of every kind. Although throughout the apartheid period white right-wingers and black extremists had talked wistfully of committing genocidal violence against the other group, the number of deaths caused by such racist extremists was mercifully few. Far worse was the escalation of the UDF–Inkatha conflict into a low-intensity civil war. Casualties soared both in Natal and on the Reef, at a tempo of up to 200 dead a week. Ironically, of all the lives lost to political violence under NP rule a good half were lost in the 1990–4 period *after* the abolition of apartheid. In effect, the ANC made a major push to dislodge Buthelezi from his redoubts and he resisted just as fiercely, now under the banner of the recently launched Inkatha Freedom Party. The ANC kept up a hail of accusation that a sinister 'third force' was behind much of the violence. It was certainly true that the police and army were disposed both publicly and privately to assist the IFP but no evidence was ever presented of a third force independent of the police and army. At the same time, however, apartheid hit squads were still on the loose, as were MK armed units, whose assassination of hundreds of Inkatha leaders was probably the largest hit-squad activity of all. In the end Buthelezi lost ground in urban areas and on the Reef but largely held his rural base.

The public sector acted in the spirit of *sauve qui peut* which, inevitably, led to increased fraud and theft. Trade unions upped their bids, safe in the knowledge that de Klerk was keen to buy off trouble, particularly among black intellectuals: this produced quite unsustainable increases in teachers' salaries. In the homelands the ruling elites happily ran up unpayable debts, confident that when the homelands were reincorporated into South Africa, Pretoria would have to take over their debts too.

Amidst this chaos the one constant was that both the ANC and NP leaders wanted a negotiated settlement. This commonality was finally to win the day. In 1990 all emergency restrictions were lifted and in December 1991 a constituent assembly, the Convention for a Democratic South Africa (CODESA), was set up to work out a transitional constitution. Most of the mainstream parties attended but only two, the ANC and the NP, really mattered. The Conservative Party, rightly grasping that what was really being negotiated was the surrender of white power, campaigned furiously against CODESA and won a crucial by-election on the issue. De Klerk's reply was a whites only referendum on the question of continued negotiation – which he won with a two-thirds majority. The ANC had to restrain its own radicals who viewed negotiations as unnecessary or even a betrayal, and who clung to the vision of mass action leading to 'the seizure of power' and revolutionary rule.

But negotiations continued. The key was the authority and personality of Mandela, now the undisputed leader of the ANC. If de Klerk could deliver the whites, Coloureds and Indians, no African dared face down Mandela. He connected the new mass ANC to its militant past. Oliver Tambo had had a stroke and Walter Sisulu had retired so Mandela alone represented the historic ANC. His release from jail had been an enormous world media event and he quickly earned the affection and respect of every section of the population. His courage, fortitude and resolution through twenty-seven years in jail could not be argued with and he had a humility, a lack of rancour and a sense of humour that were utterly winning. His popularity also far outran that of the ANC.

The other major ANC figures were Joe Slovo, whose command over the SACP and MK made him unchallengeably the leading strategic thinker; Chris Hani, who took over as both SACP and MK boss and whose courage, intelligence and charisma made him the hero of the

ANC youth and the popular choice among the ANC following; and Mbeki, the epitome of the black Englishman, whose cool diplomatic skills made him an immediate favourite with the white business circles who anxiously sought contacts with the new ANC elite. Slovo was white (and, it soon emerged, had cancer) which meant, inevitably, that the future leadership, in the post-Mandela era, lay between Hani and Mbeki.

Not only Slovo, Hani and Mbeki, but so many other top ANC leaders and negotiators belonged to the SACP that the party, realising the disastrous effect on both domestic and international opinion if a visibly communist-dominated movement came to power, decided to allow its members to terminate their membership or to 'take a sabbatical'. Mbeki and Ramaphosa both took this opportunity, Ramaphosa becoming the ANC's new Secretary General while Slovo avowed he now had only an ANC career, relinquishing the SACP leadership to Chris Hani.

Slovo, Albie Sachs and other SACP leaders also launched a 'charm offensive' calculated to highlight their concern for human rights. They expressed shock at the revelation of the Soviet labour camps, though this was clearly a calculated gambit. The truth about Soviet labour camps had been revealed by Soviet refugees in the 1930s, by Jean Paul Sartre and Simone de Beauvoir in the early 1950s and by Khrushchev in 1956, long before the further revelations of the 1980s. The SACP leadership had remained blindly impervious to all of this but now its leaders had a belated – and very public – Damascus experience. Sometimes this did not work. When interviewed by Etienne Mureinik of the Judicial Services Commission for his appointment as a justice of the Constitutional Court, Albie Sachs had to admit that he had made no move to voice any dissatisfaction at human rights atrocities which had gone on, year in and year out, in the ANC camps.

Given that there was now to be a negotiated transition, not a revolutionary victory, the ANC and SACP concentrated on pushing their cadres (often the same people) into key positions – the SACP allocating Sachs to the Constitutional Court, for example. There was a problem, though. The ANC and SACP were now two separate organisations which rapidly developed different profiles, the ANC a mass party with the support of two thirds of the electorate and the SACP a much smaller vanguard party. Many prominent SACP members were put into positions to implement ANC policy decisions against which they had voted at SACP meetings. Without exception they took the ANC line, as careerism dictated.

Slovo, like many others, did not trust Mbeki – whose reputation as a consummate player of exile politics had earned him, according to the journalist Howard Barrell, the sobriquet of 'smiling death' – and supported Hani. But Hani did not really fit into the negotiated transition model: he was dubious about a negotiated compromise and early on voiced the view that the ANC should merely seek to control the police, the army and the broadcasting service. Why have an ANC Minister of Education, he asked, when it was clear that such a portfolio could only be 'a bed of nails'? One of Hani's many attractions – quite apart from a liking for Shakespeare and Latin poetry – was that he was willing to come out and say things like that. The plan was that after Mandela had served one term as President, Hani would succeed him, uniting the ANC and SACP in his person. Meanwhile, so as not to panic the bourgeoisie, such notions had to be kept under wraps.

The solution found was for Hani to move down to the Transkei, using Bantu Holomisa's good offices to build up MK there so that it could balance off de Klerk's control of the police and army. Hani, wildly popular with the youth and not above using Xhosa chauvinism, rapidly built up a regional base in the Transkei. At the first ANC conference held inside the country he was elected in top position to the NEC. This clearly made him invincible. He had command of MK and the SACP, had the backing of COSATU, almost all of whose leaders had now joined the party, and he was the only ANC politician with a regional base to rival Buthelezi. However, another group in MK, led by the former MK commander, Joe Modise, supported Mbeki. Back in Lusaka Modise had nearly had Hani executed for insubordination and was alarmed to see Hani's star rising. It was this intense world of exile intrigue that now mattered most. Ironically, it was those who hadn't been in exile – such as Cyril Ramaphosa – who were the outsiders now.

At CODESA, of course, the ANC sat as a united bloc. At first progress was good but by May 1992 deadlock occurred over the proposed two-thirds parliamentary majority required to amend the constitution, with the NP demanding a 75 per cent majority. The ANC offered a 75 per cent figure for amendment of the Bill of Rights and a 70 per cent majority for everything else. De Klerk had delegated negotiation to a junior minister, seldom attending the talks himself, and failed to realise that, given opinion polls showing a combined non-ANC vote of around 35 per cent, this was actually a generous offer. Instead, talks broke down and shortly thereafter, in July 1992, ANC–IFP tensions in Boipatong township on the Reef exploded into a horrendous massacre of ANC supporters by what was, in effect, a classic Zulu raiding party. The ANC alleged that the violence had been stoked by de Klerk, a ludicrous notion, for de Klerk had much to lose and nothing to gain from such explosions of violence. The ANC, however, walked out of the talks and called for 'rolling mass action' to enforce its will.

Since it was clear that revolutionary action against the (still overwhelmingly strong) apartheid state was bound to fail, the ANC decided to go for the far softer target of the Bantustans. Both the Ciskei and Bophuthatswana governments were toppled, though only after an ill-judged march on the Ciskei capital of Bisho on 7 September 1992, which resulted in twenty-nine deaths. Repeated threats of a march on Ulundi (Buthelezi's capital) never came close to materialising: even Harry Gwala, the SACP and ANC leader in Natal and a self-declared Stalinist, admitted that not many marchers could expect to return alive from such an expedition.

'Rolling mass action' – strikes, protests and demonstrations of every kind – allowed the ANC to vent some of the accumulation of emotions that had built up in its decades of struggle. This was, indeed, one of the problems of the negotiated transfer of power. After all that non-whites had suffered under apartheid and the ANC's long defiance and insurrectionary propaganda, there was a strong sense of anticlimax in watching ANC leaders chatting amiably with Nat leaders. Worse, by abolishing apartheid, de Klerk had shot the ANC's fox. There was a vast cloud of pent-up excitement, anger, hope – and dawning ambition – within the anti-apartheid movement which had to be expressed. Anyone witnessing the apparently insane antics of student radicals on university campuses in this period or the impossibilist demands and wild accusations of ANC activists would struggle to explain these phenomena except as chiliastic, millenarian emotions. It was also quite clear that, whatever was said at the time and later about the importance of reconciliation, power-sharing and compromise, the ANC as a whole was focused on complete victory for itself and complete defeat for its opponents.

This was why the ANC found it difficult to believe that de Klerk meant what he said about free elections and the transfer of power: there had to be a catch. Decades of struggle had given the whole movement a strong belief that the enemy would never give in and a corresponding belief that it was in permanent opposition. There was almost a reluctance to believe that whites were really giving up their power. Indeed, long after the transfer of power ANC leaders would tend to excuse their failures by insisting that while they were in government they were not yet in power, which was still held by 'imperialism', big business or 'reactionary forces seeking to defeat transformation'. Crucially, this meant that during the negotiations to draft the new constitution the ANC stance assumed that it still needed protection against white injustice.

Hence the great oddity and irony of the constitution, a liberal document written by parties which were both passionate opponents of liberalism. For the Nats, having abandoned apartheid, were left with no real ideological principles but a far more realistic sense that the minorities would need every protection they could get from a hegemonic ANC majority. Thus both Afrikaner and African nationalists found common ground and mutual protection in the principles of liberalism and human rights, a conclusion delightedly encouraged by both international and domestic liberal opinion. De Klerk could not pretend that the NP was not a latter-day convert to such principles, though he sought to avoid apologising more than was absolutely necessary for the shameful cruelties of apartheid. For its part the ANC, once in government, was to find that the result of its earlier enthusiasm for human rights and restraints on the abuse of power was sometimes extremely awkward.

The Bisho tragedy stunned both sides and early in 1993 negotiations reopened. Rolling mass action had undermined de Klerk's authority for it showed that he was unable to take a tough line against those he was keen to negotiate with. Moreover, he had vowed to complete the negotiation process within the term of parliament, so for him time was getting short. In effect, the ANC could afford to break off talks but he could not. He would simply have to agree to their demands to get an agreement. When constitutional negotiations resumed, Slovo proposed a 'sunset clause' – a government of national unity (GNU) for the first five years after the first democratic election, and a guarantee of job security for public servants. The latter was determined mainly by the ANC's need to reassure the police, armies and civil servants of the homelands that they would not lose everything through incorporation, but it was also a huge relief to white civil servants, a key Nat constituency. The Nats happily accepted this deal but had to watch as all their other proposals – for federalism, permanent power-sharing and constraints on the power of a simple majority single chamber – were rejected.

On 10 April 1993 Chris Hani was assassinated by Janus Walusz, a right-wing Polish immigrant who, police quickly discovered, had been part of a conspiracy with the right-wing MP, Clive Derby-Lewis. There was immediate turmoil as ANC and SACP supporters vented their anger at this shocking deed but the ANC leadership made no move to break off talks. Nor did the talks break up when the extreme right AWB men forcibly attempted to occupy the building where negotiations were taking place; nor, indeed, when the PAC began a series of terrorist acts, including the mowing down of a congregation at prayer in a Cape Town church. These desperate acts, all committed by those who felt excluded from the ANC–NP deal, could not shake the determination of the principals to see the deal through.

The assassination of Chris Hani had a profound effect on the course of South African history. Immediately Mbeki became the certain next ANC leader and president after Mandela. On the principle of *cui bono*, this soon led to (baseless) speculation that Mbeki must have had a hand in the murder. The point was that Walusz had acted within a tiny window of opportunity. He had had to know which house in the anonymous suburb of Boksburg belonged to Hani and also on which day Hani would both be at home and have given his bodyguards the day off. There was no way the far right had access to such intimate details of a communist leader's life: there had to have been a helping hand from somebody within the ANC or close to Hani. There was so much uncertainty about this that Hani's widow, Limpho, an ANC MP herself, seemed unsure who could or could not be trusted within the ANC and approached the opposition Democratic Party leader Tony Leon to ask what he thought of the matter. But there was no hard evidence against any of the possible ANC accessories to the crime whereas the guilt of the far right was undoubted. Some wondered whether, beyond even a possible ANC accomplice to the murder, a foreign intelligence agency had played a role or held a watching brief.

Despite de Klerk's surrender of one sticking point after another, the work of constitution drafting could not be completed on time and so it was decided to make do with an incomplete and provisional constitution instead. This was hailed as a great triumph although no word had yet been said about the electoral system, the key to the workings of the new political system and thus the most important item in the constitution. In fact, the ANC and the NP had reached agreement on this but kept it secret. When the full document was finally released this became comprehensible, for the new electoral system – unique in the world – was in reality a scandalous political bosses' charter. It is not unusual that PR lists give power to party bosses who draw them up. What made South Africa's election provisions unusual was that there were to be no constituencies at all and no possibility for local communities to have any control over their representatives or to choose who they might be. Even when MPs resigned or died there were to be no by-elections so that political leaders would be spared even these sporadic expressions of grass roots feeling. Instead, 400 MPs were to be elected on a purely proportional basis from party lists. Any MP who disagreed with his party could be thrown out of parliament by the party bosses, who were also given the power to move people at will into and out of seats in parliament and the provincial assemblies.

Although this monstrous system vitiated many of the democratic provisions in the rest of the constitution, its cleverness lay in the fact that it held out the prospect of representation to every little political minority, whose criticisms of the system were, accordingly, muted. But the opinion polls showed that the ANC and NP would win over 80 per cent of the vote between them and the real interest in the system lay there. For the Nats it meant they could hope to remain a significant factor in the country's governance – but the system was, of course, most beneficial of all to the ANC's ruling group.

For not just a majoritarian but a dominant party to agree to a simple proportional system was unique in the world's electoral history. The reason for this was that this system was exactly what the ANC exiles needed in order to maintain control over the movement as a whole. The exile leadership, used to exercising absolute discipline over a movement with no constituencies, clearly understood that the situation was different in South Africa – a strange country for many of them, for the exiles knew the London or Moscow Undergrounds far better than the streets of Soweto. Here there was an anarchic, diverse following, loyal beyond question but out of control. In the first months that Thabo Mbeki had been back he had acquired a BMW – there were only too many willing godfathers in the white business community, happy to buy such toys for the new elite – which was promptly stolen in Soweto. The ANC network there quickly put out the word among the 'comrades', who had intimate knowledge of the criminal world, that the car should be returned. It duly was – but the incident spoke volumes. The township world was chaotic and rough, and the UDF leaders, used to such realities, were entirely too rough and ready.

The ANC and SACP leadership felt the desperate need to bring this rumbustious and sprawling constituency under control. The electoral system meant that local activists would be under the boss's thumb, excluded from the party list – or simply listed too low down – if they stepped out of line. Moreover, exile leaders, many of them white,

Coloured and Indian communists, could be put high up on the list, snug behind Mandela's coat-tails, protected by the ANC's popularity and certain to win election. Had they had to win constituencies, few of them would have survived. In white, Coloured or Indian constituencies they would have lost and in African constituencies they would have faced steep competition from popular black challengers. The system also allowed the ANC to achieve the 'right' gender and tribal balance. Thus the deal was struck between de Klerk and the ANC-SACP leadership. These were, indeed, the true godfathers of South Africa's 'miracle' transition to democracy: an Afrikaner aristocrat, himself the son of an apartheid Cabinet minister – and perhaps the most Stalinist Communist Party still extant outside North Korea and Cuba.

This deal was quickly accepted and trumpeted as a miracle, and ANC ministers were soon travelling round the world, happily suggesting that they share their miracle and show the Arabs and Israelis, the British and Irish, the Tutsi and the Hutu how to resolve their conflicts. This mainly showed that they had not understood their own 'miracle'. For was it really a miracle that the ANC had embraced the possibility of winning a battle without a fight – a battle they could not hope to win by any other means after the collapse of the Soviet Union? One has to consider that even at the end of the armed struggle the life expectancy of an MK infiltrator was only six months. By accepting peace the ANC elite accepted the fruits of power and office in a modern working country, replete with jumbo jets, computers and six-lane highways. Accepting the ministerial Merc, the big salary and the big house was, perhaps, wondrous magnanimity in the eyes of the admiring world – particularly since one could carry on calling everyone 'Comrade' to show where one's heart was. But miracle it was not.

The real miracle, if one truly existed, lay in what de Klerk had done, defying all predictions that Afrikaners would draw their wagons in a circle and fight to the last. Had de Klerk been willing to pay this price, the apartheid state could have fought on for another decade. Within a few years President Mugabe next door in Zimbabwe was to give a demonstration of just what a determined minority could do, destroying its country rather than allow majority rule. But de Klerk and the modernising Afrikaners he represented wanted to be part of the cosmopolitan Western middle class; they had no interest in re-enacting some blood-soaked piece of nineteenth-century folklore. The reason why de Klerk could give away one bargaining counter after another was that the real bet he was making was that if he made the best of what was by now a thoroughly bad job, at least his *volk* would be able to carry on living in South Africa in relative peace – the fundamental deal – and the logic of the capitalist economic system in place would carry the black elite along with it. 'It's not just the ports and the roads and the airports,' he told me when I quizzed him about this. 'Look at our big companies. We're not a satellite economy. Look at our banks, our financial infrastructure. We have built well.' Ten years on from liberation, with a burgeoning new black capitalist elite very much to the fore, one can see that while de Klerk lost his short-term bets with the ANC, he probably won his long-term bet.

Moreover, the social basis of this miracle lay not in anything de Klerk or the ANC did but in the evolution of South African society in the decades before 1994 when, despite all the obstacles, a rapidly growing black educated class emerged, when every year the fraction of GDP going to the white minority diminished, when black wages rose sharply and when the steady reality of urban South Africa became increasingly racially integrated. By the mid 1980s one could see the Group Areas Act being widely disobeyed, one knew more and more mixed couples, universities and other institutions were already desperate to recruit blacks at every level and in a thousand little NGOs and office situations one could see people of different races rubbing along on altogether more friendly and intimate terms than before. Etched in my mind are Durban jokes in the early 1980s about how to describe the rising class of Zulu yuppies: Buppies? Zuppies? By the time de Klerk spoke on 2 February 1990 a fragile but genuine social basis for the new South Africa already existed and the majority of whites felt as liberated as blacks by his statement. No more boycotts and sanctions, no more isolation, no more pariah status, no more guilt . . . When Mandela and Winnie emerged hours late for the world's TV cameras from Pollsmoor prison, African friends said meaningfully, 'You're all on African time now.' And we all laughed.

The 1994 election was a moment of great celebration, signalling the arrival of full political equality in a single South African nation. But it was also a forgone conclusion: for all its euphoria it merely ratified the deal between elites. In the event the key deviations from the script were that the NP managed only 20 per cent of the vote (de Klerk had hoped for 30 per cent); that Mandela was happy to get less than two thirds of the vote for the ANC (it won 62.5 per cent) and thus vetoed the attempt by ANC militants to deny Buthelezi his victory in KwaZulu-Natal; and the survival of the Democatic Party with just 1.7

per cent of the vote, or seven seats. With deep unwisdom the DP had elected the hard-drinking Zach de Beer as its leader and he had slumbered his way through the election, nearly sinking South Africa's liberal tradition in the process. Having survived, the DP chose a new young leader, Tony Leon. With both the IFP and the NP in the Government of National Unity, the future of liberal democracy in South Africa fell upon him and his six followers. Just as Helen Suzman had, on her own, guaranteed the continuity of that tradition between 1961 and 1974, so Leon and his little group performed the crucial task of extending that tradition into the new era of mass democracy. Within five years their numbers grew from seven to thirty-eight and after ten years to forty-nine. In the absence of any other credible opposition they managed to establish themselves as the main alternative to the new hegemonic nationalism.

Mandela became President at seventy-six, having never – as his Nat colleagues were wont to explain to outsiders – occupied elective office before in his life though, as they hastily added, this lack of experience 'was not entirely his own fault'. Indeed not: his twenty-seven years in jail had hardly been at his own behest. But Mandela spoke from the heart about the need for reconciliation and for everyone to pull together for the sake of the country. Coming from a man who had spent over a third of his life in jail and who had refused all compromise in order to be free, this was magical stuff. Moreover, the man had grace, a sense of humour and a complete lack of grandeur – when children were present he would leave the VIP enclosure to go and dance with them. The country and the world embraced him for all that. He addressed the Queen of England as 'Elizabeth' and the American President as 'Bill', and they both loved it. So did South Africans. Mandela, known to intimates as 'Madiba', became a quasi-magical figure and the 'Madiba factor' quickly became known to the world. When the Springboks won the 1995 Rugby World Cup it was due to the 'Madiba factor' and the victory the next year of the country's soccer team in the African Cup of Nations was quickly put down to the same thing.

Meanwhile, at home, he was doubly betrayed. The world had luxuriated in the pictures of Nelson walking free, hand in hand with his wife Winnie, on the first glorious day of his liberty – now as iconic an image as Neil Armstrong's 'giant leap for mankind'. But the fact was that Winnie, much admired by the ANC youth for her courageous and challenging stand during the apartheid era, was a child batterer and serial adulterer. Mandela, by his own account, was never to share a bedroom with her. Within the ANC he also seemed to be isolated.

Outside the government he was a towering figure but within it he had little power. The ANC exiles exercised complete control over his actions and speeches, and from the outset it was not Mandela but Thabo Mbeki who chaired the Cabinet, ran the government and consolidated his position by judicious use of patronage. Had ordinary South Africans known that Mandela was so disempowered that he often wandered out of Cabinet meetings long before they ended, they would have been scandalised.

The crucial battle had come early on when Mandela had wanted to promote Cyril Ramaphosa, the ANC Secretary General who had negotiated the constitution and overseen the party's election victory, to be Deputy President alongside de Klerk – and ultimately his own successor. A phalanx of ANC exiles identified with Mbeki were implacably opposed – and Mandela gave way. In the end Ramaphosa never served in the Cabinet at all and Mandela thereafter did pretty much whatever Mbeki said, for he was determined to observe the discipline of the movement which was his life and Mbeki was by now largely in control of that movement.

The collapse of communism had robbed the ANC of its programme, though for a considerable time it clung to the doctrine of nationalisation of industry. In a fashion which was to be all too typical, all attempts by local South Africans to convince the ANC that the era of nationalisation was long gone were simply dismissed out of hand – but when foreigners made the same point they were, in the end, listened to. Meanwhile from the early 1990s on an enormous effort was put into developing the ANC's Reconstruction and Development Programme. The SACP had long had the habit of developing the ANC's programme for it but this time it worked primarily through COSATU, the idea being to write a comprehensive programme covering every aspect of life in South Africa. Endless conferences, study groups and workshops laboured mightily through seven different drafts of the RDP, which soon achieved the status of Holy Writ, the Bible of the government-to-be. In tone it was left Keynesian, with the assumption that the central state would be the key driver of social change and economic development. A new ministry was to be set up under Jay Naidoo, the COSATU leader, to push the RDP through.

All this effort was merely a testament to how far the ANC was from understanding what lay ahead. No attempt was made to look at the actual situation of government finances or to work out how the RDP would impinge on the work of existing government ministries or how the necessary human resources would be found for this protean programme. Above all, no attempt was made to evaluate, cost or budget the RDP, which quickly became known as Rumours, Dreams and Promises. The ANC went into the 1994 election as certain winners but, holding the RDP aloft, made promises they had no need to make and which they could not possibly keep: their posters read simply 'ANC: Jobs, Jobs, Jobs'.

The 1994 election was in itself one of the greatest events in South African history. No one who participated in that wonderful event, when at last white, brown and black queued to vote together as equal citizens, will ever forget the experience. It was, too, one wonderful moment to see the first black president elected at the head of an overwhelming majority – and to see this accepted not just calmly but warmly and with pride by all South Africans. The ANC had fought hard and long for this moment, and although many other actors and forces had contributed to the emancipation of black South Africa, no one could deny the ANC its epochal triumph. For this was not an emancipation of the slaves granted by a William Wilberforce or Abraham Lincoln, nor even was it an independence day graciously granted by a colonial administration. This was, in the end, a huge act of self-emancipation and self-assertion, one which will ring down through history and be celebrated by democrats everywhere.

But such celebration would depend heavily on whether the ANC was able to make a success of government. One thing was already clear: robbed of its socialist agenda, robbed even of the satisfaction of abolishing apartheid, the ANC poured all the more energy into devising affirmative action programmes of every kind. The problem was that they had seen Nat governments from Malan to Botha carry out a vast programme of social engineering and they were determined to do the same. The fact that in the end this social engineering had collapsed made less impression than the sheer ambition of the thing – and the fact that Afrikaners had come into power as poor men in 1948 and emerged by 1994 as a comfortable middle class. In addition, many ANC exiles were vastly impressed by their experience of the nomen-klatura system in the USSR. The remarkable objective was adopted of trying to make every key institution demographically representative at every level – something no other country in the world had attempted. In addition, great stress was laid on gender equality so that white women were early beneficiaries of the programme, but were then dropped from it. Since there was a chronic shortage of skilled local blacks, many companies and other institutions resorted to hiring foreign blacks. Inevitably, skilled white males, finding that even foreigners were now preferred over them, emigrated in droves.

No sooner was the ANC in power than it realised that, having taken over all the homeland debts and generously written off Namibia's debt, the South African state owed R254 billion – some $80 billion – and that interest payments alone were R50 billion a year. The budget deficit was already running at 9.5 per cent of GDP and the last thing the government could afford was an RDP spending spree. Moreover, the first thing ANC ministers did was to start shaking out 'apartheid bureaucrats' from the civil service and bringing in their own people. The sunset clause meant this was an expensive business with the old guard bought out with handsome packages, only for their successors to find they did not know how to do their jobs and thus needed to hire a vast army of consultants.

Turmoil in the civil service continued for years thereafter as the new recruits went on to better things, as left-wing whites, Coloureds and Indians were turfed out in turn to make room for more Africans and as lower levels of the old bureaucracy were also put out to grass. The result was that by 2000 the civil service was 72 per cent black and this 'transformation of the public service' was regarded by the government as one of its major successes: indeed, this was usually the prize exhibit in the endless preaching of the need for 'transformation' of every institution. But the result in one ministry after another was a large and progressive loss of capacity so that the government, having promised to deliver a great deal more than its predecessors, systematically disabled the administrative machine on which it depended for delivery of anything. The result, immediately, was that even when large sums were made available for this or that RDP objective the government found it could not spend the money.

Meanwhile, business and labour, concerned at the lack of a clear economic policy, began to come up with alternatives of their own. The government's answer to both was the introduction of GEAR – the Growth, Employment and Redistribution policy introduced in 1996 and presented to the country as the ultimate programme for development. GEAR had three legs: greater labour flexibility, privatisation and greater fiscal and monetary stability. The government argued that the result would be rapid growth and many more jobs, but it was clear from the outset that the opposite would be the case. Reducing the budget deficit to less than 3 per cent of GDP meant slashing public spending, with inevitable job cuts. By then the possibility of labour flexibility had already been undermined by a series of ultra-protectionist labour laws supported by the Labour Minister, Tito Mboweni (later the Governor of the Reserve Bank), which merely encouraged employers to cut their labour force wherever possible. COSATU's vehement opposition first slowed and then halted privatisation. However, fiscal and monetary austerity were entirely possible and these were strictly adhered to. Unfortunately, the policy, modelled after World Bank-IMF packages for other African countries, could not succeed on one leg alone.

The Left – especially COSATU and the SACP – opposed GEAR from the outset and the policy is still the major stumbling block between the alliance partners, though Mbeki cunningly entrusted key parts of GEAR's implementation to SACP ministers such as Alec Erwin (Trade and Industry) and Jeff Radebe (Public Enterprise), forcing them to act against their own party's policy. Several times the alliance seemed to be on the brink of collapse over GEAR, and at one stage during Mbeki's presidency the new SACP leadership – Blade Nzimande and Jeremy Cronin – were accused of organising a fully fledged left-wing opposition against the ANC. But despite friction the alliance survived, cemented by an ambivalent consensus about the 'national-democratic revolution' the country was said to be going through, with the Left still believing this would merely be a first stage, preliminary to embarkation on full-blooded socialism. More practically, the Left enjoyed influence and patronage through the alliance which it would be loath to lose, while the ANC saw the alliance as a guarantee against competition from a party further to its left.

These early years of the new South Africa were dominated by the activities of the Truth and Reconciliation Commission, set up with the task of investigating violations of human rights during the apartheid era. It also organised hearings for the perpetrators of such violations who were offered amnesty provided they came forward voluntarily and made full disclosure, and that they had acted on political grounds. TRC hearings were organised in each province, allowing many people to come forward and tell of their sufferings and grievances, and many of its proceedings were televised. It was a huge drama, allowing the country to relive some of the horrors of the apartheid era, with tears, pain, repentance and often forgiveness on the part of the victims. It was hoped that these hearings and the TRC's final report would enable the country to deal with its past and lead to reconciliation.

This, unfortunately, did not happen. The TRC was crippled from the start by its own patent bias – it had a clear pro-ANC majority and behaved so badly towards de Klerk when he appeared that both the

TRC chairman, Desmond Tutu, and his deputy, Alex Boraine, had to apologise publicly. Neither the IFP nor DP were represented. It was, moreover, weighed down with clerics who turned the hearings into a quasi-religious occasion – and who were signally lacking in the historical, legal and research skills needed for the job. Moreover, almost no attention was paid to the 1990–4 period when most deaths had occurred. The final TRC report (2003) contained many inconsistencies and frequently ignored the findings of more expert bodies which had come up with different results. The interim report (1998) had to be held up while sections adjudged unfair to the NP were cut out, and the final conclusion laying one-sided blame on the IFP for its war with the UDF-ANC also had to be altered.

Probably the greatest justification for the TRC was that it had allowed many ordinary people to express their sufferings but it was otherwise mainly a wasted opportunity. Some whites insisted that its proceedings and findings had been a complete eye opener, though Helen Suzman pointed out that nothing that emerged there had truly surprised her and that those who professed themselves shocked simply hadn't been paying attention to what had been going on. In fact, the TRC had lost the trust of most whites as soon as its bias became evident. Desmond Tutu compounded this impression by repeatedly appealing for whites in general to repent of their guilt for apartheid – thus revealing his belief in the un-Christian doctrine of collective guilt. It was a sorry sight to watch him desperately struggling to extort an apology from Winnie Mandela for her child battering and other crimes and then, when none was forthcoming, giving her a pardoning embrace nonetheless. For the TRC was based on an obvious flaw. The notion that by getting those who have fought one another to tell the whole truth about their wrongs and sufferings one would somehow produce reconciliation and even love was a peculiarly religious conceit. As van Zyl Slabbert pointed out, anyone tempted by such notions had only to attend the divorce courts for a morning to see what nonsense they were.

In the end the TRC pleased almost no one. The ANC were furious that it had escaped from its control far enough to criticise human rights atrocities in the MK camps. Buthelezi and P. W. Botha both successfully defied TRC invitations to appear, Botha treating it scornfully as a 'circus'. Its report is largely forgotten, its conclusions and recommendations ignored. For years apartheid victims got none of their promised (and very modest) compensation and the only prosecution stemming from TRC findings was opened much later, in 2004, for clearly opportunist reasons.

What the TRC did do very powerfully was to embody and express a new political correctness which still lies at the heart of the new South Africa's political culture. In this climate it did not do to point out that the same ANC ministers who liked fêting racial reconciliation were simultaneously applying old-style job reservation to discriminate against whites, Indians and Coloureds though now, with the Population Registration Act abolished, there were no formal definitions of what constituted racial identity. The racial minorities were simultaneously told that they must try to be African and abandon Eurocentrism; and also, of course, that they weren't Africans, that appointment on merit was a reactionary and racist doctrine and that proper Africans must get the jobs and contracts.

A freakish new tribe of whites emerged who chanted these mantras louder than any African in their desperate urge to be onside with the new political correctness, who expatiated on the theme of white guilt and saw white racism everywhere – one of the new sins was 'subliminal racism'. Some even launched an initiative whereby all whites were to sign an apology to all their non-white compatriots. Dress code told a lot. The new black elite tended to deck itself out in 'traditional African dress', usually a designer version of West African styles or Nyerere-style Mao jackets which had no basis in South African tradition at all. (Real African traditional dress was to be seen only at such deeply unfashionable venues as IFP parades.) Left-wing whites, Indians and Coloureds frequently wore Afro shirts in imitation of Mandela, gave African double-handshakes and some even toyi-toyied. Most public occasions gave themselves up to this strange mix of parody and pantomime. Time and again they were saved only by the fact that Mandela himself – sincerely and quite unusually – believed in reconciliation and frequently demonstrated this at a personal level with almost unbelievable generosity. But overall the Mandela period was one of drift – when problems began to pile up for the future.

The crucial Education Ministry was headed by Sibusiso Bengu, under whom Fort Hare University had collapsed into bankruptcy. Bengu had received a difficult legacy: non-functioning township schools, unruly students, undisciplined and often poorly educated teachers, too many tertiary institutions, many in financial trouble and anyway not offering a proper education. Bengu simply took the path of least resistance. His main initiative was to offer packages so that the best-qualified teachers and university staff could leave. All too many did. Standards declined amidst rampant politicisation – it became apparent, for example, that no university vice-chancellor could be appointed unless he or she was acceptable to the ANC.

The disaster at the Health Ministry was even greater. The Minister, Nkosazana Zuma, decided to emphasise primary health care at the expense of the country's existing first-class medical institutions. The result was to do great damage to the latter without noticeable improvement in the former. Simultaneously, Mrs Zuma refused to give priority to the Aids epidemic, which had begun to achieve terrifying proportions. At first, even the fact of the epidemic was not mentioned, then government money was thrown at a ludicrous anti-Aids musical and at quack cures while meanwhile the government refused to distribute the drugs able to inhibit the disease or prevent mother-to-child transmission. Mandela became concerned and started to speak openly about the need for sexual discipline but, when told that preaching condom use was unpopular, backed off – a failure of leadership of terrible proportions. In the whole apartheid period about 30,000 people had died from political causes of every sort but the new government's head-in-the-sand attitude to Aids was soon killing that many people every few months. By 1999 life expectancy for a newborn male in Zululand was down to twenty-eight years, probably lower even than at the time of Shaka.

The Aids disaster revealed with brutal clarity how little concern the new ANC elite had for the African poor but the international community kept culpably silent. In early 1999 the World Health Organisation held its AGM, the World Health Assembly. In the corridors the talk was about the horrific situation over Aids in South Africa and whether the country should be declared a Global Health Emergency. But not a word was said from the podium. Instead, Mrs Zuma was given an award for her anti-smoking campaign – sheer cynicism, for her policies helped guarantee that many black South Africans would die of Aids long before they could be stricken by lung cancer.

Although the IFP was now in government, the IFP–ANC war continued until 1996, albeit at a lower intensity. But these early years of the new South Africa also saw ordinary crime soar to intolerable levels – in the 1994–2004 period there were over 215,000 murders. The police force was devalorised, demoralised, underpaid and undermanned, and the government simply lacked the political will to crack down on (mainly black) lawbreakers.

Crime was always the principal reason for departure given by the growing number of emigrants, though undoubtedly affirmative action and concern at deteriorating standards of education were major causes.

Naturally, whites, Indians and the young were the first to leave – by 2000 there were reckoned to be some 300,000 South Africans living in the London area alone. This emigration was immensely damaging: it meant the flight of skills, capital, entrepreneurship and managerial capacity, and on average five jobs were lost for every skilled professional who left. Moreover, the flight became increasingly non-racial, for many Coloureds and skilled Africans began to leave too. At first Mandela pleaded with emigrants not to go but when it became clear that this made no difference he adopted the 'good riddance' attitude more typical of government. For the government instinctively tried to constrain (particularly) doctors, nurses and teachers from leaving but seemed utterly unwilling to give them incentives to stay.

This emigration spoke volumes of the deep unease among the minorities, including many who had fought the good fight against apartheid but found themselves unwelcome in the new South Africa. This unease could not escape de Klerk. Nor could he fail to see that the GNU was a coalition only in name, with its NP and IFP components being overruled at every turn by the ANC majority. As soon as the constitution's final draft had been approved in May 1996 de Klerk led the NP out of the government. In opposition he proved singularly ineffective, however, accelerating the slide of minority voters to the DP.

The protracted Mandela honeymoon came to an abrupt end with the President's speech at the ANC conference at Mafikeng at the end of 1997 in which he denounced all forms of opposition – parties and NGOs – as part of a vast conspiracy against the government, integrally connected with Third Force terrorism and crime syndicates. The speech, thought to be largely the work of Thabo Mbeki, had been handed to Mandela who, with typical organisational loyalty, had merely read it out. It created such a disastrous impression among international journalists covering the conference that Mbeki wandered among them cautioning them not to take the speech too seriously. In fact, the speech seems to have had two motivations. First, Mbeki wanted to head off criticism of GEAR (seen as a retreat to the right) by playing to the paranoia of the far left but, with an Mbeki presidency now in prospect (Mandela had made it clear he would not stand again for President in 1999) he also wanted to get Mandela on record with the most draconian sentiments to make sure a more liberal Mandela presidency would not be unfavourably contrasted with his own. Even Wilmot James, head of the normally pro-government Institute for Democracy in South Africa, began to warn about threats to civil liberties under an Mbeki presidency.

The transition to the Mbeki presidency was perfectly smooth. Mbeki had done such a thorough job of driving all possible rivals out of contention that there was no alternative to him. Besides, he had already been leading the day-to-day government business during the Mandela era. As his deputy President Mbeki chose Jacob Zuma, the genial former head of ANC Intelligence who had done a great deal, together with Chief Buthelezi, to bring peace to KwaZulu-Natal in the election run-up. Zuma was chosen partly because, as a Zulu, he provided ethnic balance but also because he was uneducated, a man who had been a latecomer to literacy as a self-taught adult – and who therefore could not plausibly be considered as a rival or alternative to Mbeki.

The 1999 election saw the ANC vote increase to 66.4 per cent – but many opposition voters had been deprived of the vote by the excising from the franchise of large categories who had been allowed to vote in 1994: voters who happened to be abroad, permanent residents who were not citizens and, most of all, those unable to acquire a new bar-coded ID book in time. Given that the old ID book was still legally valid, this meant depriving citizens of a fundamental right because they lacked a discretionary document. However unconstitutional this measure may have been, the Constitutional Court duly took the government's side, as it usually did on any issue of importance. The unhappy comparison with the way Afrikaner nationalism had begun its career in government by disenfranchising the few Coloureds who still had a vote was patent. In a country where the struggle for universal franchise had been the consuming passion of the century, this derogation of constitutional rights by both the government and the court was one of the most disgraceful events of the new era.

The other main feature of the election was the collapse of the (now renamed) New National Party (6.9 per cent), which was easily overtaken by Tony Leon's DP (9.6 per cent), which had provided a far clearer alternative and more rigorous opposition. This implosion signified the end of the road for Afrikaner nationalism but also a triumph for the liberal tradition. The NNP hung on to power in the Western Cape but were now a regional party only. In KwaZulu-Natal the IFP were again returned to power – they led an uneasy coalition government there with the ANC – and this time even the ANC did not question the validity of their victory. Soon after it became clear that the NNP's local branches were deserting to the DP en masse. Then, in the run-up to the December 2000 local elections, the NNP under Marthinus van Schalkwyk decided to join the DP in the Democratic Alliance (DA). This, it soon transpired, was a major mistake by the DP. As soon as the local elections were over, the NNP leadership began secret negotiations with the ANC, eventuating in the NNP's departure from the DA. The ANC, delighted to break up the main opposition threat, gave away a few junior ministerial positions to the NNP but, thanks to the NNP, gained control of the Western Cape. The two nationalist elites were comfortable together: they were both more at home with paternalistic government than with liberal democracy, both believed in rule by the state rather than by the law and both were fundamentally *étatiste*.

The Mbeki presidency soon gave evidence of a disturbingly paranoid style. Unlike Mandela, with his strong attachment to his natal village of Qunu, Mbeki had no sense of rootedness. He had spent his entire adult life abroad, had been accustomed to address even his own mother and father as 'Comrade' and his only real family had been the ANC. This did not make for a very secure personality: 'The nearest thing he's got to a sense of constituency is the UN delegates' lounge,' as one observer put it. And indeed, he spent a great deal of time travelling abroad. Even when in South Africa he often kept a low profile and showed no taste for socialising. This aloofness and a certain intellectual arrogance communicated themselves badly and he lacked the popular touch.

Mbeki's strategy was set by imagining first what could possibly threaten him and then acting pre-emptively against such threats. Since it was obvious that the ANC could not be defeated if it could maintain racial solidarity at the polls, he quickly jettisoned the inclusive 'rainbow' notion of a common South Africanism and instead harped on the theme of 'two nations, one white, one black' and played the race card on almost every possible occasion. Within the ANC he radically centralised power: not only would he as President appoint the Cabinet, but he would now also appoint all directors-general of government ministries, all ANC provincial premiers and even the mayors of all major cities. Before long his right-hand man, Steve Tshwete, fabricated an absurd 'presidential plot' in which those rivals Mbeki had driven out of politics – Mathews Phosa, Cyril Ramaphosa and Tokyo Sexwale – were all accused of plotting against Mbeki with the connivance of foreign intelligence services.

Worse still, Robert Mugabe's defeat in the March 2000 constitutional referendum in neighbouring Zimbabwe suggested that a fellow liberation movement was about to be ejected from power. Mbeki immediately concluded that this was part of a more general imperialist assault on the liberation movements of southern Africa and that they must all stand together or go under. Accordingly, he hastened to extend support to Mugabe, frequently going out of his way to appear hand in hand with him and instructing the South African election observer team to legitimate Mugabe's subsequent parliamentary and presidential victories, turning a blind eye to the horrific brutalities and open rigging which accompanied them. Both South African and international opinion were revolted by Mugabe's human rights atrocities, so Mbeki disguised his support as 'quiet diplomacy', but only those determined not to face the obvious truth of Mbeki's pro-Mugabe position could take this seriously.

At the same time Mbeki made it increasingly plain that he did not accept the link between HIV and Aids. Even Mandela, after all, had shrunk from the unpopularity involved in attempting to tell black males to change their sexual habits and if this challenge had been too much for Mandela's enormous authority and popularity to bear, it was certainly a bridge too far for Mbeki. Aids denialism was his way out. Having gone out on a limb on this issue, Mbeki felt unable to retreat and repeatedly attempted to justify his position with bogus science. In particular he encouraged every sort of quack cure and resisted the introduction of anti-Aids drugs that would actually work. The result was prodigious damage not only to his and South Africa's reputation but to the entire ANC tradition of concern for human rights. For no ANC Cabinet minister was willing to speak up either for human rights in Zimbabwe or for the right to proper treatment of the ever-larger number of HIV-positive South Africans.

It was in these two respects that the Mbeki presidency diverged most disastrously from the path charted by Mandela. Mandela himself made no secret of the revulsion he felt at Mugabe's behaviour and he also increasingly sided with those who wanted more urgent action on Aids and admitted openly that he himself had not done enough in this regard while President. This produced a lengthy period when Mbeki would not answer Mandela's calls. For, despite Mbeki's clear intellectual ambition – his speeches were littered with literary allusions and he insisted on his own expertise in fields as diverse as Aids research and the arcane calculation of mining costs – there was a petulance and inconsequentiality to his presidency. Endless initiatives would be announced with *grand éclat* – a policy co-ordination unit here, an integrated rural development policy there – but within a short time these initiatives would be abandoned, empty, for there was no follow-through. It was as if Mbeki enjoyed giving the inaugurating speech for such initiatives but lost interest once the speech was over. The two greatest examples were his NEPAD – New Economic Partnership for African Development – and the African Union. NEPAD rested on assumptions about large-scale capital inflows on the one hand and governance monitoring on the other, both of which lacked all credibility. The AU immediately set itself the same sort of impossible targets – a single army, currency, judiciary, parliament etc. – which had discredited its predecessor, the Organisation for African Unity.

At the same time he was willing to flirt outrageously with complete nonsense, the wilder shores of Aids denialism or other half-baked pseudo-knowledge picked up during his late-night trawling of the Internet. Thus the entrance to the 'Ubuntu Village' at the 2002 World Earth Summit held in Johannesburg featured pictures of Mbeki among flowers and fronds. Inside, one was confronted immediately by two large stands both dominated by Mbeki, one about the AU and one about NEPAD: there were endless talking screens of Mbeki speeches, Mbeki photographs and the like. Sandwiched in between these two stands was the Institute of Afrikology, selling herbal cures for everything from Aids to TB, all decked out with smiling photos of a beneficent Mbeki. It was impossible to believe that this placement was an accident. International journalists covering the event could merely gawp; the by now largely slavish South African press carefully avoided mention of such embarrassments – but either way no one could take the President seriously.

The result, after less than two years, was a vertiginous drop of confidence in Mbeki who now regularly trailed 20–25 per cent behind the ANC in opinion polls. Inevitably, the hitherto unimaginable began to happen and there was increasing speculation that anybody – even Jacob Zuma – might be better. This predictably fed Mbeki's paranoia. First Zuma was required to make a humiliating public announcement that he would never challenge Mbeki for the presidency and second a two-year-long police investigation was launched into possible corruption by Zuma in connection with the huge new arms deal signed by the government. At the end of this Zuma was not charged, but a great deal of his dirty linen was hung out to dry in public: it turned out that Zuma had been financed by Indian businessmen who had sought commercial advantage from the arms and other deals. The intention, transparently, was to leave Zuma dangling as damaged goods, unable either to succeed Mbeki or even to answer the charges.

Mbeki and his chief speech writer, Joel Netshitenzhe – both of them graduates of the Marx-Lenin Institute for party cadres in Moscow –

tended to phrase all their objectives in Leninist language and had from the outset insisted that the ANC was bent on 'the national democratic revolution' or NDR, that is to say a preliminary phase of building socialism in which the patriotic bourgeoisie would play a leading role in developing the forces of production. This formulation allowed Mbeki to appeal both to the SACP and to the growing black middle class which was the chief beneficiary of ANC rule. Initially this class had been assisted mainly by affirmative action and the 'transformation process' but increasingly it benefited from 'black empowerment', that is to say schemes to push the development of a black business class by systematic preference in the allocation of state (and, increasingly, private) tenders and contracts, and by requirements that white-led companies bring in black business as equity partners, often on extremely favourable terms.

A series of industry charters were drawn up with the aim of transferring at least a quarter of all South Africa's corporate assets into black hands by 2010–13. This will be one of the most rapid and sweeping transfers of wealth ever seen, and it will put at risk both the solvency of the banking system and the strength of companies built up over many years, sometimes over a century and more. *The Economist* put the matter succinctly: 'Who will fund this colossal transfer of wealth? The total cost, according to Azzar Jammine, chief economist at Econometrix, a consultancy, could be about R700 billion ($110 billion). That is equivalent to 10 per cent of the country's money supply every year for ten years. Black South Africans do not have that kind of money, nor could South African banks provide it without risk to their solvency. The government could foot the bill, but that would add ten points to inflation for a decade and lower the growth rate from 3–4 per cent to 1–2 per cent, estimates Mr Jammine, unless the assets somehow become more productive under their new owners who often lack experience. In practice, the cost will probably be split between the banks, the government, the firms divesting shares and the blacks buying them. Overall,' *The Economist* concluded, 'the charters look like a hideously expensive way to enrich a small number of black people, many of whom will, on past form, be senior members of the ruling party.' Indeed, the BEE deals announced in 2003 alone amounted to R30 billion – but two thirds of these derived from companies owned by just two men – Patrice Matsepe and Tokyo Sexwale.

The new black bourgeoisie formed by this process was largely parasitic both on state patronage and on existing corporate structures: it tended to take over shares in already established businesses and it was far from clear whether any value at all was being added by the process or how well this new business class would fare in anything like a free market. Moreover, it was quickly clear that a small class of black super-rich had evolved and that every new empowerment opportunity tended to feature the same fortunate few names, usually of the politically well-connected or their wives. The longer this process went on, the harder it became to believe that the day would ever come when the 'national democratic' phase of the 'revolution' would be deemed to be complete and that the moment for a transition to socialism had arrived. Doubts of this kind clearly haunted the SACP, whose chief theorist, Jeremy Cronin, alarmed at the growing comparisons with Mugabe's Zanu-PF regime in Zimbabwe, which had similarly enriched a tiny compradore bourgeoisie, gave an unguarded interview in 2002 in which he spoke of 'the Zanufication' of South African politics. Mbeki forced him to deliver a grovelling public apology and retraction, though not before Cronin had been publicly attacked by Mbeki supporters using now standard terms of anti-white racist abuse.

In one sense the hasty building of a black middle class was making up for decades of apartheid when the government, on Tocquevillian grounds, had considered this the most dangerous group of all. The other main achievement of these years was a slow but steady progress towards fiscal stability. Over the first nine years of ANC rule economic growth averaged 2.8 per cent – less than half what was required to start soaking up unemployment and vitiated by a steep decline in the currency, but at least the negative growth years of the 1980s were not repeated. The budget deficit was brought down to 2.4 per cent of GDP by 2003 and public sector debt, which had stood at 64 per cent of GDP in 1994, was down to 50 per cent and falling. But domestic investment was at record low levels: throughout the first nine years of ANC rule it remained steady at 16–17 per cent of GDP, whereas it had reached 27 per cent in the 1960s. And in the whole nine years foreign direct investment was only $22 billion, or less than 1 per cent of all FDI to developing countries. In fact, even this figure is heavily inflated by the move of many of South Africa's biggest firms to list in London: thus the 2001 inflow of $6.8 billion was almost wholly accounted for by De Beers being swallowed by the London-listed Anglo-American. Far more typical was the investment inflow of just $800 million in 2002 and $200 million in 2003. This amounted to a resounding vote of no confidence in the ANC government by international investors.

By the end of the first Mbeki term these trends had produced a clearly unsustainable situation. The rule of thumb was that every departing white cost the economy five jobs and this tallied reasonably well with the loss of something like 1.5 million formal sector jobs since 1994. The worst disaster lay in rural South Africa where government policy had been particularly perverse. On the one hand the ANC had abolished the Bantustans together with all the subsidies they had entailed and had watched as one border industry after another had closed. In its place the government merely handed out increased pensions and social grants to a huge mass of dependent unemployed.

On top of this the government took a tough line with farmers. Subsidies and soft loans were ended, imports were liberalised and in every way farming became a tougher option – particularly since the government paid scant attention to reducing the rate of farm attacks, which cost the lives of thousands of farmers and their workers. It also enacted labour legislation which increased the costs and difficulties of being an employer and the Land Reform (Labour Tenancy) Act which offered the possibility of farm workers acquiring rights to the land where they worked. The farmers frantically petitioned parliament, pointing out that the result was bound to be evictions of farmworkers on a huge scale: they were ignored. The result was indeed calamitous, with over half a million farmworkers evicted from the farms.

The result, by the end of the first decade of ANC rule, was that poor rural blacks were experiencing immiseration on an unheard-of scale. Huge numbers of unemployed and desperate people were dumped into rural squatter camps, with no prospect of jobs or social betterment of any kind. The tiny middle class of the Bantustans had, within the new provinces, become even smaller. Public facilities – schools, hospitals, police forces, clinics, universities – had all decayed. Violence, poverty and social dislocation ruled the countryside. Those who wish to imbibe reality through literature will know this world through J. M. Coetzee's *Disgrace* and Damon Galgut's *The Good Doctor*.

But this was only part of a larger social disaster. By March 2003 on a narrow definition (excluding workers too discouraged by unemployment to seek work) unemployment stood at 31 per cent. On the more truthful broad definition (including discouraged workers) the figure stood at 42.1 per cent – and both figures were steadily rising. This was hardly surprising. As we have seen, the key motor of the economy for over a century has been the inward flow of foreign investment. When that slows to a crawl – and when, simultaneously, large numbers of the middle class decide to emigrate, taking their capital with them – the consequences for South Africa's economy and society can only be catastrophic. Just as the post-1985 investment strike brought down apartheid, so the post-1994 investment strike is bound to have major political and social repercussions.

Inevitably, this has also seen a considerable worsening of inequality, even though apartheid South Africa was already one of the world's most unequal societies. In any society the most efficient means of transferring resources from the have-nots to the haves is simply to increase unemployment – and this has happened with extraordinary speed under the ANC government. When it took power unemployment, on the broad definition, stood at 32.6 per cent; nine years later, as can be seen, the figure was worse by almost one-third. On top of that, room has had to be made within the social structure for the new black middle class, including the tiny elite of black super-rich. By definition some of the resources they now possess have arisen as a result of redistribution away from others. Some of that redistribution has taken place at the expense of whites, but a great deal of it derives from the absolute immiseration of many blacks. For, of course, blacks are far more likely than others to be unemployed and the figures reach even more catastrophic proportions – 55 per cent and more among black women. This in turn has inevitable consequences for the growth of Aids, not only because so many women are forced into prostitution but because in general the weak position of women in society resulting from these rates of unemployment makes it difficult, if not impossible, for them to insist on changes in male sexual behaviour.

And Aids, of course, is the other key dimension of the social catastrophe suffered by South African blacks since liberation in 1994. By mid 2003 the Aids pandemic had secured its millionth victim and the death rate of 1,000 a day was rising fast. Another 5.3 million South Africans were HIV positive and by 2010 there would be 2.5 million Aids orphans. Despite this the government was still trying by every means to delay and postpone the delivery of anti-Aids drugs. The sheer callousness of the new ANC elite towards the black unemployed and those suffering from Aids is difficult to describe, surpassing the cruelties of Verwoerd and the old Nat elite. Take the simple statistic that in 2002 91,000 babies (almost all of them black) were born HIV positive and that at the very least 50 per cent of these babies could have been saved had anti-retroviral drugs been made available, as they were, for example, in neighbouring Botswana. Even on these minimalist terms, the Mbeki government was allowing 45,000 black babies to die unnecessarily every year – far more lives than were lost in the whole period of apartheid. And their mothers, often rape victims, could have been saved too, had the right medication been available: medication which

South Africa could afford on its own even if foreign donors weren't queuing up to help had they been allowed to do so.

The combination of growing unemployment and the awful harvest of Aids deaths impacted on a black population which wanted to believe the best of the new ANC elite. But even by 1999 there were signs of growing apathy and even cynicism, and the 2000 local elections saw DA and IFP gains throughout the Western Cape and KwaZulu-Natal as ANC voters stayed at home. This led the ANC to take dramatic action, pouring money into pensions, disability grants and child allow-ances (and raising the qualification age from 6 to 12), so that these cash handouts poured into unemployed and rural communities where they were gratefully received as proof of the fruits of liberation.

While no one could argue against the humanitarian value of such spending, it did not constitute productive investment: it merely created a vast, workless and dependent clientele living in permanent poverty. But as a political stop-gap measure it was certainly effective, particularly since – as has happened almost everywhere in Africa – the ruling party was able to communicate to its grass roots the message that failure to support the party would lead to the loss of these pensions and grants. Indeed, the ANC suggested that the only alternative to its own con-tinuation in power was a return to apartheid – which in turn implied that the ANC should rule, as Deputy-President Zuma put it during the 2004 election campaign, 'until Jesus comes back'.

Whatever the failures of the government the symbolism of the triumph over apartheid remains enormously powerful and would, on its own, probably guarantee ANC victories for years to come. But the government left nothing to chance, staging the 2004 elections as part of an enormous celebration of ten years of democracy, with Mbeki's presidential inauguration carefully arranged for Freedom Day (April 27) itself. For months all the organs of state worked flat out to stimulate a mood of euphoria over the great achievement of freedom. And, indeed, there was a lot to be proud of. The country was stable, at peace and paying its way. Moreover, liberation from apartheid had given Africans a wholly new sense of self-esteem, a feeling that they fully belonged in their own country at last. The power of this self-assertion, of this new self-esteem and the-sky-is-the-limit sense of the tremendous opportunities now open at least to the educated black elite cannot be underrated, and politically this mood is and will remain extremely potent. So great was the euphoria induced by the protracted cele-brations that the government even got away with the outrageous claim that it had created two million new jobs since 1994. Inevitably, the celebration of democracy was turned into a triumphalist celebration of the ANC itself.

These two factors – the massive turning-on of the welfare tap, making South Africa the most generous welfare state anywhere in the Third World, and the orchestration of the election campaign as part of the great ten-year celebration – were the key to the ANC's resounding success in the 2004 election, where it gained 69.7 per cent of the vote, with the DA far behind at 12.4 per cent. This time the ANC won all nine provinces. Buthelezi was at last vanquished by the ANC in KwaZulu-Natal and the IFP began to fall apart. The last vestige of provincial opposition to the centre now vanished and in effect South Africa was run as a centralised state, with federal and provincial powers all but wiped out.

Mbeki's second inauguration was a virtual coronation, for he was now an undisguisably imperial figure. More power was now centralised under one man than ever before in South African history – no less than 400 people now worked in the presidential office and both the new cabinet positions and the new premierships of the provinces were awarded in very much the way an absolute monarch of old distributed offices to clients, mistresses and favourites. Many of the new office-holders were women – several of them leading Aids denialists. Indeed, one of the new women provincial premiers had distinguished herself by sacking a doctor who had dared save the life of a raped baby by giving it anti-retroviral drugs. In the traditionally male-dominated world of the ANC such women were, inevitably, wholly dependent on presidential favour.

But as the fever of celebration died away, reality began to break back in. For all the fanfare about democracy, voter turnout had fallen by more than 15 per cent from the 1999 figure and over four million fewer people voted than had done a decade previously. In many ways the ANC triumph resembled the NP's victory of 1958. Ten years after winning power the nationalist movement was still gaining and it was using the state media and government patronage to ruthless effect. In its own mind the nationalist movement was confident, apparently vindicated on every count. But in fact the Nats' policies in 1958 were both unworkable and inhumane and a great deal of unnecessary human suffering lay ahead. In the ANC's case the record was better inasmuch as it had maintained all the liberties the new order had started with – there was no parallel to apartheid repression. But the ANC was just as confident as the Nats had been in 1958, and with as little reason. For it seemed all too probable that with the ANC's disastrous failure on employment and its inhumane policy on Aids further unnecessary suffering lay ahead – on an even greater scale.

No one regretted the demise of apartheid and everyone enjoyed the new sense of liberty. But everything now depended on taxing business and the diminishing and rapidly ageing white population as heavily as could be borne in order to keep the welfare payments flowing. The price of this and of sweeping government intervention in the economy was low investment and low growth. And, as we have seen, no South African government has survived a lasting investment strike. At some point the onward march of joblessness and Aids would surely produce a politically and socially unsustainable situation, particularly since these trends were accompanied by the extensive de-skilling of society, with obvious consequences for standards of education, health, the media and cultural life. The government's own response to this situation has largely been one of denial and even of suppressing or altering embarrassing statistics. Nonetheless, in its own survey of its period in office, *Towards a Ten Year Review,* published in October 2003, there was an admission that 'if all indicators were to continue along the same trajectory ... we could soon reach a point where the negatives start to overwhelm the positives. This could precipitate a vicious cycle of decline in all spheres.'

# EPILOGUE

South Africa has a long history but it is a young country, created in its present borders only in 1910, and an even younger nation. This new nation is deeply divided not only by class, language, religion and tradition, as are many other nations, but also by colour. Moreover, in the last century (not always, as usually assumed) class and colour tended to coincide. There are not many other nations like this in the world, although with the growth of non-white immigration to Europe their number is growing.

Binding such a nation together is not an easy task. Initially, it was not even seen as a task that had to be tackled. During the Dutch era the colony was a mere outpost and the locals were not expected to participate in its life except as slaves – and even there aliens were preferred. British colonialism had stronger notions about the usefulness of the local population, but this only led to their conquest and dispossession by both the British and the Dutch. But the British conquered and dispossessed the Boers too – who then stood up and recovered. Will this happen to the African majority?

It is often said that the policy of pre-apartheid governments differed only in degree from what was to follow. This was, actually, not so. Despite all their racism and injustice, the country's pre-apartheid rulers still believed that their black countrymen were a legitimate part of the population who would, in some very distant time, have to be fully incorporated in it. Afrikaner nationalism rejected this idea and, once in power, sought to stall and even to reverse the process – and this at a time when South African society, including its African component, had undergone profound social changes. This always doomed attempt at exclusion brought forth the irruption of African nationalism on a wholly new scale and ultimately its victory.

What in the end did Afrikaner nationalism do for Afrikaners? It improved their social and economic status but ultimately led them to such disgrace that what was in 1900 the world's favourite victim group had ninety years later become its most hated ruling group. The nation was humiliated and even Afrikaans language and culture have been undermined as a result.

Initially, Afrikaner and African nationalism seemed very different. The ANC was the first South African government to promise to build a common nation – a promise met with enormous enthusiasm and gratitude by all layers of society. But with a decade now passed it is clear that the two nationalisms have much in common, particularly when in power. Both have flattered to deceive. Both have built followings on a sense of historic suffering and grievance, and both have attempted simultaneously to create a sense of victimhood and a feeling of superiority among their adherents.

This promise of a common nationhood has not materialised. Racial slurs fly around and President Mbeki has flatly reversed the initial project by insisting that there are two nations in the country, the poor black and the rich white – although this is less and less true with every passing year. Moreover, it looks as if African nationalism is bent on the same self-destructive trajectory as its predecessor. Mbeki's Aids policy has brought enormous suffering to his own people and will now always be associated with his rule. It is not impossible that he and most of his ministers will be remembered with much the same ignominy as that of their Nat predecessors. The truest gauge, perhaps, is the way in which first Afrikaner and then African nationalism sent the best and brightest fleeing from the country – and showed scant concern to reverse the flow. This was a betrayal of the country's future at the time of Verwoerd, Vorster and Botha, and it is a betrayal of the country's future now.

The tragedy of South Africa is that it has always been ruled – and still is – by elites which seek their own group self-interest rather than that of the country as a whole. Only when it at last acquires a ruling elite which thinks and feels for the whole of this beloved country will the sad cycle change. This is what guarantees Nelson Mandela a special place in South African hearts. He alone for a brief and precious moment seemed to promise at least the possibility of a common South Africanism.

To write South African history is, however, to be conscious of rhythms far longer than this recent clash of nationalisms. These are merely the preoccupations of the last hundred years and to write this history is to walk with the strandlopers, to wander with the San and wonder at their cave paintings, to marvel at the crossing of the Suez isthmus by early man. To be a historian, a soothsayer, is in truth a magical profession and while these later follies – and their terrible human cost – may upset and outrage us, we are also merely latter-day magicians, playing with the pieces and setting them out in the way that seemed right to us. What we share – and share with the simple tribesman, the most primitive settler, the humblest slave – is to love this beloved country on the southern tip of Africa and want only for its people that they wake to greet the coming sun without regret.

# SUGGESTIONS FOR
# FURTHER READING

W. Beinart, *Twentieth Century South Africa*, 2nd ed., Oxford, 2001

Ph. Bonner, P. Delius and D. Posel (eds), *Apartheid's Genesis 1935–1962*, Johannesburg, 1993

J. Daniel, A. Habib, R. Southall (eds), *State of the Nation: South Africa 2003–2004*, Cape Town, 2003

T. R. H. Davenport, *The Transfer of Power in South Africa*, Cape Town, 1998

T. R. H. Davenport and Christopher Saunders, *South Africa: Modern History*, 5th ed., London, 2000

A. Davidson, I. Filatova, V. Gorodnov, S. Johns (eds), *South Africa and the Communist International: A Documentary History*, vols 1, 2, London, 2003

A. Drew, *Discordant Comrades: Identities and loyalties on the South African left*, Aldershot et al., 2000.

S. Ellis, T. Sechaba, *Comrades against Apartheid*, London, 1992

H. Giliomee, *The Afrikaners: Biography of a People*, Cape Town, 2003

C. Hamilton (ed), *The Mfecane Aftermath: Reconstructive Debates in Southern African History*, Johannesburg, 1995

A. Jeffery, *The Truth about the Truth Commission*, Johannesburg, 1999

——*The Natal Story: Sixteen Years of Conflict*, Johannesburg, 1997

R. W. Johnson and L. Schlemmer (eds), *Launching Democracy in South Africa: The First Open Election, April 1994*, London, 1996

R. W. Johnson and D. Welsh (eds), *Ironic Victory: Liberalism in post-liberation South Africa*, Cape Town, 1998

T. Karis, G. M. Carter (eds), *From Protest to Challenge: A Documentary History of African Politics in South Africa, 1882–1979*, vols 1–4, (vol. 1 with S. Johns, vol. 3 with G. Gerhart), Stanford, 1987

—— *From Protest to Challenge: A Documentary History of African Politics in South Africa, 1882–1979*, vol 5, Bloomington and Indianapolis, 1997

J. Laband, *Rope of Sand: The Rise and Fall of the Zulu Kingdom in the Nineteenth Century*, Johannesburg, 1995

J. Lambert, *Betrayed Trust: Africans and the State in Colonial Natal*, Durban, 1995

T. Lodge, *Black Politics in South Africa since 1945*, Johannesburg, 1983

—— *Politics in South Africa (from Mandela to Mbeki)*, Cape Town, Oxford, 2002

N. Mandela, *Long Walk to Freedom: The Autobiography of Nelson Mandela*, London, 1994

P. Maylam, *A History of the African People of South Africa from the Early Iron Age to the 1970s*, London, 1995

—— *South Africa's Racial Past: The history and historiography of racism segregation and apartheid*, Aldershot et al., 2001

D. R. Morris, *The Washing of the Spears: The Rise and Fall of the Zulu Nation*, London, 1994

T. Pakenham, *The Boer War*, London, 1982

J. Peires, *The House of Phalo: History of the Xhosa People in the Days of their Independence*, Johannesburg, 1981

J. Rantete, *The African National Congress and the Negotiated Settlement in South Africa*, Pretoria, 1998

R. Ross, *A Concise History of South Africa*, Cambridge, 1999

J. Seekings, *The UDF: A History of the United Democratic Front in South Africa 1983–1991*, Cape Town, Oxford, 2000

R. C. H. Shell, *Children of Bondage: A Social History of the Slave Society at the Cape of Good Hope 1652–1838*, Johannesburg, 1994

V. Shubin, *ANC: A View from Moscow*, Cape Town, 1999

Truth and Reconciliation Commission, *Final Report*, vols 1–5, Pretoria, 1998

C. van Onselen, *The Seed is Mine: The Life of Kas Maine, a South African Sharecropper, 1894–1985*, New York, 1996

F. Welsh, *A History of South Africa*, London, 1998

J. Wentzel, *The Liberal Slideaway*, Johannesburg, 1995

N. Worden, *The Making of Modern South Africa: Conquest, Segregation and Apartheid*, Oxford, 1994

N. Worden and C. Crais (eds), *Slavery and its Legacy: Breaking the Chains in the Nineteenth Century Cape Colony*, Johannesburg, 1994

### REFERENCE PUBLICATIONS

W. J. de Kock and D. W. Kruger, *Dictionary of South African Biography*, 5 vols, Cape Town, 1983

T. Karis, G. M. Carter and Gail M. Gerhart, *From Protest to Challenge: A Documentary History of African Politics in South Africa, 1882–1979*, vol. 4, Stanford, 1987

N. E. Sonderling, *New Dictionary of South African Biography*, vol. 2, Pretoria, 1999

E. J. Verwey, *New Dictionary of South African Biography*, vol. 1, Pretoria, 1995

The website of the Helen Suzman Foundation is an invaluable free source of information on contemporary South Africa – www.hsf.org.za

# INDEX